Rich in Good Works

Mary M. Emery of Cincinnati

Ohio History and Culture

Millard F. Rogers, Jr.

Rich in
Good
Works

Mary M. Emery of Cincinnati

_____

Art Collector and Philanthropist

To
Jock + Gunhild Rose
with best wishes
Millard F Rogers

The University of Akron Press

The publisher gratefully acknowledges a grant in support of this publication from the Thomas J. Emery Memorial.

Frontispiece. Mary M. Emery with Elizabeth Livingood, youngest child of Lily and Charles J. Livingood, at Mariemont, Rhode Island, c. 1912 (Author's collection)

All inquires and permissions requests should be addressed to the publisher, The University of Akron Press, Akron, OH 44325-1703

Manufactured in the United States of America

First edition 2001

Library of Congress Cataloging-in-Publication Data
Rogers, Millard F.
      Rich in good works : Mary M. Emery of Cincinnati / Millard F. Rogers, Jr.
        p. cm. — (Ohio history and culture)
      Includes bibliographical references and index.
      ISBN 1-884836-66-6 (cloth: alk. paper)
        1. Emery, Mary Muhlenberg, 1844–1927. 2. Women philanthropists—United States—Biography. 3. Women art collectors—United States—Biography. I. Title. II. Series.
HV28.E35 R64 2000
361.7'4'092—dc21
[B]   00-056383

To Nina

CONTENTS

PREFACE

To some, she was Guppy. To others, she was the Lady Bountiful or Madame X. To most, she was simply Mrs. Emery. Little remembered today, she was well-loved during her lifetime in Cincinnati, the city of her maturity. She was less recognized nationally in spite of her many benefactions across the United States and abroad. Devoted to her family as wife and mother, and to good works after the deaths of her husband and children, her life epitomized the philanthropist dedicated to humanity's welfare. Mary Muhlenberg Hopkins, as the wife of Thomas J. Emery and as his widow and heiress of a fortune, shied from public acclaim. Even after the death of her husband, when her many philanthropies were initiated, she deferred to his memory and most often attached his name, not hers, to the various projects or institutions she supported.

This book tells the life story of a remarkable humanitarian and philanthropist. Increasing attention to the philanthropic efforts of women is evident in post-1970s research and publications. Author Kathleen D. McCarthy correctly states, in *Lady Bountiful Revisited*, that "philanthropy lies at the heart of women's history." Mary Emery's life embraced her family and church in its first part and her philanthropies in the second. She was relatively inconspicuous in Cincinnati society until her husband's death, but her second direction in life evolved from her wealth and greatly raised her profile after she was widowed. With her inheritance, she stepped into a new role as art collector and supporter of many causes. Mary's philanthropic inclinations during her husband's lifetime were meshed with Thomas's wishes, perhaps even subordinated to them. After his death, she recognized her "vast responsibility" as inheritor of a fortune. She had no surviving children, and she absorbed the remaining years of her life with the dissemination of her inheritance.

Apparently, Mary did not have any organized, systematic plan for her philanthropy. As opportunities arose, and as supplicants sought her help, she responded. She was not casual in her giving, however, and several causes appealed particularly to her. These were the Episcopal Church, medical programs for children, educational activities and those helping young people, and agencies headquartered in Cincinnati. Although a legal resident of Middletown, Rhode Island, just outside Newport, Mary considered Cincinnati her true home. It was not unexpected, then, that most of her charitable giving centered on this city, its people, its agencies and institutions. She took great pride in Cincinnati but did not confine her generosity to its city limits.

Mary Emery's giving did not seek acknowledgment of her name or person, and, in many instances, she insisted that her husband be recognized if any name were attached to a gift. She was a generous supporter of cultural institutions, especially the Cincinnati Art Museum. It benefited greatly from her generosity. Her world-class collection of old master paintings was hers to enjoy during her lifetime, but she formed it expressly as a future bequest to the museum. Mary's gifts most often resulted from requests presented to her directly or through Charles J. Livingood, her advisor. Many applicants for her charity were men and women she knew and respected, but clearly Livingood was the gatekeeper for all of Mary Emery's philanthropic endeavors.

Mary Emery first attracted my attention during my tenure as director of the Cincinnati Art Museum from 1974 to 1994, when I was in daily contact with the museum building she provided, the endowment she established, and the collection of paintings by Titian, Mantegna, Hals, Murillo, Van Dyck, Gainsborough, and others she bequeathed to that institution. It was not difficult to grasp her methodology in acquiring these masterpieces, but so many questions were unanswered about her life, her husband, Emery's acquisition of wealth, and her dedication to charitable acts and the dispersal of most of her estate. In 1974, my family and I settled in

Mariemont, a planned community initiated by Mary Emery. Thus, another connection with this lady aroused my curiosity.

I started collecting information on Mary Emery in 1975. An early article I wrote about her, published in the *Cincinnati Art Museum Bulletin*, was a brief biography. As a result of incomplete research, the article also carried a few errors. Thorough research began in earnest upon my retirement in 1994 as director of the Cincinnati Art Museum. My original intention was to write a biography of this selfless woman, coupling with it a detailed history of the beginnings of Mariemont, one of America's most important examples of town planning. When research was completed, however, I decided to separate the stories. Mary Emery's biography now stands independently.

Fictional or undocumented occurrences in her life were discounted in my research. I avoided imagined dialogue or conversations. Interviews with individuals who knew Mary Emery were nigh impossible, as she died in 1927. Mary's husband, Thomas J. Emery, who created the fortune permitting her generosity, was a particularly elusive subject for research. Archives, newspapers, libraries, historical societies, court records, and published references were searched for information on Mary Emery, her family, and her philanthropies. Although reminiscences and information from those who knew her are rare, one contact added immeasurably to my research. I am grateful for the opportunities I had to interview Mrs. Elizabeth Livingood McGuire, the youngest daughter of Charles J. Livingood. Throughout her childhood and teenage years, Elizabeth Livingood was part of Mary's surrogate family. Along with her parents and siblings, Elizabeth Livingood spent many summers near Newport, Rhode Island, on the Emery estate. She visited Mary frequently at her Edgecliffe home in Cincinnati. She shared with me many memories of events, individuals, and activities involving Mary Emery and her life in Cincinnati and Rhode Island, and she provided photographs of family gatherings that enhanced my picture of this philanthropist. I am indebted to her for her many recollections that assisted my research.

Charles J. Livingood was Mary Emery's closest confidant after her husband's death. He managed her husband's estate, advised her on business and charitable matters, acted as her secretary, and served as her surrogate son. The bulk of Livingood's papers have disappeared, except for his diaries, a few letters, and other documents remaining in descendants' hands. Copies of these were generously lent to me by Livingood's grandson, Virginius Hall, Jr. A cache of Emery documents and photographs, probably deposited by Livingood with Mary Emery's nephew, John J. Emery, was available to me through the kindness of Lela Emery Steele, the grandniece of Mary Emery. These two sets of papers, clippings, and memorabilia were invaluable in my assessment of Mary Emery's and Charles Livingood's lives.

Many individuals and institutions assisted my research, and I acknowledge with gratitude the following: Compton Allyn; Arnold Arboretum of Harvard University: Karen Madsen; Babies Milk Fund, Cincinnati: Tina Roberts; Berea College: Elizabeth Sloas; Berry College: Ruth Ash; Mr. and Mrs. Alexander R. Cari; Christ Church, Cincinnati: Ruth Avram; Cincinnati Art Museum: Terrie Benjamin, Mona Chapin, William Clark, Ran Mullins, Cathy Shaffer; *Cincinnati Enquirer:* Owen Findsen; Cincinnati Historical Society: Laura Chace, Anne Shepherd; Cincinnati Public Library; The Thomas J. Emery Memorial: Henry Hobson, Jr.; Episcopal Diocese of Arizona: Rev. Donald P. Monson; Episcopal Diocese of Colorado: Rev. Canon Cyril F. Coverley; Episcopal Diocese of Idaho: Wallace Farnham; Episcopal Diocese of Northern California: Rev. John L. Bogart; Episcopal Diocese of Southern Ohio: Rev. John G. Carson; Charles Fleischmann III; Harvard University Archives; Thomas Hogan III; Hobart College: Charlotte Hegyi; Walter Langsam, Jr.; Library of American Landscape History: Robin Karson; Mariemont Preservation Foundation: Janet Setchell, Fred Rutherford; Ruth K. Meyer; Middletown (Rhode Island) Historical Society: Mary Bellagamba; Prof. Zane L. Miller; National Society of the Colonial Dames of America: Anne Ott; National Society of the Daughters of the American Revolution: Elva Crawford; Newport Historical Society: Bertram Lippincott; New York Historical Society: May Stone; Frederick Law Olmsted National Historic Site: Linda Genovese, Joyce Connelly; Packer Collegiate Institute, Brooklyn: Marie Castator; David Reichert; St. Philip's Church, Circleville, Ohio: Rev. Steven Williamson;

St. Paul's School, Concord, New Hampshire: David Levesque; Salvation Army National Headquarters: Susan Mitchem; Saranac Lake Free Library: Janet P. Decker; Spring Grove Cemetery and Arboretum, Cincinnati; Taft, Stettinius & Hollister, Cincinnati: James R. Bridgeland, Jr.; *Town & Country Magazine:* Susan J. Bleecker; University of Cincinnati: Archives, Medical School Archives, Jean Wellington, DAAP Library; University of the South: Anne Armour-Jones; Wildenstein & Company: Joseph Baillio. To my wife, Nina, who shared my interest in Mary Emery and Mariemont and who patiently endured and encouraged this book, I express my heartfelt thanks.

Millard F. Rogers, Jr.
Mariemont, Ohio

Rich in Good Works

Mary M. Emery of Cincinnati

CHAPTER I

The Girl from New York and the Emery Family

WALKING THROUGH his darkened and steam-filled factory on December 30, 1857, Thomas J. Emery, Sr., stepped into an open hatchway, falling four floors to his death. The founder of an impressive Cincinnati dynasty of manufacturers, real estate developers, and philanthropists, and Englishman who emigrated some twenty-five years earlier, he ended his life in the candle and lard oil factory that launched his fortune and that of his heirs. One day after the accident, a Cincinnati newspaper announced in its headlines, "Death of Thomas Emery, Esq.—Melancholy Occurrence," and elaborated on the circumstances in a brief article.

> Mr. Emery had recently completed an extensive building on the corner of Vine and Water Street for the manufacture of Lard Oil and Candles, and the machinery was being put into operation yesterday for the first time. About 5 o'clock, he was in the fourth story of the building. There was considerable steam in the apartment, and this with the heavy weather that prevailed, rendered it quite dark. In walking about he accidentally stepped into the hatchway and fell through the several floors, into the cellar, a distance of about sixty feet. One of the lads working on the floor from which he fell, saw him fall through the hatchway, and ran down stairs as rapidly as possible. In his excitement he fell from the first floor into the cellar, and was much injured. When

Mr. Emery was taken up, a few minutes after the accident occurred, he was dead. Several of his bones were badly fractured, and the probability is that he was undoubtedly dead before he reached the cellar.[1]

Thomas Emery was fifty-nine years old in 1857. He had been a Cincinnati resident since at least 1832, when he began his prosperous career there. On December 19, 1832, Emery advertised for the first time in the *Cincinnati Daily Gazette*, announcing himself as a "land agent" with a downtown office. This first announcement of his commercial venture, selling land and buildings, was repeated regularly in the newspaper's subsequent advertisements. Scattered among notices selling cough syrups, rewards for runaway slaves, and inducements to purchase barrel staves, Emery's real estate focus persisted throughout 1833.[2]

From its beginnings in the late eighteenth century and into the twentieth, Cincinnati was a mecca for land speculators and real estate investors, as proved by the many advertisements in local newspapers. Residential and commercial buildings jockeyed for good locations throughout the city's core, a basin hemmed in by hills in all directions except to the south, where the river was a natural barrier. Real estate speculation prospered, as there was abundant undeveloped land, and investors could purchase land with little capital and watch it grow in value as additional speculators took advantage of the booming economy in the 1830s. Cincinnati was a merchant's city, and idle cash always sought channels for investment. Thomas Emery, the immigrant, perceived this, as did his sons in the decades after their father's death.

Emery was born in Bedford, England,[3] on December 15, 1798. Possibly he worked in a London bank as a young man before setting out for America. He was already married with two children when he reached Cincinnati by 1832.[4] Certainly he had some capital, for his enterprise as land agent required cash investments. Emery worked quickly to enlist the support of prominent Cincinnatians, men like Nicholas Longworth and Daniel Gano, recording their names and others as references in his advertisements beginning June 26, 1833, in the *Cincinnati Daily Gazette*. A measure of success came quickly, for Emery moved his office that same year to 11 East Fourth, on the city's prestigious business street.[5] There he

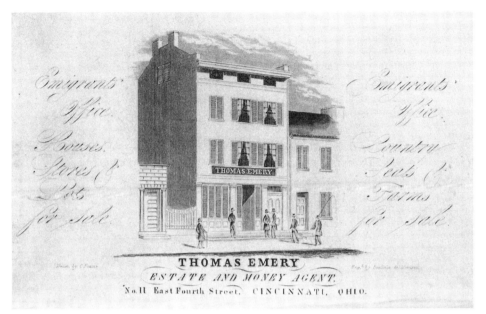

First office and residence of the Thomas Emery family, 11 East Fourth Street, Cincinnati, 1833 (Courtesy Cincinnati Historical Society)

maintained his residence as well. City directories illustrated a three-story building housing a street-level office with two floors of rooms above, the shuttered windows hung with ruffled curtains appropriate for a young, already prosperous family man.[6] This first known home for the Emery family in Cincinnati, its plain Federal-style façade opening directly onto the street, carried a large sign above the front door: Thomas Emery. There, Thomas and his wife, Kezia Brown Emery (1808/9–1876), lived with their two children who were born abroad, Kezia (1828–1900) and Thomas Josephus (1830–1906), who gave his birthplace as Newport, Wales.[7]

When Emery arrived in Cincinnati with his wife and two children, the city was devastated by a cholera epidemic, and floodwaters reached sixty-two feet above low-water mark on the Ohio River. Boats docked four blocks up from the landing at Pearl and Main Streets, and river traffic was treacherous.[8] Trade flourished in the city in spite of these calamities. A visitor to the city in 1832, Colonel Thomas Hamilton, recorded his impressions of the bustling town of over 28,000 residents where Emery established his business.

> [Cincinnati] is, apparently, a place of considerable trade. The quay was covered with articles of traffic; and there are a thousand indications of activity and business which strike the senses of the traveler, but which he would find it difficult to describe. Having nothing better to do, I took a stroll about the town, and its first favorable impression was not diminished by closer inspection. Many of the streets would have been considered handsome in New York or Philadelphia; and, in the private dwellings, considerable attention had been paid to external decoration. The most remarkable object in Cincinnati, however, is a large Graeco-Moresco-Gothic-Chinese-looking building, an architectural compilation of prettiness of all sorts, the effect of which is eminently grotesque.[9]

This "most remarkable object" was the Bazaar of Mrs. Frances Trollope, the commercial enterprise of a strange, flamboyant English lady who hoped to bring her tasteful goods and wares to a backward western town she thought was starving for sophistication.

Branching out by 1836 in other enterprises, Emery *père* joined another transplanted Englishman, Isaac A. Davenport, in the grocery, wine, and hops business, while retaining his land agency.[10] His partnership with Davenport apparently ended in 1839, when their joint advertisements ceased. Falling back on his occupation as estate and money agent, Emery pursued that trade until it failed in the recession of 1841. Apparently he suffered losses but was diligent in repaying his creditors. Thomas Emery recovered and was released from any liability, according to the Cincinnati newspaper that announced his fatal accident while recording his charitable character.

"He has since been very successful in business, and had accumulated a fair amount of wealth. Mr. Emery was a quiet and unassuming man, strictly conscientious in all his dealings, and was much respected by his fellow citizens. In his charities he was systematic and liberal. He made it a point never to refuse to give for a worthy object, or to permit himself to be asked the second time. He seemed to regard it a privilege to contribute towards relieving the wants of his fellow creatures, or to promote the general interests of the community."[11]

Between the date of Cincinnati's founding in 1788 and Thomas Emery's death in the mid-nineteenth century, the Queen City of the West, as Henry Wadsworth Longfellow had dubbed the city, expanded its grid of streets reaching up from the muddy Ohio. It continued its economic reliance on the river artery of trade and commerce that led down to the Mississippi. Merchants called her the Tyre of the West. The more unseemly title, Porkopolis, was derived from the meatpacking industry and slaughterhouses that flourished throughout the city. By 1850, with a population of just over 115,000, Cincinnati was the nation's center for the whiskey and hog markets, both dependent on corn, a major agricultural crop of the fertile farmlands both north and south of the Ohio River. And from the by-products of meatpacking came candles and lard oil, the two products responsible for the future financial empire of Emery's two sons.

Breweries and lard oil factories were so numerous that a Cincinnati historian, writing in 1851, bragged with statistics that are remarkable for the numbers that elucidate a commodity practically unknown today.

> There are probably thirty lard oil factories here, on a scale of more or less importance. Eleven million pounds of lard were run into lard oil that year, two-sevenths of which aggregate made stearine; the residue, lard oil, or in other words, twenty-four thousand barrels of lard oil, of forty to forty-two gallons each. The oil is exported to foreign countries. . . . Lard oil, beside being sold for what it actually is, enters largely, in the eastern cities, into the adulteration of sperm oil, and in France, serves to reduce the cost of olive oil. We now come to the star candles, made of the stearine expressed from the lard in manufacture of lard oil.[12]

Emery's lard oil factory was one of thirty similar industries that may have existed in Cincinnati on or near Water Street as early as 1846. Emery's location at 33–35 Water Street, one short block from the river, abutted the boat landing and was certainly at that site by 1850–1851.[13] In 1853, city directories carried the first mention of the oldest Emery son, Thomas J., who was then twenty-three years old and already a clerk in his father's factory.[14] He attended Woodward College, as Woodward High School in Cincinnati then was called, until age sixteen, when he entered the family business in a minor capacity.[15] By 1856, the company was styled "Thomas Emery and Son," a title it would bear until the agreement with their widowed mother later established a new company entity. Of the six children of Thomas and Kezia Emery, the three sons officially entered the family business in 1859.[16] That business, although initiated with a real estate and money agent focus, derived its early prosperity from candle making; and that was linked to Cincinnati's hog-slaughtering industry and its by-product of grease from animal fat. The Emery brothers acknowledged their indebtedness. "In the candle business we had a new process of distilling cheap greases; our competitors were using costly tallow and lard. Candles were high and our profits large for a number of years."[17] In a handwritten agreement between the widow, Kezia, and her sons Thomas J. and John J., with J. Howard witnessing, a partnership[18] called "Thomas Emery's Sons" was formed that would prosper throughout the nineteenth century and well into the twentieth. It would expand from lard oil and candles into real estate and housing, creating nationwide holdings and the foundation of wealth for a remarkable lady, Mary Muhlenberg Hopkins Emery.

Mary was born during the second marriage of a widow and a widower. Her parents had eastern and mid-western backgrounds, with her father's heritage extending back to a passenger on the Mayflower. Her mother descended from a pioneer of the western frontier, as Ohio was considered in the early nineteenth century. Mary's rearing and education centered in New York and Brooklyn, and this afforded her the sophistication and training a well-bred young lady might acquire in America's largest city. By the time she reached Cincinnati, she was educated beyond the usual level of her peers. Mary's sensible, middle-class family values supported her throughout her life, with her retiring nature complementing that of her husband, even as his considerable wealth registered the couple among the nation's upper-class millionaires. While Mary's family life in the East does not compare with the Emerys' colorful saga in Cincinnati, her story after her marriage to Thomas J. Emery is one of warmth and tragedy, philanthropy and compassion, riches and loneliness.

In a letter written by a suitor and clearly intended to woo a future wife, the New York merchant Richard Hubbell Hopkins (1798–1863) wrote in the early spring of 1838 to Mary Barr Denny Muhlenberg (1807–1893), a widow since 1831, urging her to sit for her portrait by a miniaturist then

*Portrait of Richard H.
Hopkins (1798–1863),
Mary M. Emery's father,
by Edward D. Marchant
(1806–1887), 1838*
(Courtesy Cincinnati Art
Museum)

working in New York City. "I have made an arrangement for my miniature, price 40 dollars, give the first sitting tomorrow if business does not
prevent. Will have it in readiness to send you in a week or ten days, and
now my dearest request you to sit for yours. I find on inquiry that
Marchant has some reputation, and is at least respectable as an artist, but
you should not pay him over 40 dollars."[19] The forty-year-old Hopkins was
a widower who had moved to New York City from Circleville, Ohio, after
the death of his first wife.[20] The widow Muhlenberg accepted Hopkins,
and on December 11, 1838, they were married in New York City.[21] Mary
Barr Denny Muhlenberg had been married before to Francis Swaine Muhlenberg (1795–1832) and was childless. She was the daughter of a pioneer
settler of Circleville and Chillicothe, Ohio, General James Denny, who
also edited and owned the first newspaper in Pickaway County.

Portrait of Mary Barr Denny Muhlenberg Hopkins (1807–1893), Mary M. Emery's mother, perhaps by Edward D. Marchant (1806–1887), 1838 (Courtesy Cincinnati Art Museum)

On December 19, 1844, Mary, the first of two daughters, was born to Mr. and Mrs. Hopkins, then living at 15 Amity Street, New York City. Mary was given the middle name of Muhlenberg.[22] Isabella Frances (1848–1935), the second child, followed four years later. She never married and remained close to her older sister throughout her life. Silhouette portraits of the two pantalooned youngsters taken about 1850 are fleshed out as solemn, wide-eyed girls posed with their mother in a tintype a few years later. When Mary and her sister were born, their father was employed as a dry goods merchant at 94 Pearl Street, New York. The Hopkins' home address, 15 Amity Street, was in the prestigious neighborhood near Washington Park. There the family remained until 1849 when they moved to 2 Albion Place. In that same year, Mary's father joined

Williams, Bradford & Company, another merchant firm, at 14 Cortlandt Street. By 1851, when Mary was seven years old, her peripatetic father moved the family to 47 Sydney Place, Brooklyn, where they remained until their move to Cincinnati in 1862.[23]

Mary presumably attended the local schools of New York and Brooklyn before enrolling for two years, from 1860 to 1862, at the prestigious Packer Collegiate Institute in Brooklyn Heights. Housed in a four-story Gothic-style building with lancet windows and crenellated stone trim, the institute on Joralemon Street was one of the finest private schools in the New York and Brooklyn areas. It provided thorough instruction for young ladies in many subjects usually reserved for male students in the mid-nineteenth century. Classes in astronomy, geometry, and algebra were offered along with elocution, penmanship, Latin, and modern languages to develop "the mental and moral powers of the pupil; to educate the mind to habits of thinking with clearness and force; and to discipline the heart to yield to the dictates of reason and conscience."[24]

Mary's scholarly interest is captured in a posed photograph she treasured throughout her life, probably made when she was sixteen and enrolled at Packer, depicting her seated with her gray-haired professor at an ornate table covered with papers and books. Mary's small paper notebook, filled with handwritten trigonometry formulae and examples, is a

Silhouette of Mary M. Hopkins, c. 1850–1852 (Courtesy Lela Emery Steele)

Silhouette of Isabella F. Hopkins, c. 1850–1852 (Courtesy Lela Emery Steele)

Mary Denny Hopkins with her daughters, Mary (left) and Isabella, c. 1854
(Courtesy Lela Emery Steele)

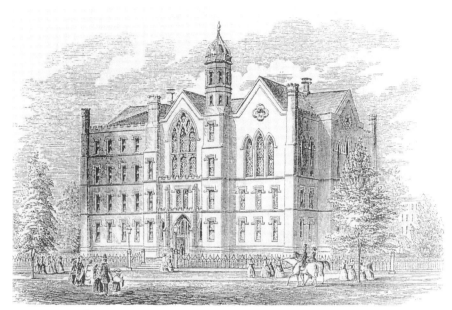

Packer Collegiate Institute, Brooklyn, New York, where Mary M. Hopkins was enrolled as student, in 1860–1862 (Author's collection)

sample of the notes required from a Packer student. Following fourteen pages of trigonometry exercises ("To find the sine and cosine of the sum and difference of two arcs" is inscribed as the heading for one page), Mary recorded thirty-one lectures on astronomy by Professor Darwin G. Eaton in her meticulous script. A lecture held on April 2, 1862, focused on planets was the final one for the class.[25]

Mary's studies in trigonometry and astronomy ended in 1862, and she and her family began anew in Cincinnati, a much smaller northern city with a definite southern outlook. As both of Mary's parents had an Ohio background, they sought closer ties with relatives there. Hopkins intended a business partnership with a relative, Lewis C. Hopkins, who owned a dry goods company at Fifth and Vine Streets,[26] then as now a prominent downtown location. The family resided with Lewis Hopkins in one of Cincinnati's best neighborhoods, Mount Auburn. Lewis presided like a squire over this hilly section of the city and presented to Cincinnati in

Mary M. Hopkins with a professor, probably from Packer Collegiate Institute, c. 1860–1862 (Courtesy Lela Emery Steele)

1866 one acre of choice land for a park, to be kept "free of buildings, and to be tastefully planted with durable trees and shrubbery."[27] In the mid-nineteenth century, Mount Auburn's large, turreted homes were considered suburban, almost countrylike in setting and distance from downtown. There, Mary's father died on April 24, 1863. Mary was eighteen years old.

Although the teenaged Mary recognized the obvious differences between her new home in Cincinnati and her New York City roots, such as population numbers, climate, and the sympathetic leanings many Cincinnatians had for the South, she must have felt the loss of friends and the academic studies she had pursued so diligently. Compared to her female contemporaries, Mary was highly educated for a young woman of the day and particularly in Cincinnati, where "Girls' schools, while not ignoring the more abstruse studies like history, philosophy, languages, and the sciences, paid particular attention to those ornamental accomplishments which peculiarly suited the feminine temperament, the ability to paint on velvet, to construct wax fruit, flowers, and trees, and to accompany [oneself] on the piano [as] of more use to the young plutocracy of Cincinnati than algebra and natural philosophy."[28]

The Cincinnati she joined was not far from the anxieties and sorrows of the Civil War, and she knew that fortifications to protect the city were constructed across the river in Kentucky. Steamboats and paddle-wheelers jostled for docking space at the cobblestone landing near the candle and lard oil manufacturing plant of the Emery family and the warehouses and factories that provided a booming economy. The elegant residences along downtown streets, such as those on Fourth that stretched ten or twelve blocks from Nicholas Longworth's Federal-style mansion, known as Belmont, to the western extremity and its townhouses, appeared similar to those in New York and Brooklyn. Mary could attend theater productions, concerts, lectures, even art classes in Cincinnati, as well as visit a museum of natural curiosities. Sculptors and painters found ready patronage, particularly for portraits. Prominent artists working in Cincinnati when Mary Hopkins arrived were James Beard (1811–1893), Thomas C. Lindsay (1839–1907), Charles T. Webber (1825–1911), and Alexander H. Wyant (1836–1892), who contributed to the eminence of the city as one of America's centers of art and culture, vying with Philadelphia, Boston, and New York. The vitality and achievements of Cincinnati were appropriate for its stature as the most populous city west of the Alleghenies at the onset of the Civil War. Mary Hopkins spent her childhood and early adolescence in the nation's largest metropolis; she left for one of the few cities of cultural substance apart from the eastern seaboard. There she would marry and live her remaining years.

CHAPTER 2

Building the Emery Empire

W HEN EDWARD, Prince of Wales, visited Cincinnati in September 1860, he attended services in St. John's Church at Seventh and Plum Streets It was then the most prestigious Episcopal church in the city. In this church, Mary Muhlenberg Hopkins and Thomas J. Emery, scion of the Emery family, were married on May 24, 1866[1] at 8:30 in the evening. Mary's wedding dress may have been her mother's, for its elegant style dates from the late 1830s. Although the bride's petite figure (she was of medium height with narrow waist and small hands) dressed in shining white satin[2] captured the attention of friends and family, Mary's demure and retiring nature never called attention to herself. This shyness continued throughout her life. An engraved card welcomed well-wishers to the Emery's home at 301 West Fourth Street from 9:00 to 11:30 following the wedding.[3] The Emerys left for Europe on an extended honeymoon lasting nearly one year, a lengthy trip often taken by wealthy newlyweds.

Cincinnati was little aware of the significance this alliance would have for the city in the twentieth century. Other events in the spring of 1866, such as the fire that destroyed Pike's Opera House, the cholera epidemic that took 2,028 lives, and the construction of the Jewish temple at Plum and Eighth Streets attracted more attention.

Just after the Civil War, J. Howard Emery, the youngest brother of Thomas, fostered family interest in land purchases across the country as

Thomas J. Emery (1830–1906), husband of Mary M. Hopkins, c. 1880–1885 (Courtesy Children's Hospital, Cincinnati)

well as real estate development in Cincinnati. By his aggressive tactics and ability to evaluate the value of a potential purchase, Howard Emery set the tone for the family's future, basing its growing prosperity on land and buildings and removing some of the dependence on candles and lard oil. Howard wrote from San Francisco to Thomas on June 17, 1866, excited about the purchases he had made in the "best part of downtown," on Post and Mason Streets. His letter began, however, with regrets that he could not attend the wedding of Mary and Thomas on May 24. "Knowing that you will be anxious to hear from me and be advised of that which I have done here, I venture to address you at Paris, although I am unacquainted with the proposed date of your arrival there. I have been shown your wedding cards by Mr. Rooks, but as yet have received none myself. I regret exceedingly that I could not have been present when you and Mary were married, but regret is useless. Give your wife my love and say that I intend writing to her before long."[4] In Turin, Italy, towards the end of their European trip, the Emery's first child, Sheldon, was born on March 18, 1867. Thomas and Mary then returned home to West Fourth Street. Albert, the second son, was born on September 21, 1868, in Cincinnati and was baptized in Christ Church, the Gothic Revival edifice at the opposite end of Fourth Street.[5] Mary became a communicant of that church sometime before 1870, and thereafter it was the most significant focus of her charitable activities until 1906.

In the 1870s, as the Emery real estate holdings grew, Mary, Thomas, and their two sons made frequent trips to Europe. Photographs were made of Sheldon in London (in 1871 when he was four years old) and Albert in Paris (in 1872), for the proud parents and doting grandmother, Mrs. Richard Hopkins. Mary's mother remained in Cincinnati after her husband's death and lived with the Emery's at 357 West Fourth Street after

Dress worn by Mary M. Hopkins at her wedding to Thomas J. Emery in Cincinnati, May 24, 1866 (Courtesy Cincinnati Art Museum)

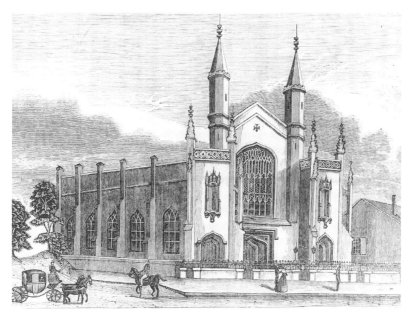

Christ Church, Cincinnati, c. 1850, Mary M. Emery's religious home during her lifetime (Courtesy Cincinnati Historical Society)

1876. Extended travel did not keep Thomas J. Emery unaware of advantageous land and building purchases. More and more in the decade of the 1870s, the Emery brothers shrewdly perceived that housing, as investment opportunities, would turn a good profit. They saw that housing, especially for those of modest means, could be reliable rentals in some apartment buildings they erected, while other renters required more amenities and better locations in their apartment choices. The Emerys were also aware that major cities like Cincinnati had far too many slums and inadequate homes for the large numbers of wage earners, immigrants, and former agricultural workers who moved to the cities after the Civil War. Emery housing at first targeted Cincinnati's low-income renters, but, as their business prospered, they enlarged the class of renters.

In the last decades of the nineteenth century, the Emery real estate empire flourished, largely due to a keenly perceived market, tight control in a family-owned-and-managed business, and prudent investments. As an

Albert (left) and Sheldon Emery, the two children of Mary M. and Thomas J. Emery, c. 1878 (Courtesy Lela Emery Steele)

eager scout for property to purchase, J. Howard Emery appeared in Denver in 1870 and recognized the potential profit in owning land in the Capitol Hill district. Forty acres bought from Henry Crow in the Emery name was later divided into residential lots, then "regarded as the choicest residence section of Denver."[6] The Emery clan held firm in their belief that good housing could be profitable for them. In 1872, the three Emery brothers refined the partnership that was formed in 1859, signing a new agreement and continuing "Thomas Emery's Sons."[7]

Cincinnati was surprised in 1877 by the audacity of Thomas and his brother John, when they built the Emery Arcade and Hotel. Erected at Fifth and Vine Streets and extending through the block to Race Street, the arcade's innovative combination of shops and hotel became a showplace. Seventy shops within a street-level arcade were clustered below offices in a skylighted building of four stories that was joined to a hotel of 176 rooms. The Emerys wisely sited their arcade at the soon-to-be commercial center of Cincinnati, adjacent to Market Square (now Fountain Square).

Brother Howard played a small role in the business by this date, only five years after he joined the partnership. His aggressive leadership in acquiring properties withered under an apparent mental illness. His sister Kezia wrote to her brother Thomas about her concern for "poor Howard" noting that she was "glad he is able to go about and that he enjoys his travels so fully." She added that she was sending "another kind of globules, recommended for softening of the brain," and offered an admonition: "I hope you and Mary enjoyed your visit to California and that the rest and recreation it afforded you will prove beneficial. I am glad to hear such good accounts of the progress of Sheldon and Albert in their studies. I know you will not allow them to apply themselves at the expense of their health." She concluded with gratitude, noting that her interest in additional real estate development was ended, now that the arcade and hotel were completed. "Dear Papa was blessed beyond most in the acquisition of property; on us devolves more the duty and obligation of spending judiciously; we have to fulfill the work left uncompleted by those who have gone before us to the heavenly world."[8]

As Thomas J. Emery's business and real estate holdings expanded dramatically in the 1870s, Mary focused on her family and on a few selected charities. Her home on West Fourth Street was close to her mother-in-law's, where her husband's brothers, John J. and J. Howard, lived until their mother's death in 1876. Children living with their elders as the Emerys did, was not unusual. Mary's mother, Mrs. Richard Hopkins, lived with her daughter from 1876 to 1893.

Mary and Thomas's home life with their children can only be surmised, but a scrapbook inscribed "Albert Emery / Xmas 1879 / from / Mama" doc-

Mary M. Emery in a mantilla, c. 1875–1880 (Courtesy Mariemont Preservation Foundation)

uments one charming episode from childhood recorded by Mary's son.[9] An evening of fun and games beginning on March 18, 1878, at "Emery's Hall," presumably the family's residence, was published in a handbill posted in Albert's scrapbook. He and another lad, J. F. Kerr, functioned as treasurer and manager, respectively, for a week-long "Grand Entertainment." Albert starred as the attorney in the theatrical production, *The Colored Witness*, with admission of five cents charged for the event that would include tricks, songs, and a magic lantern showing of a hundred pictures. Doors opened at four o'clock, and the professionally printed handbill concluded: "The Hall is perfumed with Dr. Price's Perfumers."[10] Albert's exuberant showmanship, so charmingly evidenced in this theatrical, demonstrated itself in a darker, tragic way in a sledding accident years later.

Mary's interest in art, richly demonstrated in the last two decades of her life, first evidenced itself in the year of the Emery Arcade opening in 1877, when a dedicated and enthusiastic group of ladies, the Women's Art Museum Association, single-mindedly organized themselves to establish an art museum and training school for art. The association resulted from the success of Cincinnati's representation at the Centennial Exposition of 1876, a celebratory fair held in Philadelphia and directed by Alfred T. Goshorn, a talented entrepreneur who became the first director of the Cincinnati Art Museum after its founding in 1881. Mary Emery joined the Association in 1877 and continued her membership until the group disbanded in 1886, lending her name as the wife of one of the city's leading businessmen. She did not have great wealth in her own name, and she had no art collection, but she joined other fine old families of Cincinnati in "an effort to awaken and cultivate an interest in the establishment of such an undertaking [the Cincinnati Art Museum], with Schools for training in the fine and industrial arts, and thus provide here at home the means which shall raise the general standard of taste, and in time give us our own skilled designers and workmen."[11]

As the Women's Art Museum Association encouraged interest in their goal, they sponsored lectures to educate Cincinnatians on the importance of establishing an art museum based on the model of the South Kensington Museum, London (now the Victoria and Albert Museum). They also held frequent meetings and exhibitions, such as the special viewing of works of art exhibited in May 1878 at the residence of John Cochnower, 166 West Seventh Street, with objects lent by many of the first families of Cincinnati, including Mrs. Thomas J. Emery, Mrs. Larz Anderson, Joseph Longworth, Mrs. James Gamble, Mrs. John Shillito, John Twachtman, Thomas Buchanan Read, William Fry, Thomas S. Noble, Mrs. G. K. Schoenberger, and George Nichols. Held in connection with the city's renowned May Festival, the second oldest choral music event in the United States, it was the "ladies belief [that] such exhibition would give new force to the aspirations and purposes for art in the city."[12]

Cincinnati society eagerly supported art and music early in the nineteenth century. The plan to found the Cincinnati Art Museum was a landmark accomplishment, inspired by women and consummated by men.

Mary and Thomas moved easily among Cincinnati's patricians, who were covered eagerly by the society columnists. A reporter attending a party in May 1880 at the Emery home at 357 West Fourth Street raved over the floral displays of roses, lilies, and smilax hung in festoons from the chandeliers, while admiring the "polite servants" who assisted guests from their carriages. Mary, her mother, and her sister, Isabella Hopkins, received guests in the front parlor, "making a trio of ladies of rare dignity," with Mary wearing a "toilet" of white satin with long train and joined by her husband in full evening dress. The guests that May evening, including Mr. and Mrs. Larz Anderson, Judge and Mrs. Alphonso Taft, Mr. and Mrs. George Schoenberger, and Mrs. Aaron Perry, each played a role in the art museum's future, but not at a level equaling Mary's eventual commitment.

The beginning of the 1880s augured well for the Emery brothers and for Mary. Thomas and John Emery shrewdly planned to expand their investment in Cincinnati's housing market while continuing to operate their income-rich oil and candle factory near the river. Good, low-cost housing was never plentiful in nineteenth-century Cincinnati, with overcrowding in tenements encouraged by the city's restraining topography. But, as the city extended its streets out to the suburbs of Clifton, Mount Auburn, and Walnut Hills, streetcars reached growing neighborhoods. Workers found it easier to live beyond comfortable walking distance to their factories, shops, and warehouses. By 1888, seventeen horse-drawn streetcar lines served Cincinnati. The Emerys wisely bought land and erected apartments along these arteries. Their renters were not the city's poor, but wage earners and those of modest means. Downtown remained the fashionable and handiest address, however, with Fourth Street "the Broadway of Cincinnati, running from the aristocratic East End to the railroad environed West End. Several blocks on Fourth Street are of such solid and lofty structure that they remind one of the substantial magnificence of New York."[13] On that street, in 1881, the Emery's Lombardy Apartments opened at number 322, an early example of multi-family living units rising seven floors behind an elaborate façade of applied columns and pedimented windows. Cincinnati's leading architect, Samuel Hannaford, was its designer, and the young lawyer William Howard Taft set-

Edgecliffe, Cincinnati, home of Mary M. and Thomas J. Emery, designed by Samuel Hannaford, built in 1881, demolished in 1987 (Courtesy Cincinnati Historical Society)

tled in as one of its first residents in apartment 25. The future president of the United States resided there from 1883 until his marriage in 1886.

Hannaford turned his hand again in 1881 to design the Emery's new residence, Edgecliffe, a rusticated gray stone mansion of baronial proportions (thirty-one rooms) commanding a position overlooking the Ohio River in East Walnut Hills.[14] A protecting porte cochere guarded heavy metal and glass doors that led into a white marble foyer, centered with a fountain. A spacious main parlor, a glassed-in sunroom with a spectacular river view, and a wood-paneled dining room opened off the foyer. Benn Pitman (1821–1910) and William Fry (1830–1929), Cincinnati's premier

Aerial view of Edgecliffe and grounds (*Courtesy* Cincinnati Enquirer)

wood-carvers, executed the dining suite of furniture and the wall reliefs, reputedly taking seven years to carve the oak buffet. Looking up to the skylight three floors above, a second floor balcony surrounded the atrium and opened to bedrooms and sitting rooms. Servants occupied the top-most floor, except for the carriage drivers and stable hands, who lived above the massive carriage house just inside the main gate to Edgecliffe. The grounds boasted a greenhouse to supply Edgecliffe with the fresh flowers so dear to Mary.

With the opening of the Lombardy in 1881, Thomas and John began two decades of aggressive land acquisition and construction of residential or apartment buildings in Cincinnati, as well as hotels and offices. The Palace Hotel opened on September 5, 1882, at the corner of Sixth and Vine Streets, reputedly in answer to Thomas J. Emery's perception that hotel rooms at the Burnet and Gibson were too costly (as much as $3.00

or $3.50 per day with meals). He charged only $2.00 daily for the same amenities at the Palace. Hannaford again served as architect, becoming the favored designer for Thomas Emery's Sons and conceiving a building with European flair unlike anything yet seen in Cincinnati. Its eight floors made it the tallest structure in town, while its sophisticated French Second Empire style and mansard roof evoked images of faraway Paris. Emery and Hannaford perfected the apartment building of the 1880s and 1890s, with the same architect designing at least two more buildings, the Brittany (1885) and the Saxony (1891) for his patrons. By 1891, however, the Emerys retained the firm of Johann B. and Joseph G. Steinkamp as "house" architects. One of the Steinkamp's best efforts, producing a handsome blend of classical motifs in the decoration of the façade, was the Norfolk (1891).[15] Thomas and John developed a management system that integrated all aspects of their real estate business, including land purchases, architects, construction, rentals, and maintenance, under one tightly controlled partnership. To the praise they received for their business acumen, the brothers added admiration for producing the first truly fireproof office structure in the city, the St. Paul's building. Built on the site of old St. Paul's Church in 1884, the brothers maintained their offices there until they moved to their new Mercantile Library Building in 1902. Many of the city's best buildings were the Emery's: quality structures, even luxurious by the standards of Victorian Cincinnati, with each sited to take advantage of public transportation and favorable locations.

The two sons of Thomas and Mary Emery reached adolescence in the 1880s, and Sheldon was sent to the exclusive St. Paul's School, an Episcopal institution in Concord, New Hampshire, in 1882. Albert followed one year later. With their children away and the Emery interests thriving, Mary and her husband increased their involvement with charitable causes, particularly Christ Church, where Thomas joined the endowment committee,[16] serving the church his wife would bless so magnificently in the next century. Church work benefited from Mary's time, her husband's money, and even Mary's fine soprano voice when she performed in a musicale in Walnut Hills that also engaged the young artist John Twachtman to design the evening's program.[17] In 1882, Thomas Emery's Sons also

*Sheldon Emery
(1867–1890), elder son of
Mary M. and Thomas J.
Emery, c. 1882 (Courtesy
Lela Emery Steele)*

joined the generous subscribers to a fund generated by Charles West to construct the original building of the Cincinnati Art Museum, giving $1,000 to the campaign to match West's challenge gift of $150,000. The challenge was met by Cincinnatians in only one month. The museum that would be so dear to Mary's heart decades later was assured of a home.

In 1883, the Emerys began their long record of involvement with children's health with a second-hand contact. Cincinnati, like most other cities in the nation at that time, had no hospital or medical facility especially focused on the care and treatment of children. Young patients in Cincinnati were treated along with adults in regular wards, with no specialized pediatric attention. Recognizing the need for a more sympathetic response, Mrs. Robert Dayton approached Isabella Hopkins, Mary Emery's sister, for help in starting a hospital for children. They sought advice from their Episcopal bishop, Thomas A. Jaggar, who told them to solicit their friends for help. By November 16, 1883, the Hospital of the Protestant Episcopal Church in the Diocese of Southern Ohio was formed. A large frame residence in East Walnut Hills was acquired by March 1884 as the first home of the new hospital, no doubt resulting from funds supplied by Thomas and Mary Emery.[18] The twelve beds, a housekeeper, a nurse, and volunteer services of four local physicians gave way four years later when the Emery brothers Thomas and John joined in presenting land and building for a spacious new hospital. On one acre of land in the Mount Auburn neighborhood, the Emerys raised a three-story brick building that opened on November 23, 1887. They imposed only two conditions: no patients could be discriminated against because of race, creed, or color; and the poorest patients must receive the same good care as any others. From these humble beginnings and continuing shepherding by the Episcopal Church, Children's Hospital evolved.[19] Mrs. Emery's support never waned thereafter.

Albert Thomas Emery (1868–1884), younger son of Mary M. and Thomas J. Emery, c. 1882 (Courtesy Lela Emery Steele)

Isabella Frances Hopkins
(1848–1935), sister of
Mary M. Emery, 1892
(Courtesy Lelea Emery Steele)

A sorrowful blow struck the thirty-nine-year-old Mary Emery, in February 1884 when Albert was injured in a sledding accident at St. Paul's School.

> Another serious accident resulted from the fine coasting in this city, Saturday afternoon [February 2]. A party of St. Paul's School students were coasting on the "Tebbetts Hill", so-called, near the School, and one of the number, Albert Thomas Emery, of Cincinnati, Ohio, received injuries which will in all probability be fatal. Young Emery and three fellow students were coming down the hill on a double runner, at the time of the accident, he being the rear one on the sled. By some means the sled tipped over when going very fast, throwing the boys forward upon the snow. Emery's head struck with force just above the right temple upon the point of a runner of a single sled which was being drawn up the hill, and his skull was badly fractured. Dr. Crosby and Dr. Marden were quickly summoned, and rendered all possible surgical aid. Portions of the brain matter exuded constantly, and Saturday evening it seemed as if the boy could

live but for a short time. Sunday morning Dr. Potter, of the Massachusetts General Hospital, was telegraphed for, and came on the afternoon train. He succeeded in removing several splinters of bone from the brain. A parallel case, so far as the character of the wound is concerned, is the noted one where a drill passed through a man's head, a number of years ago, the man surviving the injury. The injured boy is 15 years of age. He entered the School at the beginning of this school year, and has a brother in the School who entered the year previous.[20]

As soon as news of the accident reached them, the parents left for Concord on Saturday night, February 2, and arrived at Albert's bedside while the lad was still conscious. There they remained, while telegrams and news accounts spread westward to Cincinnati detailing Albert's declining condition, until his death on February 11.[21] Heartbroken, the parents left Concord on February 12 and accompanied the body to their home. Albert was buried in the family plot at Spring Grove Cemetery.

Children's Hospital, Mount Auburn Avenue, Cincinnati, c. 1887 (Courtesy Children's Hospital, Cincinnati)

CHAPTER 3

Death's Legacy and Charles J. Livingood

T HE DECADE OF 1880–1890 was one of prosperity and expansion for the Emery interests, especially in their real estate holdings. One year after Albert's death in 1884, Thomas helped organize the Cincinnati, Lebanon, and Northern Railroad, serving on its board of directors. Lard oil and candle sales increased handsomely, and a new and expanded factory site was found in 1887,[1] abandoning Water Street for the area called Ivorydale, north of the city and near the soap works of the Procter & Gamble Company.

The family circle decreased when J. Howard Emery dropped from the partnership due to mental illness. Traveling as a salesman of Emery candles, Howard bought properties wherever his sales contacts took him. Kansas City, Denver, and San Francisco were targeted, with purchases in those cities alarming his brothers. But, as early as 1877, Howard showed signs of mental illness, and an agent hired by the Emerys was sent out from Cincinnati to confer with him. He reported "the astounding information that Howard had become at least temporarily demented."[2] His illness ended his land acquisition activities that once brought important properties into the Emery empire, and, in 1886, Howard Emery died in an English sanatorium. But as one Emery's life ended, it seemed that another's would ensure the continuation of the dynasty. Sheldon Emery, having entered Harvard University in 1884 with the class of 1888, failed to graduate and

Charles J. Livingood (1866–1952), photographed at age 28 by Landy, Cincinnati, February 6, 1892 (Courtesy Elizabeth Livingood McGuire)

returned to Cincinnati sometime during his 1886–1887 year while enrolled in the law school.[3]

The surviving son of Mary and Thomas J. Emery was expected to enter the family business after graduation from college. Having failed in his educational accomplishment, the shy twenty-one year-old joined Thomas Emery's Sons as a chemist and lived at the family home, Edgecliffe. The city's cultural opportunities attracted him, and he joined the Literary Club, a men's group dedicated to weekly meetings and scholarly papers prepared and read by members.[4] His work desk was ready for him in the St. Paul's Building, and his father would prepare him for his future responsibilities. He was then the only male member of the generation after his father and uncle. In 1889, his Uncle John was unmarried and lived in New York City, distancing himself from his brother in geography but not decision making. The two financiers and developers wrote daily to each other, conferring and agreeing on every acquisition or construction project. Their partnership was close. It relied not only on blood relationship but also on respect for the other's keen moneymaking abilities.

John J. Emery's intended bachelorhood ended with the death of his nephew Sheldon Emery, the only heir to the family fortune, on October 26, 1890. Returning to Cincinnati after attending a wedding in Detroit and a business meeting in Dayton, Sheldon fell ill and was treated unsuccessfully by the family physician, Dr. T. C. Bradford. He died at Edgecliffe in his mother's arms. "A young man of most exemplary habits, strongly endowed with all of the energy and careful, discriminating ways of his father, the senior of that firm that has done so much for the building up of Cincinnati, the Thomas Emery's Sons. Sheldon Emery died last night [Sunday, October 26] at 6 o'clock at the family residence, Edgecliffe, after an illness of two days."[5]

The local newspapers immediately reported "a natural curiosity in the city to know what will become of the large Emery estate, now that the only heir is dead."[6] A poignant "Memorial," published by the Literary Club and read at their meeting on November 15, 1890, reported Sheldon's retiring "mental and social habit," noting that he was "beginning to take upon himself the successful management of large business affairs, for which opportunity had been afforded in his father's office."

Following Sheldon's burial at Spring Grove Cemetery under the Emery monument, letters and telegrams were sent to friends and relatives with the sad news. A Harvard classmate of Sheldon's, working in the snowdrifts of the Colorado Rockies as a surveyor, received one of the announcements and wrote to the grieving mother on November 11, 1890.

> My poor Mrs. Emery:
>   You will pardon, I know, my addressing you thus, for surely my heart at this moment goes out to you as to my own Mother, a heart full of sorrow and deepest sympathy. Oh, if only I dared believe that I might be of the smallest comfort to you now—the least part of what you have been, sometimes unwittingly perhaps, to me in my darkest hours! I indulged this hope in the message of yesterday, brusquely expressed though it was. Your letter, reaching me so late, seemed to require a speedy answer. I hastened to the nearest station and tried to say what I would now: that you have only to command me. I might hope to make myself useful (pardon this cruel intrusion of business!), but whatever

becomes of the proposition I shall ever cherish the memory at such a time you thought of my welfare.[7]

With these comforting words, Charles Jacob Livingood, perhaps not so unwittingly, signaled the beginning of a new career that brought him employment with the Emery interests and eventually a place by the side of Mary M. Emery as advisor, manager, surrogate son, and dear friend. Following the death of Thomas J. Emery, and for the last twenty-one years of Mary's life, Livingood was a solicitous, caring presence who guided her in almost every endeavor she undertook. The life story of Mary Emery is intertwined, after 1906, with that of Charles Livingood.

Livingood's heritage, education, and interests prepared him well for his future role. His family descended from Jakob Lowenguth, an Alsatian who emigrated to America in 1710. Charles J. Livingood's father was a prosperous lawyer and real estate developer in Reading, Pennsylvania, where Charles was born on February 6, 1866. Educated in the city's public schools and at Shortlidge's Academy in Media, Pennsylvania, he entered Harvard University in the autumn of 1884 in the class of 1888.[8] "I took the Academic course graduating 'cum laude' in English Literature, History, and Philosophy. Under such men as Bocher, Hart, Briggs, Wendell, Macvane, Hill, Moore, Childs, Taussig, Boyce, my regular studies included the Languages, Literature, Art, Political Economy, History, Psychology, and Philosophy but I also got much from William James, Shaler, and best of all, both in class room and out from George Herbert Palmer. I owe much too to Norton, Edward Everett Hale, and Phillips Brooks."[9]

In a recollection delivered as a paper read before the Literary Club fifty years after graduation, Livingood told of the two professors he most admired, the eminent Hale and Brooks. "It is significant that both these men took an humble place as college preachers even though attendance on chapel was voluntary or perhaps because of this very fact. There were many vacant pews mornings in Appleton Chapel in my day but never on Sundays or the weekday mornings when either Brooks or Hale preached. Indeed, Brooks is reported as saying that he would rather be an influence in a college than become a Bishop."[10]

Two other professors who impressed Livingood were Charles Eliot Norton and Charles Herbert Moore. The former encouraged Livingood's study of art, although formal instruction in the field of art history as known and taught in the twentieth century was missing from the curriculum. In his autobiographical paper read before the Literary Club of Cincinnati, Livingood complained of Norton's "desultory, destructive comments on the colors of our neckties and took all inspiration away from us by saying that the poetry of the day was merely the twitterings of birds and that architecture, especially modern buildings, gave him a pain. He did not say where. He himself was notoriously up in the clouds in his thoughts about Art, a great admirer of the insane, always wrong, John Ruskin." Professor Frederic Ward Putnam's lectures in anthropology and archeology introduced Livingood to the study of early man, an interest he would pursue throughout his life. Little did the college freshman dream that the site of his professor's earlier excavations (the prehistoric Madisonville site east of Cincinnati) would be the very spot where Livingood's most significant collaborative work with Mary Emery would be realized in the next century.

At Harvard, Livingood participated in Hasty Pudding performances and developed a facility for languages, especially French. While the class of 1888 included sons of eminent families such as Adams, Choate, Cabot, and Paine, Livingood's friendship with Sheldon Emery led to his life's work. The two men lived in adjoining houses on the Cambridge campus, and together they spent vacations hunting and fishing in the Maine woods. Following graduation, Livingood encouraged his father to support him for a year's period of European travel and study. In December 1888, he enrolled as *étudiant de lettres* at the Sorbonne. In Paris, his fluency in French admitted him to lectures by noted professors and led him to a first meeting and eventual friendship with the French poet and Nobel laureate, Frédéric Mistral (1830–1914). Livingood lovingly recollected his Sorbonne period as "my golden days," picturing the buildings he saw from his window in the Gran Hotel du Perigord on an engraved bookplate used in his extensive personal library. By February 1889, he was convinced that his poor eyesight limited his study, and he embarked on a ramble through Italy, France, and Spain, finishing with a visit to the Paris Exposition.[11] Livingood's *Wanderjahr* introduced him to villages and housing projects of interest especially to his father, who had erected more than three hundred homes in the Reading area and no doubt thought that his son would return, perhaps with a law degree eventually, to assist in the family real estate ventures.[12]

His return to the United States was reluctant. His eyesight was failing, so he thought outdoor work might be helpful. First he tried the electrical business and, in the spring of 1890, he became a surveyor in the plains and mountains of Colorado. Soon he was cured of his eye problems.[13] On the way west to his new job with the Denver and Rio Grande Railroad, working on the construction of the Moffatt Tunnel and Colorado's Utero Canal, Livingood stopped in Cincinnati to visit his friend Sheldon Emery. An offer of employment with Thomas Emery's Sons probably occurred then, for Livingood referred in his sympathy letter to Mrs. Emery about "the proposition" and his appreciation of her thinking of his "welfare." While visiting Mrs. Emery and Sheldon, he enjoyed an introduction to a leading citizen of Cincinnati, future president William Howard Taft, who was encountered "pushing a baby carriage—and in the buggy was Robert A. Taft, now U.S. Senator."[14] Moving on to Colorado, the rigors of work on a surveying team soon encouraged the twenty-four-year-old to look elsewhere.[15] He began work in November 1890 with Thomas Emery's Sons, a blessing for him and for Mary Emery.

Livingood's employment with the Emerys started at the bottom of the ladder in a large-scale real estate and development company, earning him a modest salary as an assistant outside man under John H. Hall. For the next fifteen years, he supervised the papering and painting of flats and the collection of rents. The Cincinnati landscape changed as neighborhoods sprouted magnificent apartment buildings—the Alexandra, Haddon Hall, Cumberland, Navarre, Clermont, and Verona—all erected by Thomas and John J. Emery, with Livingood assuming more and more managerial responsibilities. The widespread Emery empire required many of Livingood's quickly learned supervisory skills, and his travels ranged from a ranch of 100,000 acres in the Texas panhandle to a small town near Portsmouth, Virginia, to a housing development in Denver, all while he kept an eye on the numerous Emery holdings in Cincinnati. He lived with

Mary and Thomas Emery at Edgecliffe through 1891, then moved to a boardinghouse at 133 Broadway in 1892, and a shared apartment at 65 West Fourth Street from October of that year to April 1893.[16] These four rooms on the third floor were practically indistinguishable from an under-graduate's housing at Harvard—the walls hung with plaster casts of the Acropolis *Venus Tying Her Sandal* and a photograph of the Leaning Tower of Pisa, dark oak bookcases crammed with matching sets of books, Orien-tal rugs scattered over sisal carpeting, class pictures on dressers, and a bust of Praxiteles's sculpture, *Hermes,* from the Olympia Museum. "Here's to 65—God bless her," Livingood wrote on a photograph illustrating the apartment he shared with two friends, known only as White and William.[17]

In the last decade of the nineteenth century, Mary and Thomas Emery continued their relatively private lives, with Mary turning more actively to her church. In 1891, a liberal movement of sorts at Christ Church enlisted her and her sister's signature on a letter questioning the voting policy that permitted only pew holders to vote for the vestry.[18] Mary again spoke out regarding the government of her church in 1898, when a group of forty-five parishioners, the largest in church history, met and urged the hiring of a new rector, with Mary submitting a three-part plan to raise pew rents and make them equal in cost, to form a committee to solicit funds to retire the deficit, and to reconsider the merger plan with St. Paul's Church. By her initiation of this proposal, Mary Emery showed she could be fired with enthusiasm and common sense. At this time, Christ Church was the "richest Episcopal church in the West."[19] Its members included many of Cincinnati's leading families, the Larz Andersons, the William Cooper Procters, and the Thomas Emerys, to name a few of the 1,200 parishioners. To memorialize their lost sons, Mary and Thomas Emery pre-sented to Christ Church in 1892 a bronze baptismal font in the form of a kneeling angel.[20] This sculpture and Mary's reform plans supplemented the Emerys' substantial financial support of the church in the century's last years. The selection of Frank H. Nelson as rector of Christ Church in 1899 positioned this kindly, hard-working minister to be future spiritual advisor to Mrs. Emery, his influence second only to Livingood's after 1906.

Apartment of Charles J. Livingood, 65 West Fourth Street, Cincinnati, 1892–1893
(Courtesy Cincinnati Historical Society)

Nelson, born in 1869, was a contemporary of Charles Livingood and grad-uated in 1886 from St. Paul's School, where Sheldon and Albert Emery attended. Finishing at Hobart College in 1890, he matriculated at the General Theological Seminary, New York City, and became an Episcopal priest in 1897. St. George's Church, New York, was his first assignment before his calling to Cincinnati. By then, Christ Church was the preemi-nent Episcopal church in the city, larger and wealthier than both St. John's and St. Paul's. Nelson married Mary Eaton, the daughter of the Cincinnati portrait painter Joseph Oriel Eaton, in 1907, and headed Christ Church until his retirement in 1939.[21] During the years of his min-istry until Mrs. Emery's death, he quietly encouraged her gifts to many Episcopal philanthropies.

The 1890s noted a contact, minor to be sure, between Mary Emery and the Cincinnati Art Museum, but one heralding her future interest in col-

lecting art. The museum's assistant director Joseph Henry Gest
(1859–1935) may have dreamed that the wealthy mistress of Edgecliffe
might some day become a serious, dedicated art collector when he wrote
in the autumn of 1892 and apologized for the week's delay in responding
to her letter inviting him to call and see "the two paintings and the watercolors". He added: "I am quite sure we shall be glad to have them."[22] Presumably these were proposed gifts for the museum, open only six years in
its new Romanesque Revival style building designed by Cincinnati architect James McLaughlin and sited in Eden Park, not far from the Emerys'
Edgecliffe home. The proposed but unknown gifts were initial, tentative
entries in the costly and high-powered arena of collectors and dealers that
Mary Emery would experience only after her husband's death. But most
importantly, this first exchange of letters began a professional relationship,
even a warm friendship, with Gest (who would become director in 1902
and serve until 1929) as patient advisor and Mrs. Emery playing Maece-
nas.

Mary's interest in collecting art was minor before 1907, although hesi-
tant forays were made with a few purchases, unknown today. Only her
acquisition in 1870 of Alexandre Calame's *Sycamore Trees*, primarily to
decorate the walls of Edgecliffe, is recorded. Her choice of this Swiss
painter's work does not foretell the selection of masterpieces in her collection formed in the twentieth century. Gest was tantalized with the possibility of helping form a collection of outstanding merit in Cincinnati, but
he was cautious in recommending artists or dealers. "Mrs. Thane Miller
telephoned to me this morning concerning a Mr. Howland who seems to
have used my name as endorsing certain pictures he is offering for sale. I
think she said you had bought something. I am sorry if this be the case,
unless the pictures commended themselves to you by their own merit, for I
have not the faintest recollection of having seen them, nor do I recall Mr.
Howland, and I certainly did not authorize the use of my name."[23] The
walls of Edgecliffe, "the best decorated residence in Cincinnati," according to a reporter who visited the home in 1896, were impressive for their
colors, not for their art. After praising a painted ceiling by Vollmer (the
only art mentioned) the writer visited room after room, first recording the

*Joseph Henry Gest
(1859–1935), director
of the Cincinnati Art
Museum (1902–1929)
and principal art advisor
to Mary M. Emery,
c. 1930 (Courtesy Cincinnati
Art Museum)*

small vestibule or reception room in "modern Colonial style, in monotone ecru effect." The hall was covered by aluminum leaf, painted over with red and finally covered with a stenciled pattern. The Emerys' music room, the largest room in the house, was in "Renaissance style in soft green and cream tones, with only occasionally accessory colors, such as are given in delicate flowery tracery and the two small figure panels on the ceiling." In the reporter's last view of the Moorish-style library, he praised the Spanish tile fireplace and the "look of the Alhambra."[24]

Recognizing that the loss of Sheldon Emery precluded a male inheritor of Thomas Emery's Sons, at least until—and if—the recently married John J. Emery produced a son who could head the company, the two brothers and their wives, "knowing the uncertainty of life . . . and with the acquiescence of their wives," executed an agreement with terms that settled the estates and survivors' interests in operating the company after the death of one partner. The 1895 agreement stipulated specifically "that in case of death of one of the Emerys [Thomas J. or John J.] the survivor is to have the full charge, control and management for the benefit of himself and the representatives of the deceased of all of the firm or joint property for the term of five (5) years after the death of the deceased."[25] Just as the present partnership was based on trust and respect for each other's expertise in developing their real estate and manufacturing enterprises, the future of the partnership would be under the control of the remaining Emery brother.

Careful planning characterized the Emerys' business philosophy. Their real estate strategy was to buy unimproved land, await a growth spurt in population in that area, and build to rent. One Cincinnati real estate expert stated that Thomas Emery "was the best-posted man on real estate values and possibilities, as well as the lay of the land, of any man in the city, and that the ink was never dry on a deed for property they bought before a spade was throwing dirt for a cellar."[26] By the turn of the century, the Emerys were the largest property owners in Cincinnati. They held on in periods of economic panic, persistently purchasing property to improve, always buying, never selling. Thomas and John also recognized the need to have competent managers and associates, requiring of them daily progress reports, supporting the almost daily exchange of letters between Thomas in Cincinnati and John in New York.

Although Cincinnati was central to the Emerys' business, and the company's holdings spread from east to west in the United States, the brothers recognized opportunities in Europe to sell candles for good profit. Global expansion held no terrors for the Emerys. Thomas stated in a newspaper interview in 1900 that business in Europe was good. He foresaw the ability of Cincinnati companies to compete worldwide, given the city's access to good transportation. Surprising the reporter, Thomas said that his Emery Candle Company sells more candles in Germany than in the State of Ohio, and candle sales in London surpass Cincinnati's. His home town was "the best point in which they [businesses in Cincinnati] could be located" to sell in Europe.[27]

Memories of their lost sons spurred both Thomas and Mary to donate funds to provide services, buildings, or programs to benefit children. The Protestant Episcopal Hospital in Mount Auburn, a gift of brothers Thomas and John Emery, was an impressive example of their generosity. Thomas was not as generous as Mary would be after his death in 1906, yet their joint gift of facilities for the Fresh Air Farm and Society epitomized the focus of later benefactions. Sometime before the annual meeting of the society in 1897, the members were informed by Mrs. Larz Anderson that a "gentleman friend who had long been a close watcher or looker of the society's movements, and interested to a degree of helpfulness, desired to purchase for the organization a Fresh Air or convalescent home of its own, or rather purchase some old farm suitable in adaptations and availabilities as to locations, size, farm and meadowland, woods, etc. not probably to exceed some twenty-five acres (ten of which must be in woodland) all of which necessarily must fill the best desires and needs of the Society as set forth by them."[28] The friend was Thomas J. Emery, and soon a suitable farm in the village of Terrace Park, fifteen miles east of Cincinnati, was purchased by him and deeded to the Fresh Air Farm and Society on January 24, 1898. He then became a trustee of the organization, a post Mary assumed after her husband's passing. In the warm months, the farm functioned as a refuge for indigent women and their children, mostly brought in from riverfront areas of Cincinnati and other poor neighborhoods. They were guests on a working farm but contributed some services in housekeeping, raising vegetables, and tending orchards and livestock. The Fresh Air Farm and Society embraced concepts of improved housing and care, however impermanent or briefly experienced, that would persist with Mary Emery in later years. A large brick farmhouse in solid Victorian style was the centerpiece of the property in a rolling, wooded landscape. For the opening on May 20, 1898, the Little Miami Railroad carried six passenger cars with visitors and dignitaries, including Mr. and Mrs. Emery, out to the farm to dedicate it and unveil a bronze plaque in the farmhouse entrance hall memorializing the Emery sons with engraved words foretelling Mary Emery's philosophy in giving.[29]

> We need not be missed if others succeed us
> To reap down those fields which in Spring we have sown.

He who plowed and who sowed is not missed by the reaper
He is only remembered by what he has done.

As the decade ended, there were sad events as well as pleasant ones for the Emerys. Thomas's sister Kezia, the oldest sibling, died in Italy on August 28, 1900, mourned by followers of the many Italian causes she supported.[30] A happier event a few years earlier was the wedding, on December 3, 1896, of Charles Livingood, now well established in Thomas Emery's Sons and already close to Thomas and Mary, to Lily Broadwell Foster, member of a distinguished Cincinnati family.[31] In the ten years that followed, Livingood's role in the company expanded while Thomas and Mary Emery embraced him as a son.

CHAPTER 4

The Widow Mary Emery

CINCINNATI RETAINED its sinewy vitality in 1900 as the new century dawned. It had dynamic industries in carriage-making, soap and meat by-products, brewing, printing inks, furniture, and yeast. Its level of culture exceeded that in most large American cities. An art museum in its handsome building in Eden Park and a symphony orchestra playing in Music Hall were hardly equaled in Chicago, Detroit, or St. Louis. Carry Nation came to Cincinnati in 1901 to fight the saloons that lined downtown streets, and the first reinforced concrete skyscraper in America rose on Fourth and Vine. Thanks to Boss George Cox, who ran Cincinnati's City Hall and politics, corruption and patronage reigned throughout the wards. Attractive neighborhoods were annexed to Cincinnati, places like Hyde Park, Bond Hill, and Roselawn. The city's prosperity and conservative character meshed with Thomas and John J. Emery's business philosophy: careful, calculating, and cognizant of people's needs.

President Theodore Roosevelt, as successor to the assassinated William McKinley, faced an age of business excesses and formidable trusts when he took office in 1901. The Emerys' Cincinnati pride blossomed when Nicholas Longworth II, member of the prominent Longworth family, married the President's daughter Alice in 1908. Roosevelt's zeal for social reforms appealed to Thomas Emery, for the latter was a reformer of sorts, a champion of African Americans, of orphans, and of the less fortunate. His efforts never approached Mary's, however, in scope and funding, although the seventy-year-old tycoon frequently answered the call with a "liberality and public spirit of one of the Queen City's foremost business men." He provided quarters in his Phoenix Building for the burned-out Cincinnati Gymnasium, and when the gymnasium's committee called on Thomas Emery, he "received the gentlemen cordially and, in the course of the conversation that ensued, told of the immense amount of good he had received when a former member of it. At that time Mr. Emery was quite an athlete, and stated that it was the proudest moment of his life when he could 'chin' himself on the parallel bars with one hand."[1]

Thomas's health, usually robust, began failing in 1901 when he suffered a tumor and operation on his jaw. This condition prompted winter excursions to North Africa, accompanied only by his valet, where he sought the dry Algerian desert at Biskra, southeast of Algiers. Emery claimed that the climate there permitted him "to escape the keen winds and frosts of America [and] in the city of Algiers the luxuries and amusements of European cities can be had."[2] Mary seldom travelled abroad with her husband after 1900 but remained quietly at home, making social calls and tentatively considering an art acquisition or two. Appealing to her were bronzes by America's most prominent sculptor, Augustus Saint-Gaudens (1848–1907), exhibited in 1902 at the Cincinnati Art Museum. The prices were reasonable, ranging from fifty dollars to $1,200, but she retreated from acquiring an example.

Thomas Emery's letter to "My Dearest Wife," written from Biskra, Algeria, in February 1902, records the close working partnership shared by him and his brother as well as his complaints about John J. Emery's attitude. The letter indicates, too, his willingness to give Mary some glimpse of his strategy as real estate investor.

> I have yours of 30th enclosing your father's letter of 1838. Do you wish it retd [sic]? It is a very good letter but not at all expansive for a letter written just before marriage. To travel in the days before RRS [railroads] was a different affair from present journeys. In all our buildings and purchases of land in Cinti, Joe [his brother, John J.] has always been consulted and he has approved. I was therefore surprised to hear him object to our building many flats. It is only

because they are profitable that we have built them. They pay 10½ to 12% in
this way with the Int [interest] on the [indecipherable] we shall get our money
back in 7½ to 8 years! If the good times continue for only five years we shall
have gotten so much of the cost that we can afford to meet a very low market
for rents. Joe highly approved of the Biagg [?] purchase, and when it was not
confirmed he equally approved the purchase of the lot on which Haddon Hall
[one of the Emerys' apartment buildings] is being erected. We all agree that we
cannot continue to build as we have been doing for the simple reason that
Cinti cannot support an indefinite number of flats. The lease of College [?] he
disliked. All this was open to him; he approved and wrote that the shops
underneath would bring in short time $4,000 each. We only calculated on
$3,000. The advance of taxes received after the lease was made. All supposed
that the appraisement of RE [real estate] was fixed for 10 years so that when
$73,000 was added to the valuation of College property, it was a surprise to
everybody. This advance makes the lease undesirable; and had we supposed
such a thing possible we never would have entered into the enterprise.

A short time ago we were in treaty to lease of Davis Anderson corner of
4th and Main. He raised the price and we dropped the matter. It is certainly
no pleasure to build and have the care of so much RE and I have resolved to
build no more for several reasons.

Joe's persistent desire to enter into stock purchases now that prices are tow-
ering so high above normal rates has kept me constantly holding back. The
purchases that we made one to three years ago were all profitable and other
that we did not make owing to the supposed risk would have been also very
good.[3]

With a few more griping comments about his brother, Thomas concluded that "The rest has done good as to Diabetes, and my jaw very little,
my cold is well and by dispelling the bus [business?] matters as above I
hope to improve my health still more." He signed off "With lots of love
and kisses." Thomas Emery's absence from his wife for business or recuper-
ative reasons was not unusual, for he was a traveler often anxious to
inspect his scattered properties. Mary and their children traveled together
with him to Europe and in the United States during happier years; but
after the death of her son in 1890 and her mother in 1893, she seldom left
Cincinnati. Late in 1901, however, Thomas sought an estate on the outskirts of Newport, Rhode Island, especially for his wife's enjoyment. Newport's setting on the ocean, its colonial history and architecture, attracted

the very wealthy at the turn of the century, encouraging its establishment as America's most fashionable summer colony. It was not favored by Cincinnati's elite, however, who preferred northern Michigan and Maine. With the acquisition of a house and acreage in Middletown, then a suburb adjacent to Newport, Mary found a beloved second home where she would spend the warmer months, usually May through October, until her passing in 1927.

On December 6, 1901, Thomas J. Emery purchased in his wife's name the estate of Silas H. Witherbee on Honyman Hill in Middletown, a few miles outside of Newport, paying $17,500 plus $2,182 in expenses for buildings and eighteen acres. He titled it "Mariemont," combining two French words. "Marie" honored his wife, and "mont" signified the hill where the estate's main house stood.[4] A reporter for the *New York Times* wrote, "[He] expended a small fortune in altering and repairing it. The estate is by no means as imposing as several of the summer cottagers' places, but is such a one as a person of Mr. Emery's temperament might long for."[5] Early the next year, Thomas rented the "Taggart cottage on Broadway for the season" and began the extensive renovation of the shingled house, built about 1875, once part of Honyman Hill farm.[6]

Over the twenty-six years of Mary's ownership, the estate expanded to sixty acres in six different parcels of undulating hills and farm fields adjacent to the garden paradise she created around her summer mansion.[7] Plans for the gardens and vistas to the sea were designed between 1902 and 1908 by the eminent firm of landscape architects, Olmsted Brothers, then located in Brookline, Massachusetts. Olmsted's elaborate drawings for gardens, planting diagrams, walks, and other parts of the estate were followed by plantings of rare trees, formal flower gardens, and paths and lawns, all tended by a battalion of Portuguese gardeners working under head gardener Andrew L. Dorward.[8] A driveway of raked pebbles led to the house through an imposing gate, with banks of rhododendrons lining the approach. Pedimented windows, classical columns, fan lights, and the gambrel roof of the three-story residence follow the Colonial Revival style in America, unlike the palatial "cottages" in Newport belonging to the Vanderbilts, Belmonts, and Berwinds. The Emerys' choice of suburban

The residence at Mariemont, Rhode Island, summer home of Mary M. and Thomas J. Emery, 1908 (Courtesy Mariemont Preservation Foundation)

Middletown, not Newport's fashionable streets, and their reluctance to participate actively in the season's social events, demonstrated their retiring nature.

For four summers preceding Thomas's death in 1906, the Emerys and their servants enjoyed country living at their Rhode Island estate. From its tranquil, then-rural setting, there were ocean views in the distance. Summer life at Mariemont, although supported by servants and groundskeepers, contrasted with the social demands in Cincinnati and the crowded urban ambiance of Edgecliffe, their stone mansion in Cincinnati's Walnut Hills neighborhood. By 1902, Rhode Island was the legal residence of Thomas and Mary Emery, as indicated in Thomas's "last will and testament," and Mariemont became the center of Mary's summer activities, as well as the Livingood family's.

In 1902, Mary and Thomas modestly expanded their support of Cincinnati charities, particularly Christ Church and its Girls' Friendly

View of living room, hall, and drawing room at Mariemont, 1914 (Courtesy Mariemont Preservation Foundation)

Dining room at Mariemont, 1914 (Courtesy Mariemont Preservation Foundation)

Garden view at Mariemont, Rhode Island, 1908, designed by Frederick Law Olmsted Brothers (Courtesy Mariemont Preservation Foundation)

The Addison Walk at Mariemont, Rhode Island, 1914, designed by Frederick Law Olmsted Brothers (Courtesy Mariemont Preservation Foundation)

Garden view at Mariemont, Rhode Island, 1914, designed by Frederick Law Olmsted Brothers (Courtesy Mariemont Preservation Foundation)

Garden pergolas at Mariemont, Rhode Island, 1914, designed by Frederick Law Olmsted Brothers (Courtesy Mariemont Preservation Foundation)

Bowling green at Mariemont, Rhode Island, 1914, designed by Frederick Law Olmsted Brothers (Courtesy Mariemont Preservation Foundation)

Mary M. Emery with the Livingood family (left to right: unidentified man, perhaps Chalmers Clifton; Isabella F. Hopkins; Josephine Livingood; Mrs. Emery with Elizabeth Livingood; Charles J. Livingood; and John J. Livingood) at Mariemont, Rhode Island, c. 1915 (Courtesy Mariemont Preservation Foundation)

Society, donating a house on the Ohio River near New Richmond for vacationing working girls. Proud of this gift, the Emerys chartered a boat that summer and steamed up the river with guests to inspect the new facility.[9] One year later, while Thomas Emery was still a trustee, Charles Livingood joined the board of the Fresh Air Farm and Society, a not insignificant indication of his growing assumption of duties in the Emery interests. In 1904, the Fresh Air Farm in Terrace Park held a service in the presence of the Emerys, with a memorial to their two sons, Albert and Sheldon Emery. Mary's philanthropic interests centered on the Episcopal Church, while Thomas's were focused on the needy and the less privileged. He was ever an advocate of the African-American, his interest stemming from Emery family support of the noted Cincinnati abolitionist Levi Coffin and the Underground Railway station he operated before the Civil War.

By 1903, Thomas began a friendship with Booker T. Washington (1856–1915), the president of Tuskegee Institute, Alabama, and he welcomed the educator to Edgecliffe for dinner in May. Typical of Thomas's reticence to discuss the event or attract publicity, he told a Cincinnati reporter he "considered what transpired at the dinner a private matter and would not divulge the object of Mr. Washington's visit further than to say that it was in the interest of Tuskegee Institute."[10] That interest surely involved financial support Emery might offer Washington, for the Tuskegee educator traveled widely and frequently to raise funds for his school, which catered primarily to agrarian blacks with a strong work ethic. Washington's persistent theme that hard work produces results appealed to Thomas Emery, who admired Washington's observations on the wealthy: "The more I come in contact with wealthy people, the more I believe that they are growing in the direction of looking upon their money simply as an instrument which God has placed in their hand for doing good with."[11] Although Booker T. Washington was renowned nationally and advised Presidents Theodore Roosevelt and William Howard Taft on issues affecting African-Americans, he found Cincinnati segregated, as it remained throughout Thomas and Mary Emery's lives. Hotels, restaurants, and theaters did not serve nonwhites, except in the poorest seats for stage performances. Trains from Cincinnati to the South were governed by Jim Crow regulations, with coaches set aside for blacks.

Cincinnati's YMCA was segregated, the Ohio Mechanics Institute forbade enrollment of blacks, and the Children's Home on Ninth Street permitted nonwhites to remain within its walls only for twenty-four hours before they were sent to the Colored Orphans' Asylum.

Thomas Emery advocated equal rights for all, even in the face of majority opinion in Cincinnati and the nation. He refused a request to support the Ohio Mechanics Institute in 1904 unless they admitted "Negroes . . . on the same terms as white students." His petitioners tried a second time, but were rebuffed then, too.[12] The most important observer of black history and society in Cincinnati was an African American, Wendell P. Dabney, editor and publisher of the *Union,* a weekly newspaper catering to the black residents of the city. He wrote twenty years after Thomas Emery's death, extolling the family's compassion:

> In letters of gold the name of Emery should be emblazoned upon the hearts of all Cincinnatians. The founder of that name came, and his life was an exemplification of the golden rule, that divine inspiration which has animated the soul of every truly great man since the birth of reason, the dawn of civilization. Thomas Emery had two sons, Thomas J. and J. J. Emery. They were of that English stock whose blood ever fired at oppression, whose heart ever warmed to charity. Their recognition of the brotherhood of man caused them to refuse donations to any cause that recognized the color line, and so their princely gifts to institutions carried with them the admission of colored people.[13]

By 1903, Charles Livingood, married and with two living children, enjoyed a growing closeness with the Emerys, especially with Mary. Part of Livingood's appeal to Mary, now in her late fifties, was his curiosity and interest in subjects she liked: travel, the arts, and literature. Throughout his maturity, Livingood enjoyed travel and new settings. He bounded off to Kentucky in the summer of 1903 to walk the turnpike from Maysville to Lexington, hiked by his father in 1840. Explorations of this sort faded in later life when his travels were supported rather luxuriously, but Livingood never lost a zest for seeking out new trails, a recommended church, or a memory-laden inn.[14]

Letter writing was one of Livingood's strengths, a skill he practiced by typewriter as well as by hand, usually writing in a precise, legible printing instead of longhand. His letters frequently were lengthy discourses recording his observations in a conversational, easy style. In one diary-like letter to Mary Emery, written while visiting Europe in 1905, he addressed her for the first recorded time as "Guppy," the affectionate nickname uttered by one of Livingood's children, maybe in an attempt to pronounce "god-mother" or "grandmother."[15] Livingood, his wife, and two children stayed in Menton, France, for a few months while he was recovering from exhaustion.[16] From that French Riviera location, the family sallied forth to visit selected medieval sites, while Livingood relived his student days in France.

In February 1905, a newspaper article expressed Cincinnati's concern for Thomas J. Emery's health, reporting that he was stricken with rheumatism while vacationing in Palm Beach, Florida. It was rumored that he was a victim of "locomotor ataxia," but brother John responded to the press that the illness crippled him only temporarily. The attack was serious enough, however, to bring John J. Emery from New York to Cincinnati, dispatching John H. Hall, an employee, to assist Thomas in returning to his home. Upon arrival, Thomas was "lifted from the train into a carriage."[17] Livingood wrote from Menton, France, of his concern. "My dear, dear Guppy: We are too distressed to have such discouraging news about Mr. Emery's condition, and cannot understand why such good treatment and care as he is receiving is not bringing him around more quickly. It must be an awful affliction to him to be so restless and yet so helpless. We are truly, truly sorry for you all and only wish we could help in some way. You do well to have the two nurses, especially the man. If only the bad weather were over for good with you. But I fear not. Certainly this has been a remarkable winter."[18] The ominous condition of Thomas Emery, so distressing to Livingood in the first paragraph, gave way to three pages of gossipy discussion of his meeting with the Italian composer of *Cavalleria rusticana*, Pietro Mascagni, then presenting his new opera, *Amica*, at Monte Carlo. "The play itself is intensely dramatic though the theme is old. Mascagni's music is robust, impassioned, sustained to a degree that surpasses even that wonderful quality in Cavalleria. There are many reminiscences of that opera, especially in the choruses which are superb, so strong and sure, but of course no Intermezzo of which I don't doubt Mascagni is as sick and tired as we are."

Always an avid correspondent, Livingood wrote not only to Mary Emery during his lengthy stay abroad in 1905, but he sent pages to Isabella Hopkins, Mary's sister, about his travels in Provence as well as those in Italy. At *I Tatti*, near Florence, the home of the art historian Bernard Berenson (1865–1959), a member with Livingood in the Harvard class of 1888, Livingood and his wife dined with the Berensons. Livingood's letter to Miss Hopkins, addressed as "Tante Belle," reflected on the house and its setting, detailed observation being a focus of Livingood's personality, with comments on his hosts and their lifestyle.

> I am sure you will want to hear something about Bernhard Berenson or "Bee Bee" as your friend Senda calls him, for he is without doubt the most celebrated member of the class of '88.
>
> We were invited at once to lunch with them, and found their villa (a most curious name "I Tatti", which even they do not know how to account for) most charmingly situated between Settignano and Fiesole, on one of those lovely slopes overlooking the Arno Valley. I was surprised though that they took a place which did not command a view of Florence itself. But perhaps Berenson wanted an absolute change when he came home to do his real thinking preparatory to writing.
>
> I don't know whether you realize it but he is really the most eminent critic on Italian art today. You see his judgments quoted everywhere and few of his dicta confuted or quarrelled with (although he himself says he has many professional enemies who just delight in picking him up). He has not only written the three very informing and original handbooks (not guides) on the three Schools of Northern Italy, in which he has concerned himself most, but a number of special treatises.[19]

Livingood correctly assessed Berenson's importance as an art historian, expert, and author. During the first half of the twentieth century, Berenson was universally regarded as the leading authority on Italian Renaissance art. His advisory role with art dealers, frequently rendering opinions on attributions to specific artists, touched Mrs. Emery's collecting only after 1915. By that year, her collecting interest was well established. She sought Berenson's expertise through dealers only for her paintings by Luini and Tintoretto.

Travel abroad filled many months for Thomas Emery, who vacationed without Mary on those occasions when he sought the dry desert of Algeria. Their estate near Newport easily lured them away from Cincinnati's humid summers. Mary's vacation away from the city continued until her death, and at times the press commented on her regular absences. A society editor commented in 1905 "Mrs. Emery spends much time away from Cincinnati, and it is always a rare pleasure she bestows upon her friends when she asks them together."[20]

Mary Emery and Thomas spent the summer of 1905 together at Mariemont. Seeking relief from his ailments, Thomas then sailed for Europe on October 26, going first to Paris and then on to Algiers and the oasis at Biskra where he found the "baths peculiarly beneficial."[21] Apparently, Mary argued against the journey, having "a premonition that ill might overtake her husband on this foreign trip, and when he was arranging to depart for the Old World pleaded with him to travel in America instead, offering to accompany him on any trip he might choose to make here. Her friends say she informed Mr. Emery of her forebodings, but that he laughed them off, declaring it to be only a fancy, unworthy of consideration. He believed that he would be benefited by the journey, and took the trip alone against the earnest advice of his wife, the only person accompanying him being his valet."[22]

The premonition proved correct. Thomas Emery arrived in Algeria in December 1905. Improving somewhat in North Africa, he wrote home that he was feeling better and able to walk upstairs without assistance. However, his condition worsened in early January. Thomas Emery and his valet, Alphonse P. Ruick, made their way from Biskra to Cairo, where they intended to board the *Celtic* for their return to the United States.

The alarming, sudden news of Thomas's illness first reached Mary Emery in a cable on Sunday, January 14, telling her that he was not well and was returning to the United States on board the *Celtic* that sailed January 25. A second cable was received from the valet, sent the same day, noting that Mr. Emery was not seriously ill. Hard on its heels was a cable, on January 15, saying that he was dangerously ill, followed by a message on Tuesday, January 16, that Thomas J. Emery had passed away the night before.

Ruick's testimony for probate courts in Middletown and Cincinnati recorded the sad events just prior to Thomas J. Emery's death on January 15, 1906.

> Alphonse P. Ruick being first duly sworn says: That he resides in the City of Brooklyn, County of Kings, State of New York; that he was personally acquainted with Thomas J. Emery of Middletown, Rhode Island, who at one time was a resident of Cincinnati, O.; that he met said Thomas J. Emery in Paris, France, in the month of November A.D. 1905; also in Algiers in Africa in the month of December, A.D. 1905, also in the City of Cairo, Egypt in the month of January 1906; that for about a week prior to his death, said Thomas J. Emery was not feeling well; that he affiant, was at the same hotel with said Thomas J. Emery; that on January 15, 1906 said Thomas J. Emery having grown much worse consented to go to the hospital in Cairo, Egypt; that he affiant, assisted said Thomas J. Emery in getting to the hospital and went with him to the hospital; that in the afternoon of the same day, said Thomas J. Emery grew worse and that at about ten o'clock P.M. of said day, he, affiant, was notified that said Thomas J. Emery had died; that he immediately went to said hospital, saw the body of said Thomas J. Emery, recognized his body and saw that he was dead.
>
> Affiant further says that he then proceeded to make the necessary arrangements for the body of said Thomas J. Emery to be transported to New York City in this country, the United States of America, and that he, affiant, returned to New York City on the Steamer Celtic, the same steamer which transported the body of said Thomas J. Emery to New York. Affiant knows that the body transported was that of said Thomas J. Emery, the same having been encased in his presence.[23]

Mary Emery's loneliest years began with the death of her husband. She was accustomed to losing her family, as one by one they left her—two sons, her mother, and her husband. Her brother-in-law, John, would guide the family riches and assist her as she waited in New York for the return of Thomas's body from Egypt. With Mary's approval, John J. Emery arranged for the body's shipment, concluding the formalities that permitted embalming in Cairo and the release from Islamic law that required burial within twenty-four hours of death.[24] The Cincinnati newspapers speculated anxiously about the arrival date of the body, the casket's design, and the funeral preparations. Accompanied by the valet Ruick, Thomas's casket was received in New York by Mary and John Emery and shipped to Cincinnati.[25]

The "Sarcophagus from Land of Nile" intrigued readers of the Cincinnati newspapers as it was delivered to the family's undertaker, C. Ross Lodwick, on February 13 and described in detail as if a Pharoah's tomb had been opened. "It resembles a great oblong urn, consisting of two compartments—the upper or over part, and the lower part which bears resemblance to a false floor tightly soldered down covering the remains of the dead. This oblong urn is composed of light but durable metal, fashioned into picturesque shape, resembling in upper outlines the upper part of a Chinese pagoda, and rest upon four legs, one at each corner, these legs ending in a design of an animal head."[26] The massive casket or coffin, seven feet in length and four feet in height and width, was received by a delegation led by Emery's attorneys, Drausin Wulsin and Herbert Jenney, and opened. Accounts of this ceremony relished details about the embalmed remains, "found well-preserved, the whole being a tribute to Egypt's ancient cunning in the art of embalming. Mr. Emery's countenance showed much of the expression familiar to his friends, appearing as if in peaceful sleep."[27]

On February 16, the funeral of Thomas J. Emery was held at the family's residence, Edgecliffe, with the Reverend Frank H. Nelson, rector of Christ Church, officiating. A simple, brief service of only fifteen minutes, with no music or choir, with about three hundred friends, neighbors, and employees attending, preceded interment at Spring Grove Cemetery.[28] The most prominent guest attending the service was Booker T. Washington, who stayed at Edgecliffe and was given "the finest suite of rooms. The housekeeper has received orders to have the rooms in readiness for the negro educator, who will be received on the footing of equality which the whites of Ohio have to a considerable extent admitted the negro."[29]

With the demise of Thomas J. Emery, Cincinnati's enlightened and successful entrepreneurs lost one of their leaders. His death, however, initiated through his widow, Mary Muhlenberg Emery, a new era of philanthropy for Cincinnati, America, and Europe.

CHAPTER 5

Stranger to Selfish Ambitions

First Philanthropies

THOMAS J. EMERY, entrepreneur and landowner, was dead. Thomas Emery's Sons continued, however, under brother John's leadership, with John manipulating the business from his New York headquarters under terms of the earlier agreement with Thomas. The Cincinnati office was staffed with faithful employees, including Robert Mecke, John H. Hall, and Charles L. Burgoyne, who had been with Thomas Emery for many years. Speculation as to the size of Thomas's estate and its beneficiaries spurred the press to write more about the man after death than it had during his life. Thomas was publicity shy, and this heightened the public's interest.

> He always refused to give anyone a biographical sketch, and the picture of him which appears in The Enquirer is the only one extant, and was taken in London 15 years ago. Mr. Emery never took any part in politics. He had no legal residence in Cincinnati, but called Newport, R.I., his home, and there he built a magnificent house, equal in every way to his stately home on Edgecliffe Road, Walnut Hills. The millionaire capitalist was not inclined to take much interest in public affairs, devoting all his time to looking after his immense real estate holdings here and elsewhere. He was a man of few friendships. His intimates were General A. T. Goshorn, Herbert Jenney, the attorney, and

Drausin Wulsin, his legal advisor. For more than 25 years Mr. Emery, Mr. Goshorn, and Mr. Wulsin met every Sunday afternoon, when they were in the city, but the trio of good friends was broken by the death of General Goshorn several years ago.[1]

Emery's Rhode Island neighbors, awed by estimates of $25,000,000 to $35,000,000 as Thomas Emery's wealth and assets, expressed amazement that one of the "richest men in the world" had lived in their midst since 1902. Emery was not a recluse, but he was not seen frequently around Newport. Shrinking from social events, traveling extensively, and tending to his business across the nation, he was not among Newport's bons vivants.[2] His charitable interests were limited, although he contributed to his church and a few other causes. Unlike many of his contemporaries, such as the steel magnates and rail barons who had stained their reputations by their shady, even criminal, business practices, Emery's accumulation of wealth was coupled with a responsible conservatism. His wealthy status never was ostentatiously displayed nor was his innovative entrepreneurship based on self-promotion or publicity.

Caustic views of the rich appeared frequently during the lifetimes of Mary and Thomas Emery. Thorstein Veblen (1857–1929), American economist and critic of the wealthy classes for what he perceived as their wasteful, indulgent living, could not legitimately tar Thomas with the brush of criticism he applied to others. Veblen's railing attack on the wealthy in *The Theory of the Leisure Class* against their "obligatory leisure" certainly was warranted for some in the late nineteenth century. Another writer who scorned the rich, Gustavus Myers (1872–1942), joined Veblen's diatribes against capitalism and the American magnates of the nineteenth and early twentieth century with venomous attacks on the Vanderbilts, Astors, and Morgans in his *History of the Great American Fortunes*, first published in 1910. Even Nicholas Longworth (1782–1863) of Cincinnati was singled out for criticism, but Myers made no mention of Thomas or John Emery. He assaulted Russell Sage and his fortune-making but wrote approvingly of his widow's philanthropies.[3] Mrs. Russell Sage, who embraced a large program of philanthropies after her husband's death in 1906, was the sole heir of her husband's estate except for a few minor bequests.

Russell Sage's fortune of $65,000,000 was bequeathed to his wife, Margaret Olivia Slocum (1828–1918), with no restrictions as to its use. Mrs. Sage's special interests were social betterment of all types. Acting on the advice of Robert W. deForest, her friend and close advisor, she formed the Russell Sage Foundation in 1907 to carry on her good works. DeForest embraced many philanthropies, including those that promoted improved housing for the poor. This interest led him to champion new laws in New York State to raise building and housing standards. Mrs. Sage's foundation was an unusual venture, a new frontier, as there were only eight foundations in all of the United States at that time. Mary kept a close eye on this new endeavor[4] and recognized the worth of a competent manager in Charles J. Livingood, just as Mrs. Sage relied on Robert deForest. An assessment of Mrs. Sage was written nearly thirty years after her death, in November 1918.

> Mrs. Sage was nearly seventy-eight years old when her husband died. Photographs of the time show a strong, kindly, serene, intelligent face, a presence of dignity and graciousness. She had warm sympathies and a wide range of interests. Sometimes she acted quickly, impulsively, but her larger gifts were carefully considered. She sought advice, but she had vigorous opinions and made her own decisions. Pressure she resented. Even more she resented any suggestion that a donation might perpetuate her own name. A proposal of that sort was likely to end the applicant's chances. Many of her endowments, on the other hand, bear the name of Russell Sage, for she intended them to be memorials to him.[5]

Probably the best-known philanthropist of Thomas and Mary Emery's time was Andrew Carnegie (1835–1919), who expounded ideas of sharing of wealth and followed his own advice, distributing an estimated $325,000,000 during his lifetime. Born in Scotland, Carnegie rose from poverty as an immigrant to become America's richest industrialist. His wealth was derived largely from iron and steel manufacturing, and by 1901 he sold his interests to the United States Steel Corporation. Carnegie's dedication address on December 5, 1895, for the new library he funded in Pittsburgh stated a credo that would be followed by Mary Emery.

> To one to whom surplus comes, there comes also the questions: What is my duty? What is the best use that can be made of it? The conclusion forced upon

me, and which I retain, is this: That surplus wealth is a sacred trust, to be administered during life by its possessor for the best good of his fellow-men; and I have ventured to predict the coming of the day the dawn of which, indeed, we already begin to see, when the man who dies possessed of available millions which were free and in his hands to distribute, will die disgraced. He will pass away "unwept, unhonored, and unsung," as one who has been unfaithful to his trust. The aim of millionaires should be to deserve such eulogy as that upon the monument of Pitt: "He lived without ostentation, and he died poor." There must sometimes be surplus wealth, then, and it is our duty to use this for public good.[6]

Thomas Emery during his lifetime did not embrace Carnegie's admonition, and it was left to his widow to fulfill it. In life, Thomas was generous to a few causes, but he was primarily a builder of wealth, not its dispenser. Mary's desire to employ her wealth for social betterment, however, challenges the assumptions of Veblen and Myers as well as those of the mid-twentieth-century American economist John Kenneth Galbraith, who wrote disparagingly of the rich in *The Affluent Society*. "Few things have been more productive of controversy over the ages than the suggestion that the rich should, by one device or another, share their wealth with those who are not. With comparatively rare and usually eccentric exceptions, the rich have been opposed. The grounds have been many and varied and have been principally noted for the rigorous exclusion of the most important reason, which is the simple unwillingness to give up the enjoyment of what they have."[7]

Mary Emery demonstrated not only great generosity in dispensing her fortune during her lifetime, but she provided for future philanthropy in her husband's name after her death. Mary's black-edged note paper, used for personal letters after 1906, bore the Emery family's coat of arms and Latin inscription, *fidelis et suavis* ("faithfulness and agreeable nature"), that exemplifies her character. Any intentions Thomas J. Emery had for the distribution of his wealth, other than modest provisions indicated in his last will and testament, became his wife's decisions.

The public relished facts, and even rumors, about the probate of the will. This information was second only to the newsworthiness of his death.[8] As the news was published about the will's provisions, the Middletown, Rhode Island, town fathers resented their misunderstanding of Thomas's worth, while others continued their speculation on the estate's value.

> The Cincinnati capitalist who was taxed in Middletown on only $1,500 personal property was worth nearly $30,000,000. Mr. Emery came to the quiet country town about three years ago and asked to be taxed for $1,500. In order that the matter of his legal domicile in the town where there was no inheritance tax might be emphasized, he asked that he be given some minor office such as fence viewer. The fact that he was a man of great wealth did not come to the attention of the assessors till he died. In his will he especially enjoined his agents and executors not to disclose the value of his estate. The authorities of the town feel that in this instance they lost considerable in the way of taxes. The authorities of the town, who feel they lost a golden opportunity, say Mr. Emery even objected to the valuation of $1,600 at which he was assessed.[9]

Moving as quickly as possible to act on the will, Cincinnati attorneys Drausin Wulsin and Herbert Jenney, representing the estate of Thomas Emery and his wife, filed a petition with the Probate Court of Middletown on February 5, 1906, that Thomas's will be proved and allowed, with Mary recognized as sole executrix. The court scheduled its hearing for February 21, and the two witnesses to the handwritten will that Thomas Emery signed on July 20, 1904, affirmed in the presence of seven selectmen of Middletown and Probate Clerk Albert L. Chase that the deceased was in sound mind when he executed it.[10] The salient provisions of the will did not include a valuation of the estate, for that was left to a separate listing of assets. Thomas wanted no publication of the will's wording, for "The printing of such matter serves to gratify morbid curiosity."[11] Thomas's sister-in-law, Isabella Hopkins, was recorded as executrix if Mary could not serve.

In the will's nine sections, bequests included awards of $20,000 to each of his brother's children and to his sister, Julia; many employees at the Ivorydale factory were to receive varying numbers of shares in the company; house servants were to be paid $40 for each year of service; his attorneys were bequeathed $12,500 each; and various Cincinnati organizations were given bequests of $2,000 to $10,000.[12] The final and ninth statement in the will provided the largesse for Mary M. Emery's remarkable good works of the next twenty-one years. "The remainder of my estate both Real and personal I devise and bequeath to my wife Mary M. Emery."

Mary's future as the inheritor of great wealth was influenced by several factors realized as the will proceeded through the probate process. First, the operations of Thomas Emery's Sons were to be managed by the surviving brother; that is, with Thomas's death, John J. Emery was in charge for at least five years, unless the survivor and the deceased's representatives agreed on any divisions of property or amendments to the 1895 agreement signed by the two brothers and their wives.[13] This arrangement ceased in 1908 with the death of John Emery. Second, Mary's children predeceased her and her husband, so there were no direct heirs after her death. And, third, she had at hand in 1906 the counsel of her oldest son's classmate, Charles J. Livingood, who had served as an employee of the Emery interests for sixteen years. He was admired by her late husband enough to be rewarded in his will, and, most important, Livingood had become a surrogate son. He had a unique closeness with Mary no impersonal attorney or banker could provide.

No official appointment of Livingood as Mary Emery's manager or representative was made. It seemed to be understood, as if he were an heir apparent. The death of her husband was a great loss, and it removed the helmsman from Mary's life. Mary's role before her husband's death in 1906 was as wife, mother, and pillar of her church. Her husband's affluence removed her from domestic duties, and, although she was a modest contributor to causes she and her husband endorsed, she had little financial independence. After Thomas's death, and supported by Livingood's guidance, she moved dramatically into a new role as philanthropist, art collector of national significance, and founder of a world-renowned planned community.

The Emery business could be directed and managed by brother-in-law John and the trusted staff in Cincinnati, but Mary's inherited fortune and its use now were pressing considerations needing careful shepherding. What should be done during her remaining years? She could have multiplied her fortune by doing nothing, of course, and she had no obligation to embark on a path to give away her wealth. But her philanthropic focus for the next twenty-one years became apparent almost immediately after her husband's death.

Years later, Mary Emery wrote to the American author, Dorothy Canfield Fisher (1879–1958), and recorded herself as a longtime acquaintance of the Canfield family, a "friend of the third generation." This important letter explained the situation that led to two decades of good works. Mary's letter was written in response to Fisher's of November 15, 1922, now lost, that "so overpowered me that I had to have time to 'mull it over'—hence this very tardy reply."

I agree with you in regretting that your father did not write his "Memoirs." They would have been of great interest to his children and grandchildren as well as to his very numerous friends. My situation is very different, with no posterity. However, if I had a belief in Special Providences, I would think my life had been ordered to give me strength and leisure for the disposing of a great financial trust.

First, my married life with a strong, sane business man who kept me in touch with his interests and affairs as much as a woman can be who was not a working partner. Then the closing of the lives of my two sons, my only children, leaving me without any obligations to posterity after the death of my husband, whose will put into my hands the disposition of the fortune he had accumulated. How could a woman so situated make a success of such a vast responsibility?

There came into my life a man, the friend of my oldest son, who took his, Sheldon's, desk and my husband's office. For fifteen years he was trained there and learned the methods that had succeeded in establishing a successful business. This man has been to me a son, a helper, and an advisor in everything I have been able to do. To him I owe the inspiration and knowledge that has made possible my gifts of every kind.

Illness during the past years has made me a recluse and given me time to ponder, which is denied those who are living in a social world with its many distractions and obligations. This condition has been one of detachment from "Hope and Fear set free."

Ambition for my children was denied me, yet I had them long enough to know and sympathize with all youth and its struggles in this world. It seems as if I had been really taken out of a life such as most people have, and thus given leisure which few have, by the elimination of responsibility for those usually so near to everyone, and in looking back on past years I can say as I did before that I feel I must have been led by a power that has made it possible for me to accomplish what I have done, with and through the help that has been given me and which I could never have achieved by myself.[14]

Mary Emery envisioned her philanthropic course as a duty and pleasure. Her remarkably frank letter to Fisher exposed the intended use of her wealth. She permitted little time to elapse after the will was probated to initiate in 1906 several major gifts. Livingood's assistance with these may have been slight, but his influence grew, providing him with his principal occupation and livelihood after this date.[15]

Her first use of the Emery fortune occurred when she notified the Christ Church Vestry that she would advance funds to purchase two lots east of the Parish House on Fourth Street that might provide room for an addition to the building finished in 1899. When it was discovered that the walls of the Parish House would not sustain an addition, she offered to demolish it and build a new one (even though the building was only seven years old) using the three lots. This would be realized in 1909.[16] Her second benefaction confirmed her deep interest in art and support of the Cincinnati Art Museum when she provided a fund to ensure free admission to the Museum on Saturdays.

> As an expression of my husband's interest in the people of Cincinnati, and in appreciation of the value of your art collection, I desire in the name of my husband, Thomas J. Emery, to endow the Cincinnati Museum Association with the sum of one hundred thousand dollars ($100,000), the principal to be invested by your Association as part of the endowment fund, the income only to be used for the purposes of your Association, this endowment to be on condition that, beginning with Saturday, the second day of February, a.d. one thousand nine hundred and seven, and forever thereafter, the public shall have admission, free of charge, on Saturday of each week, to all parts of the Museum to which they are admitted on other days on payment of a general admission fee, the gift to be known as "The Thomas J. Emery Free Day Endowment."[17]

Her letter to Joseph Henry Gest, director of the Cincinnati Art Museum, outlining her offer, began a long exchange of correspondence between Mary and the man who would become her principal advisor on her art collection. Gest (1859–1935) was the second director of the art museum, succeeding Alfred T. Goshorn, close friend of Thomas J. Emery, in 1902. A graduate of Harvard and a museum staff member since 1886, Gest also served as president of Rookwood Pottery and head of the Art Academy of Cincinnati, then in its heyday. Beginning in 1907, he would encourage Mary Emery in the development of her collection of old master paintings, a persistent interest of hers for the next twenty years.

The year 1907 was an active one for Mary's generosity—a testing of the waters, it seemed. In that year, she expressed a freedom in dispensing the wealth that had not been hers until recently. She offered the city (but was refused) a gift of $50,000 to preserve the old Lytle home on East Fourth Street, hoping to convert it into quarters for the Historical and Philosophical Society (now the Cincinnati Historical Society).[18] She was not alone in this cause, for her fellow petitioners included Charles Phelps Taft and John Kilgour, equally prominent citizens. In refusing Mrs. Emery's offer, city council impertinently suggested that she donate the funds instead to the University of Cincinnati for "the proper disposition of her gift."

More receptive were two New York institutions, Adirondack Cottage Sanatarium in Saranac Lake and Hobart College in Geneva. These two were unfamiliar institutions to Mary, but they were represented by two clergymen, rectors of Christ Church, who figured importantly in her life. These men were undoubtedly the instigators of the gifts, underscoring the significance of personal relationships and the interests of friends and advisors in Mary's donations. One of the nation's highly regarded tuberculosis treatment centers was operated by Dr. E. L. Trudeau in Saranac Lake. An initial contact sometime before 1906, apparently with Thomas J. Emery, produced no results in obtaining funds for a reception and medical pavilion for patients. Mrs. Emery, however, contributed anonymously a check for $25,000 through the Reverend Alexis Stein, former rector of Christ Church, to build the needed pavilion. By October 1908, the new building was finished, equipped, and named "The Sheldon and Albert Medical Building."[19] The Emery name was not affixed to the structure: her children's first names were enough. Mary's other gift in New York to Hobart College was given through one of its alumni, the Reverend Frank H. Nelson. It provided the funds to construct a new gymnasium, a "building given by Mrs. Emery in memory of an 'amiable child' and named Williams Hall."[20] At the impressive dedication ceremonies on November 15, 1907, the absent Mary remained the "unknown donor" who made the gymnasium possible, and Nelson accepted the accolades for his role in obtaining the needed sum.

In 1907, the first year after Thomas J. Emery's death, Charles J. Livingood emerged as Mary's guide, mentor, and secretary. The latter title was a designation he seldom used as the years progressed, however.[21] Requests for funds arrived in Mary's mail shortly after her husband's death in 1906, and Livingood served as a trusted intervenor, always solicitous and protective of his principal's time and interests. He did not miss an opportunity, however, to travel extensively, certainly at Mary's expense, to gather information for her or to consummate arrangements on her behalf. Pursuing one of Thomas Emery's unrealized interests, and at Mary's direction, Livingood visited Paris in 1907 and secured a building site, architect, and plans for a home for working girls, to be known as Cercle Concordia. In Livingood's negotiations, Mrs. Emery remained the anonymous benefactor who gave $250,000 and was called "Madame X."[22] Livingood acquired an ancient nunnery on the chosen site, had it demolished, and began construction for the new home. It was finished two years later and dedicated by the United States ambassador to France, the Honorable Robert Bacon. Mary Emery never visited Paris after the death of her husband, so she never saw the completed building. Personal visits to sites of her benefactions, apart from those in Cincinnati and Newport, were seldom, if ever, made. She was not alone among the American rich in receiving requests, of course, and occasionally she was the target of extortion attempts. A Columbus, Ohio, man threatened to kill her if she did not send him $5,000 by March 1, 1907. He was arrested and convicted for using the mail to attempt to extort money and sentenced to sixty days in jail.[23]

In the autumn of 1908, the Board of the Ohio Mechanics Institute in Cincinnati approached Mrs. Emery for financial support and were awed by her offer to fund the construction of a new building. The amount of the proposed gift, $500,000, exceeded any she had made or promised in the two years since her inheritance. Also, fresh in the institute's memory was

Reception and Medical Building, Adirondack Cottage Sanatarium, Saranac Lake, New York (later Trudeau Sanatorium), 1907–1908 (Courtesy Saranac Lake Free Library)

Thomas J. Emery's refusal in 1904 to contribute because of OMI's admission of Caucasian students only. Mary apparently had no such compunction.

> In appreciation of the work undertaken and carried on by your institution in educating skilled workmen and training young men and young women for useful industries, a work which was highly appreciated and approved by my husband, Thomas J. Emery, and as you have explained to me that you are in need of funds to erect a new Ohio Mechanics Institute building on the property you have acquired at the north-east corner of Walnut and Canal Streets [now Central Parkway] . . . and as I desire to assist in the further development of your worthy institution, and to secure to the Cincinnati music-loving public a hall suitable for some of its purposes, I hereby offer to donate to your institution the funds necessary for the erection of a building on the lot referred to suitable for your purposes for educational uses.[24]

The institute, founded in 1829, was one of the oldest technical schools in the United States. As an outgrowth from slightly earlier models in Scotland and England, it taught "useful" courses in mathematics, mechanical drawing, and engineering, among others, and provided a strong cadre of employees for the city's industries. Only night classes were offered until 1898. Its Tudor Revival style building opened in 1909, an immense brick and stone structure that filled the block on the street that once was an old canal. The structure was designed by Harvey E. Hannaford, son of the renowned Samuel Hannaford, who had worked extensively for the Emerys. This imposing building had as its centerpiece an auditorium named in memory of Thomas Emery. It was completed in 1912.

Noted for its exceptional acoustics, Emery Auditorium served as home for the Cincinnati Symphony Orchestra from 1912 to 1936.[25] Mrs. Emery was a longtime supporter of the orchestra, joining many prominent and wealthy Cincinnatians, including Mrs. Charles P. Taft, Julius Fleischmann, Melville Ingalls, Jacob Schmidlapp, and Mrs. Nicholas Longworth II, as shareholders and annual contributors.[26] Mary's generous offer to fund the new Ohio Mechanics Institute building provided an elegant home for the orchestra she loved, a setting smaller than the Music Hall but slightly closer to downtown Cincinnati. Not only did Mary Emery secure new quarters for the orchestra, but she was a major guarantor through annual operating support ($5,000 per year for five years, beginning in 1908). Cultural philanthropy in Cincinnati found ready donors among its patricians, and although Anna Sinton Taft is usually regarded as the preeminent patron of the orchestra during the first quarter of the twentieth century, Mary Emery's impressive support, including a new home for the symphony, equaled Anna Taft's generosity.

Mary Emery's dollars often flowed simultaneously to several philanthropic projects. While moving on the Ohio Mechanics Institute request, she committed to a new Parish House for her beloved Christ Church. Perhaps she was spurred by the memory of her disappointment years earlier when her suggestions to repair and remodel the church were declined by the vestry, or maybe she remembered the vestry's lack of encouragement of her husband's and then-rector Isaac Stanger's attempt in the 1880s to

Ohio Mechanics Institute and Emery Auditorium, Cincinnati, designed by Harvey E. Hannaford, 1909 (Courtesy Cincinnati Historical Society)

obtain suitable buildings in downtown Cincinnati for the expanding church.[27] She was clearly in control now of the church's development because of her money, her close friendship with the Reverend Frank H. Nelson, and Livingood's role in the vestry.

Christ Church's Gothic Revival building of 1835 and its 1899 Parish House dominated the east end of Fourth Street, bordered by elegant mansions. The warm red brick, crockets, and corbels of the two buildings were repeated in the new Parish House of 1909 that replaced the outgrown, slightly older structure.[28] One week before the dedication, Mary hosted a banquet for about four hundred men and women who had worked on the project, from the architects Alfred Elzner and George Anderson to the humblest laborer.[29] On January 30, 1909, the blessing of the Parish House in memory of Thomas Emery was performed by Episcopal bishop Boyd Vincent, assisted by speakers that included former rector Isaac Stanger

Christ Church,
Cincinnati,
with Parish
House,
1899–1908
(Courtesy Christ
Church)

and present leader of the church, Frank H. Nelson. Each of these men and their religion were woven inextricably into the lives of Mary and Thomas Emery, increasingly so after Thomas's death. Mary's benefactions for her Episcopal faith clearly expanded in the twentieth century and were capped by generous provisions in her will.

Next in her philanthropies, Mary enlarged a service for destitute mothers and their children that originated with the Episcopal Diocese in Cincinnati. Known as the Maternity Society when founded in 1882, it expanded into a nursing service in the 1890s and evolved in 1909 into the first prenatal clinics in the city. Many of Cincinnati's prominent socialites were involved in the clinics' administration, including Mrs. Larz Anderson, Mrs. Julius Fleischmann, Mrs. Bayard L. Kilgour, Mrs. George Warrington, and Mrs. Lee Ault. Pediatric care in Cincinnati was practically unknown in 1909, when Dr. Benjamin K. Rachford inaugurated a dispensary and began distributing milk to poor mothers and their children. Mrs.

*Christ Church, Cincinnati, with
new Parish House, 1909 (Courtesy
Christ Church)*

Emery's compassionate nature rallied to Dr. Rachford's cause. She became the largest benefactor of the program that continued as the Babies Milk Fund. Her interest was conveyed by Livingood to Dr. Rachford.

> Mrs. Emery has carefully considered the opportunity you presented to her this morning for doing good among the extreme poor who come to our clinic. Realizing that you give your personal attention to the Dispensary work done there by your assistants and that therefore you are convinced that in no better way can the extreme poor be helped than enabling them to obtain certified milk for their sick babies at as low a cost as possible, Mrs. Emery begs me to say that she would like the privilege of standing behind you personally in your effort to give out milk of this character the coming year at a price so attractive that your patients will not be induced to buy at the grocers where they can possibly save money but get inferior stuff.[30]

The benefactor of the Babies Milk Fund, Mary Emery, continued her support during the remainder of her life. Mary lived to see that agency evolve in 1915 as a Community Chest affiliate, incorporate in 1919, and operate numerous health stations for children throughout the city by 1927, each with full-time physicians and nurses.

In the nineteenth century and for many decades into the twentieth, Newport was a busy naval station with coast artillery and many military units stationed in and around the city. Newport's military officials struggled for years to obtain a recreation and club facility for the sailors and soldiers to use when on leave. Although Mrs. Emery's gift of $250,000 to construct an Army-Navy YMCA was not announced until the cornerstone festivities, her intentions were known to the secretary of the Army and Navy Departments, William B. Millar, by the summer of 1909, according to a Newport newspaper article. But typically reticent, Mrs. Emery wished to remain anonymous until the building was dedicated. Land was acquired and an architect, Louis E. Jallade (1876–1957) of New York City, employed to design the palacelike building that would rise across Washington Square from the historic Colony House, constructed 1739–1741. Unfortunately, six eighteenth-and early nineteenth century buildings were demolished to make way for the Army-Navy YMCA. On November 9, 1910, the cornerstone was ready, the guests assembled in their chairs near the rostrum, and the military units formed around the perimeter. The large crowd heard from Mrs. Emery in a letter read by Secretary Millar.

> The International Committee of Young Men's Christian Associations has accepted my gift of a clubhouse at Newport as a memorial to my sons, Sheldon and Albert Emery, and has promised to keep it open for your pleasure and comfort, thus affording you a better rallying place than you have for your leisure hours while here. It has been my privilege in Newport and at the Training Station to see and study the faces of you young men, drawn in such numbers from all parts of the country, and I am convinced that you will appreciate a clubhouse such as this, preferring it as a place of resort. If so, I trust the Newport building will bring happiness and profit to all of you. Then this memorial will be greatly blessed to me.[31]

When the YMCA was completed and opened a year later, the architect delivered the key for the building to its donor, to which Mary replied that the doors would never be locked, as she now held the key. Jallade, a high-

Army-Navy YMCA, Newport, Rhode Island, designed by Louis E. Jallade, erected 1910–1911 (Courtesy Webb Chappell)

ly regarded New York architect, figured prominently a decade later as designer of the church for Mary's planned community, Mariemont, Ohio.

Reviewing an overwhelming number of requests for funds, Mrs. Emery and Livingood sifted through the letters, some expressing great need, others brazenly attempting to extort money for questionable causes. The Babies Milk Fund prospered under Dr. Rachford's supervision, and Mary increased her support to $2,000 per year for hiring nurses and distributing milk.[32] Interest in children's welfare was not limited to Cincinnati projects, for her generosity began to reach across the nation by 1910. The schools started by Martha Berry in Rome, Georgia, in 1902 found a responsive patron when Mrs. Emery learned of their good work in teaching children from poor or illiterate backgrounds. In 1910, she donated funds for a two-story frame and stucco building, Emery Hall, to house seventy boys and their teachers. Livingood attended the dedication in the autumn of 1910 and presented a silver cup as a track trophy. The hall functioned as student housing until shortly after World War II, when fire damaged it, and it was demolished by 1948.[33]

Mary Emery, by her sixty-sixth year, 1910, demonstrated a broad interest in humanitarian projects, mostly focused in Cincinnati. While some of these received funds for a limited, finite purpose, many projects continued to request support from Emery resources and were extended year after year. She did not balk at this, it seems, but rather enjoyed her ability to maintain contacts with various charities. As World War I approached, Mary embarked on her most costly, long-lasting benefaction: A planned community to be called Mariemont, taking its name from the Emery estate in Rhode Island.

CHAPTER 6

Mariemont, Ohio

Mary Emery's New Town

I T WAS typical in Mary Emery's era that women seldom participated in the business dealings of their husbands. Nor did she, as heiress to her husband's estate, claim any business rights or privileges beyond the terms of the will. She was not oblivious, however, to the benefits of good housing as practiced by Thomas Emery's Sons, both for investment as well as compassionate purposes. Realizing that the Emery fortune was derived partially from real estate, particularly residential housing, she envisioned a model project with many apartments and townhouses designed for citizens of low or modest incomes. The idea may have been hers alone, but it seems more likely that it derived from her husband or from Charles Livingood. Regardless of its true originator, it was her wealth and acquiescence that made possible the creation of a remarkable example of town planning. It would be unlike anything seen before in the United States, although there were several American examples of planned communities of varying size, intention, and success already in existence. She named it Mariemont, honoring her beloved estate in Rhode Island.

Mary Emery's new town was developed mainly by Livingood and designed by his chosen town planner, John Nolen. In its housing and facilities, Mariemont intended to relieve somewhat the congested housing conditions in Cincinnati and to provide a model (although Livingood said he disliked the term, he used it several times to describe the concept) for other planned communities to emulate. Mariemont would offer high-quality rental apartments for "wage-earners" and "workers," but would appeal also to "all classes of people" with building lots that might be purchased for individual homes. The village would contain stores and shops, schools and parks, at least one church, and a complete infrastructure of streets, sewers, and utilities.

Mary embarked by 1910 on her most significant and costly philanthropy, assigning Livingood the task of visiting and studying planned communities in Europe and the United States. For the next three years, Livingood sought towns and cities that were built as housing experiments. English examples attracted him, especially Port Sunlight, Letchworth, and Hampstead Garden Suburb. He studied Bourneville, Harborne Tenants, and Ealing in England, and Krupp colonies in Germany.[1] The Garden City concept of Ebenezer Howard (1850–1928) impressed him, expressed so handsomely at Letchworth in 1903. He attended various conferences on town planning and visited European and American models in 1910–1913. In 1933, he acknowledged in his diary his indebtedness to several inspiring models.[2]

In 1913, Livingood's assignment was completed, just before World War I engulfed Europe, consuming millions of lives in four years of destruction. The next step, selecting an appropriate location for the new town, was particularly sensitive. Where was land available in or near Cincinnati for such an experimental undertaking? Could land purchases be kept secret, thus negating exorbitant prices? How many acres would be needed for the new town? With few answers and no assurances, Mrs. Emery's agent acted. Livingood looked no farther than some sparsely settled farm fields about ten miles east of the downtown and overlooking the Little Miami River. Mary Emery's village would rise on land once inhabited by prehistoric Indians, by pioneers settling on the Miami Purchase in the eighteenth century, and later by Ohio farmers who tilled acres of corn, potatoes, and tobacco on fertile soil. An ancient brick house, one of the oldest in Hamilton County, stood near the crossroads of the two narrow highways that split the property that Mrs. Emery eventually acquired. This simple

Portrait of Mary M. Emery by Effie C. Trader, 1908 (Courtesy Cincinnati Art Museum)

Federal-style structure had been the home of the Ferris family since the early nineteenth century. It would be the backdrop for the groundbreaking ceremony in 1923, featuring the chatelaine of a new community based on the best principles of town planning and urban design. Curiously, the chosen location contained the important Madisonville archeological site under the control of Harvard University, Livingood's alma mater.

By 1915, Livingood made his selection, 250 acres of farm land, ravines, and woods about ten miles east of Cincinnati and bordered by the Little Miami River. This acreage in Columbia Township was dotted with a few houses and farm buildings. Thirty owners were noted on the deeds to the property that Mrs. Emery eventually would purchase. Fort Ancient culture Indians once occupied the bluffs above the Little Miami River, from about 1000 to 1400 A.D. Until about 1600, the Shawnee Tribe resided there. Colonization followed passage of the Northwest Ordinance in 1787, with sales of enormous tracts going to entrepreneurs like John Cleves Symmes. That same year, Symmes conveyed nearly 640 acres, comprising the present boundaries of Mrs. Emery's land acquisitions, to Major Benjamin Stites. Members of the Ferris family settled in the region, with Eliphalet and Joseph Ferris building brick residences on their rich farm land. Eliphalet's house, probably begun in 1802, became the center point of Mariemont.

Mary Emery's land purchases began in 1915 and were made secretly through a screen of agents in Chicago and Cincinnati manipulated by Livingood, and suspended only in 1916–1918 during the nation's involvement in World War I. Each parcel of land was scrutinized by Livingood before his agent negotiated with the owner, but it was essential to acquire contiguous properties within the boundaries designated for Mariemont's construction. The shield for Mrs. Emery as purchaser worked admirably, for the many rumors generated by the sales never identified the new owner until the Mariemont project was announced to the public in 1922.

Livingood was devoted to plans for the new town during the negotiations for land. By August 1918, he had in hand a survey of the purchased acres. By October, he had sketched his layout of the nascent community on his survey sheet, marking positions in colored pencils for streets, buildings, and types of neighborhoods.[3]

Two years later, a "mysterious visitor" called at the Cambridge, Massachusetts, office of America's preeminent town planner, John Nolen (1869–1937).[4] Nolen was away on that September day in 1920, but his associate, Philip W. Foster, received the caller. He soon learned from a survey spread before him that the visitor contemplated the design and construction of a new community. Nolen's office was the patron's choice for its design. This account of the secretive visit summarized the patron's intention.

> The gentleman produced a map with all names carefully erased, and stated his errand in substance as follows: To discuss a scheme for the development of some property as a small community to house people employed in near-by factories. The major portion of the site had been acquired, but various parcels of land were still outstanding, and for that reason he wished to keep the scheme, its location, and his own identity secret.

*John Nolen (1869–
1937), town planner of
Mariemont, Ohio, and
America's preeminent
urban designer, 1916
(Courtesy Barbara Nolen
Strong)*

The community was not to be known as a "model" village, as he disliked
the word model. But all developments were to be along the highest lines, and
his desire was to produce a result that would be followed as an example
throughout the country. The village or town was to be for all classes of people,
and would have some special features, one being a development on a cooperative basis for pensioned employees.

Our visitor, having had some training as an engineer, had worked up an
interesting scheme in crayon. He was anxious to find some one to take on the
planning who would have new and advanced ideas and high ideals, and not be
governed by "cut and dried" customs. He was definitely afraid of getting some
one too old or too busy to really give the scheme the necessary thought and
attention. His selection of Mr. Nolen was the outcome of years of frequenting
city planning conferences, judging the outstanding planners by their addresses
and accomplished work.

At the close of the interview, which apparently had been satisfactory to
him, he stated, in strict confidence, his name—Charles J. Livingood.[5]

Thus began the five-year employment of town planner John Nolen, an accomplished and talented designer responsible for other planned communities, including Myers Park, Charlotte, North Carolina (1911); Union Park Gardens, Wilmington, Delaware (1918); and Kingsport, Tennessee (1919); plus a number of redeveloped cities.

John Nolen completed the master plan for Mariemont, first published in July 1921. Carefully delineating Livingood's requirements for specialized housing and the placement of various public buildings, Nolen's plan served throughout the entire building program with few changes. His design positioned streets, parks, churches, gardens, and shops, spreading 759 house lots over 253 acres. A population of 5,000 was envisioned. Mrs. Emery's Ohio village stretched out from a major town square pierced by diagonal axes. There were secondary cores for a smaller residential neighborhood square, blocks of row houses and apartments, an assortment of parks and greens, a quaint Norman Revival church, and an industrial section separated from the residential portions. Handsome Georgian Revival buildings were envisioned for the town hall, post office, and library, while a mammoth row of shops replicating those in the "Rows" of Chester, England, was intended for one side of the main square. Consideration of the residents was evident in the plans for a large hospital, a convalescent center, cottages for retired workers for the Emery estate, and a recreation complex complete with pool, tennis courts, bowling alley, and various rooms for meetings.

The interactive process of proposing and counterproposing, approving and rejecting, acted out between Nolen and Livingood seldom involved Mary Emery, although she was informed regularly about the project's progress. Occasionally, specific parts of the Mariemont proposal were presented to her for approval, such as selection of street names. But Mary never entered the day-to-day decision process that fell to others, especially to Livingood. However, she was Livingood's "principal" (a term he used frequently in referring to her in his dealings with architects and contractors) and the lifeblood of the new town, Mariemont. She was its proprietor, owner, and only financial backer. Her admiration for Livingood's abilities, his charm, and his almost familial relationship gave him special

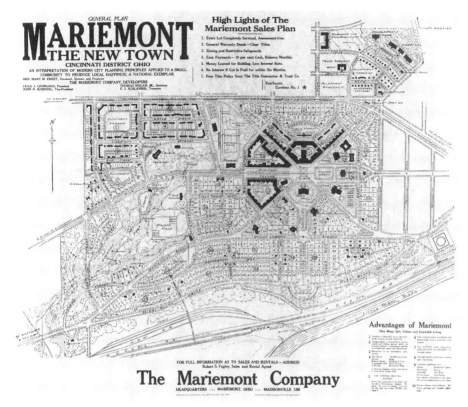

John Nolen's general plan for Mariemont, Ohio, first published in July 1921 (this version, c. 1927–1928) (Courtesy Mariemont Preservation Foundation)

authority and privileges. He relished the role, lived well, and remained dedicated to Mary and her mission.

Speculation and rumors flying around Cincinnati about the massive land purchases east of Cincinnati at the Mariemont site ceased when Livingood and Nolen participated in a well-staged announcement party before the city's prestigious Commercial Club on April 22, 1922. Mary Emery was not present at the all-male gathering. Nolen's lecture and slides vividly outlined the project of building a new town on farm land that would serve as an example of town planning at its best. The patricians attending the meeting, as well as the public, were well acquainted with

Mary's philanthropic record, but Cincinnati's newspapers spread the tale of land purchases and her dream of a "Workers' Mariemont" across their front pages.[6] Her compassionate nature and service to others once again were demonstrated in this remarkable project. The final magnitude of the Mariemont initiative, however, was unknown to any of its major players: Nolen, Livingood, or even Mary Emery herself.

Mary's daily routine in 1922 must have continued as it had for many years. Her extensive library provided hours of enjoyed reading, her Victrola filled the music room at Edgecliffe with entertainment, and she received callers. Livingood called each morning at her Edgecliffe home when she resided in Cincinnati, giving her his progress reports on the new town and acting on her past and future philanthropies. She enjoyed any information on her new enterprise, Mariemont, especially through published materials. An article on the new town appeared in the *American City* in October 1922, probably written by Nolen, but it carried no attribution. Describing Mariemont as a "demonstration town," the writer emphasized that it was not intended as a philanthropy, that it should pay an adequate return on its investment, and that similar projects will follow its lead.[7] However, because Mary Emery conceived of Mariemont as improving the housing problem and subject to her generous funding, the new town may be judged a philanthropic endeavor. Unfortunately, Mariemont never repaid its investment to its founder, nor did it serve exactly as a model for other developments.

Livingood ruminated over the many decisions ahead for the new town, and he determined that a special corporation was needed to control all aspects of Mariemont's construction and sale of lots. Thus was born the Mariemont Company on December 1, 1922, with Mary Emery as the only stockholder except for a single share for each of the trustees.[8] Funding for Mariemont after this date was funneled from Mrs. Emery to the company, and control of all the property (formerly held in her name) was transferred to it. This new agency would guide every aspect of Mariemont's planning and execution under Livingood's presidency. The other trustees included Mary's minister, Frank H. Nelson, and those long associated with Livingood in the enterprise. Mary's support of Mariemont tended to channel

Mary M. Emery, photo-graph by Henry H. Pierce, c. 1910 (Courtesy Lela Emery Steele)

her benevolence more narrowly after 1922, but she reached out regularly to various causes.

Mariemont, Ohio, was envisioned by Livingood from the start as a lit-tle English village, a town of cozy neighborhoods with many amenities, inspired by the need, he said, to provide inexpensive housing for workers of modest means and others of greater affluence. The chosen architects and their architecture would be conservative, employing a style mostly Tudor or Georgian Revival. By 1923, the village's infrastructure was designed and Livingood's choices of architects were listed. Much remained to be done, however, before construction could begin.

Livingood's attention to duty, however, never seemed to interrupt his frequent vacations and rest cures. Crucial decisions were deferred as Livingood and family embarked for Europe in February, not to return until

October 1923. He excused himself due to stress and overwork, sought rest at elegant hotels and spas, and delayed progress on Mrs. Emery's largest enterprise. Nolen and the team in Cincinnati were patient through it all.

With Livingood away for several months, Mary's business affairs were in the hands of Thomas Hogan, Jr., Livingood's able assistant and secretary of the newly formed Mariemont Company. He was methodical and loyal, certainly knowledgable about Mariemont's direction, but he lacked the special relationship with his employer that Livingood enjoyed.

By 1923, Mrs. Emery was white-haired and portly, infrequently encountered at social or cultural events in Cincinnati. She was attended by a full-time nurse, Helen Baird, who remained with her until Mary's death in 1927. Mary's sister, Isabella, who lived with her at Edgecliffe following their mother's demise, was her closest companion. The servants went about their tasks, and as some of them were married with children living on the grounds, a child's voice in Edgecliffe could brighten her day.[9]

In the spring of 1923, the public groundbreaking for Mariemont placed Mary Emery, a generally private person, in a limelight unlike any she experienced until then. Livingood remained in Europe "eating the lotus, reveling in Beauty and cussing myself for having overdone, for my old Doctor here says my whole system is in a pretty bad way,"[10] and he missed the ceremony scheduled for April 23, 1923, on the lawn of Ferris House. Mrs. Emery's limousine, driven by her longtime chauffeur, Charles Singer, deposited her near the simple platform of planks laid out for her benefit. There, with a silver spade in her hands and clutching a bouquet of roses, Mary Emery officially inaugurated her village with a turn of earth. She was watched by a group of one hundred men, women, and children. Cincinnati's newspapers, and even a newsreel cameraman for Pathé News, recorded the event and heralded "the cynosure of all sociological eyes . . . a great experiment . . . to be reared according to sound economics as well as philanthropic solicitude."[11] Mary was seventy-nine years of age. One writer, some years later, estimated her wealth at this time between $30,000,000 and $40,000,000.[12]

Shortly after Livingood returned from Europe in the autumn, he invited town planner Nolen to visit Mrs. Emery and himself in Newport. The

Groundbreaking ceremony for Mariemont, Ohio, April 23, 1923 (front row, left to right: Helen Baird, Mary M. Emery, John R. Schindel, Thomas Hogan, Jr., Reverend Frank H. Nelson) (Courtesy Mariemont Preservation Foundation)

meeting, on September 25–26, 1923, may be the only face-to-face encounter between town planner and founder. Livingood's discussion with Nolen covered operations at the new town in Ohio, with details sparingly shared with Mrs. Emery. Nolen thoughtfully sent his hostess a book by Edgar Allan Poe in appreciation of her hospitality, prompting an acknowledgment from Mary: "In spite of your admonition not to acknowledge the graceful compliment you pay me by suggesting that I would like the story of Poe's Domain of Arnheim, I must express my appreciation and thank you for giving me the inspiration it suggests. A marked book is more intimate than a conversation and I have taken to heart one of Poe's conditions of bliss, viz, 'to have an object of unceasing pursuit'—of course that is what Mariemont represents and therefore I must be in a 'condition of bliss!' Many thanks to you for opening up the vista."[13]

The end of October found Mary back in Cincinnati. In another month, construction began on the nondenominational community church, the first building to be erected in Mariemont. It was certainly Mrs. Emery's decision that the church hold precedence in the construction sequence. Although she did not attend the ceremony on November 12, 1923, groundbreaking was supervised by Livingood, who used the same silver spade his patron wielded in April. Architect Louis E. Jallade's Norman Revival stone edifice, anchoring the neighborhood of townhouses and apartments, required several years to complete, but it became the village's crown jewel.

The Mariemont town site was a sea of mud in the winter and spring of 1924. Mrs. Emery's planned community swarmed with workers as the Dale Park section, the first location for construction of Mariemont Company homes, was begun. Mary's nephew, John J. Emery, newly arrived from New York and world travels, visited Cincinnati to inspect the family's enterprises. On April 1, he joined the ceremony with Livingood to begin the first residential units, townhouses designed by Richard H. Dana, Jr. Mrs. Emery was not well enough to attend, but her brother-in-law's son presided in her stead. As a close blood relative, John J. Emery later figured in the molding of the Emery commercial empire into a new, more powerful corporation.

Construction activity peaked at Mariemont in 1924, when most of the originally intended housing units were underway or completed. By November, three hundred of these were built, several hundred children packed the new elementary school erected by the Mariemont Company, and 250 families moved into the new town. National attention in this suburban enterprise was spurred by an article in the *New York Times Magazine*, illustrated with renderings by one of the commissioned architects, Hubert Ripley.[14] The author sagely predicted Mariemont's promise and virtues. Other writers on the unique village intoned Mary Emery's name frequently, appropriately crediting her for the financial underpinnings of the project, and sometimes lauding her for the humanitarian idea of offering well-designed and relatively inexpensive housing for low-income families.

The earliest drawings published in the *New York Times Magazine* and other periodicals illustrated an assortment of styles for public buildings—

Mariemont Memorial (later Community) Church by Louis E. Jallade, constructed 1923–1927 (Courtesy Mariemont Preservation Foundation)

primarily "sham" architecture in Tudor and Georgian Revival styles. No style dominated another, nor was any style restricted to any section of the town, but the intended city hall, post office, and block of stores on the main square were grand in scale and dominant in their placement. Residential buildings were depicted more diminutively, more in keeping with Livingood's intention to repeat, at least partially, a quaint English village. As Livingood was master in all day-to-day matters pertaining to Mariemont, he had the final word on building styles. He selected the architects and chose the locations for buildings to fit into Nolen's plan. The appearance of Mrs. Emery's new town depended, then, on Livingood's perceptions, but conservative architects experienced in revival styles were likely to appeal to her taste as well.

The year ended in America's newest community with a Christmas celebration in fresh snow, with Mariemont's children waiting for the arrival of

Santa Claus, who joined them on the evening of December 24 at the lighted Christmas tree on the green in front of the Mariemont Memorial Church. After carols were sung, the rector of Christ Church, Frank H. Nelson, spoke to the children about the holiday, and the Packard limousine of Mary Emery brought her to the party. The first Christmas in the new town ended with a turkey dinner she provided for everyone.[15]

During the winter of 1924–1925, an army of construction workers labored to finish the townhouses, single homes, and other buildings of Mariemont , a town that now covered 420 acres. Mrs. Emery's investment through funds she funneled into the Mariemont Company increased to $4,000,000.[16] There is no evidence that she wavered in her support of the project, in spite of the mounting financial drain on her resources. Only Livingood knew the true extent of her support vis-à-vis other demands on her wealth, and he reduced expenditures significantly for the village only after Mary's death. Until then, the architects, engineers, and laborers worked on, an army estimated to exceed 1,000 men.

Only the meticulously detailed diary of village engineer Warren Parks recorded the infrequent visits of Mary Emery to her new town. Otherwise, practically nothing is known of her appearances in Mariemont. Since groundbreaking in 1923, she seldom journeyed to the site, but on April 12, 1925, the fine spring weather lured her, along with her nurse, Helen Baird. Unfortunately, her impressions are not known. Her aversion to publicity precluded any attention to her opinions, although the press certainly hoped to garner some statement from her and her reaction to the rapidly growing new town.

The Mariemont Company, thanks to Mary Emery, increased its capitalization to $6,000,000 in 1925.[17] Feeling a crunch for more building funds, and realizing that lots were not selling as readily as planned, the founder's deep pockets were needed to keep the venture solvent. In relation to the expected return from rents and sale of lots, the investment in infrastructure and construction was enormous. Still, the scheme for Mariemont was not considered as a philanthropy, and this was the official, published position. By 1925, Mrs. Emery surely realized that there would be little return to repay her investment, though she had hoped the returns would gener-

*Townhouses by Edmund B. Gilchrist, Plainville Road, Mariemont, Ohio, begun 1924
photograph by Nancy Ford Cones (Courtesy Mariemont Preservation Foundation)*

*Houses, (St. Louis Flats) by Charles Cellarius, Dale Park section, Mariemont, Ohio,
begun 1924 (Courtesy Mariemont Preservation Foundation)*

*Houses by Carl A. Ziegler, final group housing erected in Dale Park section,
Mariemont, Ohio, begun 1924 (Courtesy Mariemont Preservation Foundation)*

ate other planned communities through similar funding programs. The
company's promotional brochure preached the non-philanthropic nature
of the founder in its opening words. "Mariemont is not a philanthropy or
in any way paternalistic. Its sponsor, Mrs. Mary M. Emery, herself a life-
long resident of Cincinnati, is simply showing in a very practical way her
interest in the proper development of home life and home ownership by
providing an ideal place for home building. The Mariemont Company
will do part of the building, and when all the lots and buildings have been
disposed of, a good start having been made, the public, seeing the advan-
tages, will make Mariemont one of the most thriving of Cincinnati's suburbs."[18] Renters recognized these points, and one even wrote of her pleasure to Frank Nelson, who conveyed the message to Mrs. Emery, who was
addressed in the letter as "Mother Two." "I have this cozy lovely home and
all my friends and relatives do likewise and they praise Mrs. Emery for
doing this all; and all I pay is $35.00 for this darling little lovely home and
such lovely fresh pure air [and] all of my children look and feel fine

now. . . . Sometimes I long to meet Mrs. Emery and thank her. I could kiss her for making it possible for poor folks to live so nice."[19]

Nolen lost touch with Mariemont in 1925. His duties were reduced, now that his town plan was completed. Livingood felt his services were no longer needed. Nolen made his last official visit to Mariemont on October 20, 1925. Two days later, he spoke to the Ohio State Conference on City Planning in Dayton and extolled the new town. It was his farewell to a project he considered among his finest. "Mariemont is laid out on modern town planning principles, and is said to be the most comprehensive development of its kind in this country. It is neither philanthropic nor paternalistic, but a development on normal American lines, except that everything has been scientifically planned in advance, and that the owner limits profits, and will share the town's success with those who live in it. When completed, Mariemont will illustrate how people of moderate means can live well near great cities."[20]

That optimistic tone of Nolen did not shield him, however, from his dismissal in December as the new town's planner. His official termination was conveyed in a letter from Livingood that ended a five-year association.[21] The trio of Nolen, Livingood, and Mary Emery, who advanced town planning principles in America in the creation of a remarkable suburb, was disbanded.

CHAPTER 7

Mary's Alms

Later Philanthropies

S ULTRY CINCINNATI was abandoned in the summer months by the
city's prominent and wealthy families, with many having homes or
cottages in northern Michigan and Maine. The Emerys picked the Newport area, however, for their summer haunt. Beginning in the late spring
of each year, usually in May, Mary Emery and the Livingood family,
accompanied by selected servants from Edgecliffe, made the nine hun-
dred-mile trip to Middletown, Rhode Island, then a country suburb of
Newport, in a private railroad car retained by Mrs. Emery. It was an
overnight journey that started in Cincinnati's Grand Central Union station, Third and Central Avenue. The route for the trip had several
options, but the usual end of the line was Wickford, just below Warwick,
Rhode Island, where a change was made to a less elegant railroad coach.
Elizabeth Livingood McGuire recalled how impressed she was with the
rail carriage's red plush seats, the windows that opened, and the steam-
boat, *The General*, that awaited the train to take them to Newport. The
arriving party was met at the dock by carriages for the entourage and bag-
gage, carrying them up into the low hills and through the stone gate into
the landscaped grounds of Mariemont.[1]

Seacroft, purchased by Mary for the Livingood family's use in the summer, was located directly across the road from Mariemont. Its lawns and flower beds were less formal, in keeping with the homeyness of the three-story house and its wide verandas filled with comfortable wicker furniture. The views to the sea and toward Newport were especially fine from Seacroft, giving an openness to the summer home's exterior that belied the crowded clutter of its Victorian interior. Each summer when the Livingoods resided with Mrs. Emery, the lawns and trails were settings for outdoor games, Indian tepees, and costumes when the children were very young, and tennis on the clay court as they reached adolescence. Mary's season tickets to Newport's tennis tournaments and horse shows were turned over to the Livingood family for their enjoyment.

Two of Mary Emery's benefactions in 1911–1912 focused on the environment. She acquired land near the University of Cincinnati for a bird preserve and purchased a botanical garden in the western section of the city. A few acres on Evanswood Place, a wooded region in Clifton not far from the campus, was designated as a study and preserve for the Unive-

Seacroft, guest house at Mariemont, Rhode Island, 1908–1910 (Courtesy Mariemont Preservation Foundation)

Children of Lily and Charles J. Livingood (left to right: John, Elizabeth, and Josephine) at Seacroft, Rhode Island, 1908 (Courtesy Mariemont Preservation Foundation)

rsity of Cincinnati. It was placed under the supervision of Harris M. Benedict, professor of botany at the university. He had fought for three years to achieve this goal, and Mary responded generously.[2]

In the spring of 1912, Mary's interest in nature, and especially gardens, prompted her acquisition of Tuchfarber's Botanical Garden, a small tract of eight acres in Westwood, whose owner had fallen on hard times and could not meet mortgage payments. Just as the property was about to be sold to subdivision builders, Mary Emery stepped in and purchased it through her agent, John Hall. Livingood's hand was involved, of course, in studying the land and its future use. She intended to hold it until a public board could be established to operate it, perhaps through the University of Cincinnati or the Cincinnati Park Board.[3] Eventually, she chose the latter agency, and the Westwood garden became part of the city's park system.

When Livingood completed his careful study of planned communities in Europe and the United States, America was coping with the newly instituted income tax, Woodrow Wilson had succeeded William Howard Taft as President, and the Federal Reserve Bank system was inaugurated. For the first time, Americans were subject to a federal tax on their incomes because of the sixteenth amendment to the United States Constitution. It imposed a top rate tax of six percent on incomes over $500,000 per year. State income taxes were practically nonexistent at this date, however. The effects of taxation on Mary's income were negligible, it seems, for she continued to support numerous charities and causes, embarking in 1913 on an endowment for medical education at the University of Cincinnati, an interest she would later expand. Mary's close friend, Dr. Benjamin K. Rachford, for whom she initiated the Babies Milk Fund, encouraged her to establish a department of pathology in the medical school. She responded to him, writing, "Desiring to give some permanent aid in the constant battle against disease, I wish to endow a chair in Pathology in that department of the University of Cincinnati known as the Ohio-Miami Medical College, of whose pressing needs and opportunities you have kept me advised."[4] Mrs. Emery provided $125,000 to establish the new department. In gratitude, the university named it in her honor, an unusual instance of her acceptance of any recognition that labelled her in connection with her gift. Her love of children and interest in their welfare streamed through her life's benefactions, a memorial to her own sons.

Mary also responded to a request from ex-President Taft to donate to an Episcopal school, the University of the South, in Sewanee, Tennessee. Taft vacationed and played golf in Augusta, Georgia, also a favored spot for Mary. Following his loss to Wilson in 1912, he wrote persuasively to her. "It [the university] spreads a refining influence that is most valuable for the community at large. This is what has given me an interest in the matter, for, though I am not an Episcopalian, I am very fond of the church and like to do what I can to help it . . . and I thought of you in that connection. I have written a letter to Mr. Livingood asking an interview for the Bishop with you."[5] Mary's response at the urging of an old friend was generous. A new nurses' home, called the Emery Annex, resulted, but was not constructed until 1916.[6]

In the spring of 1913, before she left for Newport, Mary considerately remembered the office employees of her husband's firm, Thomas Emery's Sons, by divesting herself of 1,884 shares of the Emery Candle Company to benefit officers and workers. That company was one of the earliest ventures of "Old Tom" Emery. It remained a rich source of income for the Emery family well into the twentieth century. Mary's provision for the company's employees at that date was a rare occurrence in labor relations. Seldom were employees given gifts of this magnitude by their employers in the early twentieth century.[7]

Berea College in Kentucky enjoyed several contributions that began with Thomas J. Emery's first gift in 1898, apparently for no specific purpose, and his widow followed this lead in 1907 with a second donation. Her two largest gifts, however, were made in 1914, when she gave funds for the library's endowment, and in 1916, when she pledged the money to build the new Domestic Science Building.[8] She remembered her student days at Brooklyn's Packer Institute by endowing a pension fund with $50,000 to honor a favorite teacher, Adeline L. Jones, who died in 1912.[9] The Emery family's longstanding interest in the welfare of African Americans linked Mary Emery with other distinguished Cincinnatians such as Jacob Schmidlapp and James N. Gamble as the principal financial supporters of the Home for Colored Girls, 649 West Seventh Street, which opened in December 1914.[10] Whether it was temporary housing for the less fortunate, or preparations to create a model village, a focus on homes and good living conditions were never far from Mary Emery's or Livingood's thoughts.

A biography of one of Cincinnati's most eminent physicians, Christian R. Holmes, reports how Mary's commitment to Dr. Holmes's work joined her dedication to medical research and care. She wrote to Holmes, "My gratitude to your learned profession . . . and my desire to further its powers . . . lead me to make the following offer. . . . a well-designed and equipped building near a good hospital being an essential for the proper performance of a medical school . . . I promise for myself and my executors . . . $250,000."[11] Mary's promised gift was contingent on the raising of matching funds by July 1, 1915, to build a structure next to the general hospital, placing it under the control of the medical department of the University of Cincinnati. No doubt, Mary's good friends, Drs. Rachford and Holmes, were instrumental in the exact wording of her gift's terms. As a donor and patron, Mrs. Emery seldom required matching funds for her gifts, but in the rare instances where this was in order, the usual wealthy contemporaries came through. In this case, Dr. Holmes telegraphed Mrs. Emery at her Newport home that $255,000 had been raised by July 1, and that the principal contributors were William Cooper Procter, Mrs. Charles Fleischmann, and Mr. and Mrs. Charles Phelps Taft.[12] By the time of the new school's dedication in 1918, Mrs. Emery had contributed an additional $55,000 to equip the facility.[13]

The biographer of Dr. Christian R. Holmes, writing in 1937 about Mrs. Emery's support of the new hospital, offered some interesting observations about Mary's views of medicine. His information probably came from Holmes or Rachford, her close acquaintances. It was claimed that Mrs. Emery was an ardent follower of homeopathy. This was not uncommon in Cincinnati during Mrs. Emery's lifetime, for nearly two-thirds of Cincinnati physicians were homeopaths. Four doctors who treated Mary and her family were all rated as homeopaths. Homeopathy, the medical system based on the teachings of a German physician, Dr. Samuel Hahnemann (1755–1843), was introduced to the United States in 1825. Its practice maintained that illnesses should be treated by attenuated doses of medicine. The biographer described Mary's reaction to advice from Dr. Holmes. "Whenever her personal ills required advice beyond theirs, she sought another homeopath in Philadelphia. Rachford (whose wife with her sister had grown up in Mrs. Emery's garden and called her 'Aunt Mary') and Holmes were regulars. The latter persuaded her some years later to consent to a visit from four of his faculty. She took their advice for a month—then returned for better comfort to Philadelphia."[14]

It is true that Mary frequented Philadelphia, often with her sister, Isabella, as when she wrote to Joseph Gest in December 1915 with a request that he come and see some paintings in another outstanding private house, the Widener collection.[15] Mary was cognizant of other major collections being formed and competing with her for the masterpieces coming on the market, and Widener's was one of the best. This may have been the time for one of the homeopath visits alluded to by Holmes's biographer. Although Mary Emery certainly opened her heart to children's causes, even linking them on occasion as memorials to her lost sons, her interest in medical facilities and services was not dependent only on her love of children.

Midway through 1915, Mary sent a check for $5,000 to a city-wide campaign known as the Federated Charities, later to become the United Way, and with this gift she initiated a single campaign for multiple purposes and charities. This method of raising money soon became a common one for cities. While Mary's contribution originally was an anonymous one, she wrote in a quoted letter to the drive's chairman, Frederick Geier, a leading industrialist of Cincinnati, that her name could be used. Mary's check for $5,000 comprised eight percent of the total to be raised from the entire city. She approved of centralized giving to support welfare projects in Cincinnati and made this point in a letter to Geier.[16]

In the autumn of 1915, she turned once again to a philanthropy she first found appealing in 1910, the Berry Schools in Georgia. The schools needed a farm settlement for boys, Mrs. Emery was told by the persistent Miss Berry, requiring new barns on the school's rural campus. Mary's check for $16,000 met the cost. Seldom did she correspond with the recipients of her contributions, other than an initial letter conveying the funds, but she maintained an active exchange of letters with Martha Berry, the schools' founder, up to Mary's death in 1927. For Miss Berry's part, her letters often camouflaged her appeal for continued financial support. Nevertheless, Mary responded graciously with pledges and payments made on an annual basis.

Livingood devoted more and more time to the Mariemont real estate venture, yet his patron's charitable gifts elsewhere continued unabated. Mary Emery's pledge of $250,000 in 1915 to the Endowment Fund Association of the University of Cincinnati requested that it be used for the construction of a building for the medical school. Her gift was instrumental in initiating future and matching donations from others, and it extended her strong support of medical activities at the city's university.[17] Another educational institution was enriched by Mrs. Emery in 1916, Berea College in Kentucky. Established in 1855 near Lexington as a liberal arts four-year academic institution, Berea College served students primarily from poor regions of Appalachia. It focused its programs on agricultural and vocational courses.

Berea's president charmed her for a $50,000 gift in his polished, dignified request that followed a visit he made to her summer estate:

> As I explained to you at Newport, we have been slowly developing plans for a simple adequate equipment of Berea for its great task in bringing our three million mountain people out of the woods. Through the help you then gave us and by other means, we have made purchases of land and by advice of the Olmsted Brothers and others we have made plans for segregating our five departments—the foundation school, the vocational school, the academy, the normal school, and the college—so that each may have its own precinct and develop its particular type of education to best advantage. We shall thus have for the students of each department the close personal touch of a small school and at the same time, the enthusiasm and the great economy of a large institution. . . . Now the question is, Mrs. Emery, how much would you give to have Berea thus equipped?

The president concluded, "Your friendship has already been worth more to Berea than you are at all likely to realize." The new Domestic Science Building on Berea's campus was earmarked for the resulting gift of $50,000.[18]

Cincinnati acclaimed the generosity of Mary and her good friend, Anna Sinton Taft (1856–1931), when they rescued the Cincinnati Zoological Park in 1916. By then, the zoo was a failing institution, heavily in debt and ready to be sold by its owners, the Cincinnati Traction Company. The zoo was much loved by Cincinnatians and owed its life to an enterprising, German-born emigrant to Cincinnati, Andrew Erkenbrecker, who made his fortune in manufacturing and selling starch. He organized a bird society in 1873 and opened the city's first exhibition of birds and animals in 1875. Erkenbrecher's zoo never prospered, and it was acquired by the Traction Company in 1901. Just as grounds and animals were to be sold, the two philanthropists stepped in, certainly after Livingood scrutinized the organization and its operating costs, and provided the purchase price of $250,000. Each lady contributed $125,000 and agreed to assume any operating deficits if the citizens of Cincinnati would raise $125,000 for working capital. Mrs. Taft and Mrs. Emery carefully protected their generous provision for the zoo's continuance when they required, as a condition of their purchase, that the sale of the zoo would result if the deficits proved to be too large or impractical, with all sales proceeds going to the Cincinnati Museum Association. But the zoo prospered under the new owners and its new board of trustees, finding its next owners in 1932, when the City of Cincinnati bought it from the Emery and Taft estates.[19]

Mary's compassionate interest in the welfare of orphans and minorities expanded her late husband's support of African-American agencies when she promised in the autumn of 1916 to build a three-story "stone front" building for "the benefit of unfortunate negro girls, the gift being contingent upon a fund sufficient to equip and maintain the institution for two years being raised."[20] The Evangeline Booth Home, a rescue facility managed by the Salvation Army, was assisted by an advisory committee of prominent Cincinnatians, including Livingood, James Gamble, Bishop Boyd Vincent, and Jacob Schmidlapp. This home, like all of the charities supported by Mary, was screened by Livingood before a gift was arranged. In many instances, Livingood was expected to serve on the agency's board of trustees.

America entered the war in Europe in 1917, sending troops to France and ships across the seas to help the beleaguered Allies. Mrs. Emery's life continued largely unaffected by the war, except she refrained from purchasing paintings throughout 1918. Livingood was too old to serve in the military, yet he participated in many volunteer agencies to support the nation's war effort, such as the War Education Committee, the National YMCA War Council, and the Red Cross. For all of these he helped raise funds, but he still steered Mary's charitable giving. Even though she was increasingly frail and seldom encouraged visitors, writing to the museum that neither she nor her sister were equal to "even visits of our friends," Mary Emery helped her church by donating land for a new chapel designated to celebrate the Christ Church's centennial.[21] She also provided funds for a new building at Cincinnati's Children's Home. This agency started life as an orphanage and shelter in 1859, and was led from its inception by a distinguished group of Cincinnatians, including members of the Gamble, Fleischmann, Procter, Taft, Crosley, Geier, Rowe, Coombe and Burchenal families. By 1915, the home outgrew its downtown location on Ninth Street and obtained a rural site on Madisonville Road, on the city's east side. Buildings were then designed by Alfred O. Elzner, a noted Cincinnati architect who later would be part of the Mariemont team. The Emery Building resulting from Mary's gift housed a chapel, dining room, and space on the second floor for twenty-five children.[22] The Children's Home joined a growing list of children's causes benefited by Mrs. Emery, whose interest in children's welfare never subsided.

The carnage ended in Europe on November 11, 1918, with the signing of the armistice. Cincinnati rejoiced in the restored peace and welcomed home her doughboys. Although her philanthropic activities were curtailed somewhat by the war's worries, Mary Emery continued the generous program of dispensing her great wealth as soon as World War I ended. In 1918, she remembered a small Episcopal church in Circleville, Ohio, where her father had once served as senior warden. Her gift of $10,000 was enough to build a new parish house.[23] For Dr. Christian Holmes's hospital in Cincinnati, when funds were short, she sent $50,000, although he asked only for $25,000.[24] The need for a large and well-equipped central YMCA in downtown Cincinnati resulted in the Italian Renaissance-style palazzo she funded in 1917 and saw completed in 1918.[25] Designed by local architects Elzner and Anderson, the YMCA building cost $565,000. Although others contributed to the final cost, Mary was the principal donor.

In late August 1920, Mary Emery reaffirmed her support for the University of Cincinnati and its medical facilities by offering a large endowment to establish a department of pediatrics. Her letter from Newport pledged $250,000 to endow the Benjamin Knox Rachford Department of Pediatrics at the Ohio-Miami Medical College (then the university's medical school): "[It is] my hope in this way to show my appreciation of the great service rendered to this branch of medicine by my friend, Dr. Benjamin Knox Rachford of Cincinnati."[26] Mary's affection and support for medical programs at the University, through her friendship with Drs. Rachford and Christian Holmes, were demonstrated earlier by her gifts of $125,000 in 1913 to establish a department of pathology and $250,000 in 1915 to benefit Holmes's cause. An enduring, but unrecognized, influence on her philanthropy was her interest in children. Once, in later years, Mary Emery spoke of the loss of her sons when she described to Livingood's daughter, Elizabeth, that a necklace of coral beads with a clasp of two angels' heads represented her two boys, Albert and Sheldon, in heaven.[27]

Late in the fall of 1920, Mrs. Emery was awarded a Doctor of Laws degree at the centennial celebration of the University of Cincinnati's Ohio-Miami Medical College.[28] The degree, partly awarded in appreciation for her benefactions, rightly recognized her as Cincinnati's most important philanthropist. She was the first woman to receive an honorary degree from that institution.

It is clear that Mary Emery's charitable giving was not deterred by parsimony, for her generosity continued unabated throughout the years after her husband's death in 1906. It is perplexing, however, that no attempt seems to have been made by Livingood to estimate the ultimate costs Mrs. Emery had to bear for Mariemont's land purchases, design and plans, architects' and engineers' fees, construction costs, and the other expenses this grandiose undertaking demanded. Mrs. Emery was not concerned about her financial obligations, even for Mariemont, it seems, for she continued to support various charities, sometimes modestly, and sometimes very generously.

During 1921, she wrote to Livingood of her wish to add to the endowment of the Ohio Mechanics Institute in Cincinnati, requesting him to select securities in the value of $500,000 "and turn them over to the Treasurer in due course when you think proper as an endowment, the income only to be used for the purposes of the Institute."[29] This gift was not announced until after Mary Emery's death in 1927, although the income earned on the endowment was recorded as annual giving by the institute from 1921 to 1927. Mary's reticent nature once more shunned the publicity that surely would result from so large a benefaction. She was quiet about small gifts, too, as demonstrated when she donated $500 to help

Central YMCA, Cincinnati, by Elzner & Anderson, 1918 (Courtesy Cincinnati Historical Society)

send a promising young Cincinnati artist, John Weis, a pupil of her friend Duveneck, to Europe for further study. Livingood wrote to Gest that he heard "that John E. Weiss [sic] was planning to study abroad and explained in confidence that he [Gest] was even helping to pay the way of his associate although neither of them have very much money. Mrs. Emery heard of this and wishing to do now what the Duveneck Foundation will eventually do wishes to have the privilege of aiding so talented and promising an artist as John E. Weiss. She therefore desires to make a gift of $500 to be her contribution to the money needed by Mr. Weiss for this period of study abroad."[30]

Before embarking for Europe in mid summer of 1921, Livingood and his family spent a few days in July at the Manoir Richelieu, a favorite hotel in Quebec Province, near Pointe-à-Pic where they eventually built a summer residence along the St. Lawrence River. He wrote Mrs. Emery about Andrew Carnegie's canniness in setting up his estate, no doubt to encourage her to do the same, but he added that Carnegie had "few good paintings."[31] That same month William Howard Taft, recently appointed chief justice of the United States Supreme Court, vacationed at his summer home at Pointe-à-Pic and wrote to his friend, Mary.

> I owe you an apology for my long delay in acknowledging your kind telegram of congratulation on my appointment. Your friend and my friend, Albert Halstead [a childhood friend of Sheldon and Albert Emery in Cincinnati], handed it to me. On an occasion like this, where one has good fortune, and receives such a distinction, the greatest pleasure is the expression of kindly sympathetic interest and rejoicing on the part of one's real friends, among whom, my dear Mrs. Emery, I am proud to claim you. I sincerely hope that you have recovered from your illness from which you were suffering when I saw Miss Belle Hopkins in Boston, now near a year ago, and through whom I sent a message to you.[32]

As Mrs. Emery wrote checks for Mariemont's final land purchases in 1922, Martha Berry's persistent cries for financial help for her school in Georgia were partly salved by an annual contribution. Miss Berry knew how to play to Mary, recognizing her abiding interest in children and their welfare. "Unless I journey out into the world and tell the simple story of the school, I don't seem to accumulate sufficient funds to run the school, and I am very anxious to spend the month of June here at the schools. We are planning to hold an institute for country teachers during two weeks in June. These teachers will come from seven counties and a great many of them are young girls teaching their first country school. It is very much like the blind leading the blind. We will charge them just enough to break even, for the sole purpose of the institute is to help the teachers help thousands of little children."[33]

The Berry Schools continued to receive contributions during most of Mary's remaining years, a rare case of regular or continuing donations rather than one-time gifts. Good causes, with ongoing needs, she felt, were to be supported not once but repeatedly.

In Livingood's absence, charitable requests flooding Mrs. Emery's mail were put aside except for those already known and supported, such as

Martha Berry and the Berry Schools in Georgia. In most compelling language, Miss Berry never ceased her appeals to her generous benefactor. Her letters to Mary embellished the schools' financial needs with heartstring tugs, telling her that her schools held "nearly six hundred boys and girls now and growing every day. It seems to me that investment in the youth of our country is the best investment that we can make."[34] Martha Berry did not confine her requests for funds to Mary Emery, even urging that John D. Rockefeller be solicited by both of them. While Miss Berry was vacationing at the Hotel Bon Air in Augusta, Georgia, a resort frequented by Mary in the winter, she wrote of a fruitless attempt to enlist the Standard Oil baron: "It brought back to me so vividly the time you had me visit you there, and how we worked to get Mr. Rockefeller to help. He said he would pray for me. I feel that if his prayer did not help, the daily prayers of the boys and girls have brought great results."[35]

Pleased to hear that Miss Berry's Schools were free of debt and in need of her annual gift, Mary forwarded her pledge payment through Thomas Hogan's hands and renewed a four-year commitment.

Mary Emery was not a prolific letter writer, if one can judge by the surviving examples, but the occasional note in her handwriting always conveyed her gentility and thoughtfulness. In a letter to Martha Berry, she is charmingly naive in thanking Miss Berry's schoolboys for sending her some peanuts: "Tell them I tried very hard to eat them until I took them to the kitchen where the cook told me they must be roasted! I left them in her care."[36] The Berry Schools in Georgia again sought financial aid by enlisting a former schoolboy, then living in Cincinnati, to seek Mrs. Emery's help in the summer of 1924. "I am enclosing a letter which I have received from Mr. Livingood. You see there is no hope. Isn't it too bad. I shall just have to beg money elsewhere to keep up Emery Hall. I know that Mrs. Emery would have been glad to help and she wrote that the matter had been left to Mr. Livingood. When you see him, please fill him full of Berry."[37]

The Emery family's demonstrated interest in African-American causes was reprised by Mary, probably in 1925, when she contributed $25,000 to the Negro Orphans Asylum of Cincinnati. This organization, founded in

1844, was given $30,000 by Thomas Emery and his brother sometime in the late nineteenth century to construct a new building.[38] This handsome, three-story brick structure provided housing and care for orphans in the racially-divided city. Mary's generous gift continued the commitment of her husband and brother-in-law to children's welfare.

Mary Emery's self-effacing, retiring nature deepened with declining health as she entered her eightieth year. On January 26, 1925, her lawyers assembled in Cincinnati and witnessed her signature on her last will and testament. The three Cincinnatians who attested to the document were old friends, John B. Hollister, Charles Phelps Taft II, and Henry Hamilton Wiggers. Mary's will appointed Charles J. Livingood, "my friend," as executor and Robert A. Taft, son of William Howard Taft, in his stead if Livingood were unable to act. As a legal resident of Middletown, Rhode Island, Mary's wishes were listed in a detailed statement of ten pages.[39] The first codicil, bearing the same date, added trustee responsibilities to Livingood. Mrs. Emery employed prestigious lawyers to advise her, and leader of this group was Robert A. Taft (1889–1953) one of Cincinnati's most prominent citizens, and eventually to be known to the nation as Mr. Republican. Hoping to seal the acceptance of her will when submitted to the Probate Court, Mary penned a letter on Edgecliffe stationery to the court: "Knowing that often a person's Will is subject to question, first as to the maker being competent to draw a will and second that undue influence has been exerted on the subject of the Will—I wish to assure you that I have given grave consideration to all the matter contained in this my Will presented to you for Probate and have only altered foregoing documents at this late date owing to the coming of age of all my nephews and nieces. Kindly allow my Executor to carry out specifically my wishes as contained in this my Last Will and Testament and greatly oblige."[40]

The terms of her will were confidential, of course, and not known by the public until her death. However, one important item was announced to the press by Livingood. The will established the Thomas J. Emery Memorial, a foundation that would continue her charitable works as her estate's "residuary legatee and devisee." Named for her late husband, the Memorial resulted from Mrs. Emery's long-standing practice of commemo-

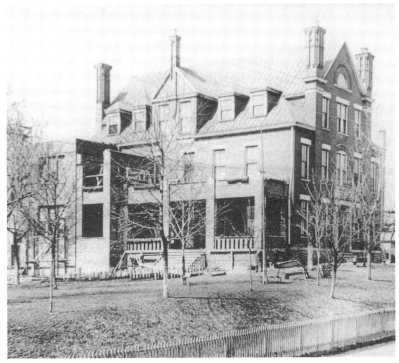

Colored Orphans Asylum, Cincinnati, c. 1926 (Courtesy Cincinnati Historical Society)

rating her spouse in many of the good works she undertook. It is not known when the concept of the Memorial occurred to her, or even if she was its sole initiator, but it was included in the will and modified slightly by a codicil.[41] Livingood released the announcement of the Memorial's formation on April 16, and the local newspapers promptly covered it.

> A unique method of trusteeship has been evolved by Mrs. Mary M. Emery, founder of Mariemont, according to announcements made yesterday by her personal representative, Charles J. Livingood. This trusteeship has been incorporated under the laws of Ohio to administer the entire residuary estate of Mrs. Emery, and is to be known as The Thomas J. Emery Memorial. It will be a perpetual memorial to the memory of Mrs. Emery's husband, the late Thomas J. Emery. It is unique also in that it is established during the lifetime of Mrs. Emery, and she may thus watch its development while it carries on the

Robert A. Taft (1889–
1953), "Mr. Republican,"
son of President William
Howard Taft, and one of
Mary M. Emery's lawyers, c.
1925 (Courtesy Cincinnati His-
torical Society)

many benevolent institutions already established by her, at the same time ini-
tiating new ones.[42]

Speaking for Mrs. Emery, Livingood stated that she "simply wishes to see
continued the kind of charitable and benevolent activities that have
enlisted her interest all these years." Mary Emery directed in her will that
the funds from her residuary estate should be placed with the Memorial to
create an endowment and invested to produce income. Mary's directions
for the Memorial's future use were specific. "Income therefrom shall be
used for the physical, social, civic and educational betterment of residents
of the United States, preferably those in the State of Ohio, on humanitarian lines. . . . The general purpose of this Memorial shall be to secure a
citizenry which will be more sane, sound and effective because of more
satisfactory initial conditions of environment and education."

The future disposition, therefore, of all of Mary Emery's assets was
determined in 1925. She established the Thomas J. Emery Memorial, her

art collection was assigned to the art museum, and her last will and testa-ment was written. Her tenuous health and recovery from a gall bladder operation required constant attention from a physician, according to Eliz-abeth Livingood McGuire, and, at her Newport summer home, she was the only patient treated by a doctor who lived at her estate.[43] That physi-cian, Johnson McGuire, was a young intern in the summer of 1925. His medical services were obtained through the University of Cincinnati, where Mary's support opened many doors. Tending to Mrs. Emery was not difficult, and the physician's employment by Mrs. Emery had a happy end-ing in the eventual marriage of Dr. McGuire and Livingood's youngest child, Elizabeth, some years later.

CHAPTER 8

The Edgecliffe Collection of Paintings
1907 to World War I

T HE CINCINNATI Art Museum in 1907 was one of the nation's principal art galleries. Founded in 1881 by spirited citizens, by 1886 it had its own building, a large Romanesque Revival edifice designed by Cincinnati architect, James McLaughlin, crowning a hill in Eden Park. It had a distinguished group of trustees and supporters, the business leaders of the city, following the model of patrician leadership established at the other important art centers at this time: the Metropolitan Museum of Art (founded 1870), Boston's Museum of Fine Arts (founded 1870), the Philadelphia Museum of Art (founded 1876), and the Art Institute of Chicago (founded 1879). With the exception of the Metropolitan Museum, none of the other cities could boast a museum building as elegant as Cincinnati's. The collections of the Cincinnati Art Museum were slight in their importance, however, but gifts and purchases of arms and armor, American Indian art, African sculpture, and paintings by many of Cincinnati's finest artists gradually filled the galleries, along with plaster casts of Greek and Roman sculpture.

When Mrs. Emery announced in 1906 her generous gift to endow a free admission day for museum visitors, art collectors in Cincinnati were almost nonexistent except for Mr. and Mrs. Charles Phelps Taft. True, there were a few paintings of significance in private hands or an occasional marble portrait bust by Cincinnati sculptor Hiram Powers (1805–1873) gracing a parlor here and there, but no one besides the Tafts persistently acquired European or Asian works of art. Only a few Cincinnatians had the money, not to mention the taste, to engage in collecting on the grand scale of Anna and Charles Taft. In 1907, Mary Emery entered the collecting arena. For the next twenty years, she and the Tafts were the principal art collectors in Cincinnati. Mary Emery focused her collecting exclusively, on paintings, while the Tafts sought French enamels, Chinese ceramics, and a few examples of decorative arts, as well as old master paintings.

Rich and famous Americans of Mrs. Emery's day competed with each other as collectors. They decorated their palatial homes or impressed their neighbors and, quite frequently, they began collecting to fill voids in the young museums in their native cities. Beginning collectors were influenced by their education, their peers, their interests and taste. Most often, they sought what was well known and admired, purchasing "safe" paintings and other works of art they had read about. This was the initial course of Mary and her contemporaries. The Barbizon school of French painters, including Corot, Dupré, Rousseau, and others, was very popular as Mary began to collect, and her first acquisitions were by artists of this school. Canvases by old masters, especially the great names like Rembrandt, Titian, Velázquez, and Hals, later were eagerly sought as well. Masters of the British school were so popular in the early twentieth century that their prices frequently exceeded those for greater painters. For example, Mrs. Emery paid $120,000 in 1910 for her group portrait by Frans Hals and $140,000 in the same year for Sir Henry Raeburn's *Elphinston Children.*

Collectors of art in Mrs. Emery's day had several avenues available to them in building a collection. They could travel to the art centers of London, Paris, and New York to seek dealers from whom they might purchase important paintings or objects. In those cities and many in Europe, they could familiarize themselves with other works of art during frequent museum visits, sharpening their critical eye. Collectors could purchase at auctions, either in person or through an agent, but travel and communications were complicated. Mrs. Emery and her American contemporaries usually preferred buying from dealers who catered to their clients with visits, bringing the paintings and sculpture directly to their homes to be lived with for a while as a purchase was contemplated.

The leading dealers vied fiercely with each other. Knowing the tastes of their clients (as well as their financial resources), dealers avidly courted collectors like Mary Emery, who clearly preferred to have the dealers come to Edgecliffe with their proposed purchases. Photographs frequently were studied by Cincinnati Art Museum director Joseph Gest and accompanied by his opinion before Mrs. Emery saw the original painting. In addition to Gest's opinion, the advice of Cincinnati's dean of painters, Frank Duveneck (1848–1919), was sought, along with that of his colleague at the Art Academy of Cincinnati, L. H. Meakin (1850–1917). Mary was not a gallery goer, nor was she a regular visitor of art museums in Europe and

Frank Duveneck (1848– 1919), American painter, teacher, and dean of the Art Academy of Cincin- nati, c. 1915 (Courtesy Cincinnati Art Museum)

Lewis H. Meakin (1850–1917), American painter and teacher at the Art Academy of Cincinnati, c. 1915 (Courtesy Cincinnati Art Museum)

America after the death of her husband, so her art connoisseurship relied heavily on that of others. Books, art magazines, and advice from Gest and Duveneck joined the information given her by the dealers to guide her decisions in collecting.

Except with the most knowledgeable, well-read collectors in Mrs. Emery's day, the art dealers (assisted by a few scholar-historians of art, mostly Europeans, whom they employed) were expected to educate their clients with handsomely printed booklets that accompanied prospective purchases. Most collectors relied on expert, third-party recommendations. Mrs. Potter Palmer sought advice from the painter Mary Cassatt, Isabella Stewart Gardner looked to Bernard Berenson, while Mary Emery wanted Frank Duveneck's word. Mrs. Emery also relied on the endorsements of Italian art scholar Berenson, the Harvard classmate of Livingood, who was considered the major authority in his field. Some European scholars or art historians often were bribed by the dealers for their opinions. But in Gest's case, his close relationship with Mrs. Emery and her support of the Cincinnati Art Museum complemented his innate integrity in advising her, even if, on occasion, he based his advice on little research or knowledge of art history.

Mary acquired most of her paintings from two dealers, the firms of Scott & Fowles and Duveen, without much more research than what was printed in the dealers' flamboyant paragraphs with their occasionally incorrect attributions. Remarkably, in those times there were many outstanding works of art on the market, some of them well published, and wealthy collectors made few mistakes. Mary Emery's collecting pursuits and procedures were typical of most art collectors in her day. And, as a female, she was not alone, for she belonged to a small group of rich women with an acquisitive eye, awareness of the art market, and generous intentions.

Before her husband's death, only one painting of any consequence hung on the walls of Edgecliffe. This work, a canvas by the Swiss painter Alexandre Calame (1810–1864), *The Sycamores,* was purchased in about 1870 from the collection of one Andrew Burt.[1] The lengthy gap between 1870 and Mary's earliest entry as a serious collector of fine paintings in 1907 was closed when she bought one or two paintings by highly regarded, fashionably acceptable Barbizon school artists. These first acquisitions of two canvases by Constant Troyon (1810–1865) and Jules Dupré (1811–1889), a large pastel by Leon Augustin Lhermitte (1844–1925), and a typical work by the Hague school master Jozef Israëls (1824–1911) were conservative choices, to be sure. Safe choices could be expected. Her first acquisitions were typical for their times, and Mary wanted to be sure she was in step with her peers. That same year, she commissioned Emil Fuchs (1866–1929) to paint a portrait of her late husband. The portrait remained with her until her death, when it passed to the Cincinnati Art Museum along with the Edgecliffe collection.

After 1907, this small group of paintings expanded purposefully, but with no predetermined philosophy or collecting goal at the beginning.

Portrait of Thomas J. Emery (1830–1906) by Emil Fuchs, 1906 (Courtesy Cincinnati Art Museum)

Later in life, however, Mary answered public inquiries with a statement explaining her reasons for creating the collection. She followed simple guidelines or procedures, she said, when acquiring paintings. No artist would be duplicated, although she broke this rule occasionally. Dealers often were told this was the reason she could not consider a purchase. The oil medium was her preference, and only with the Lhermitte pastel did she stray from this dictate. Mrs. Emery purchased one to eight pictures in each of the twenty years left to her, with only a few years missed. She was not driven by an insatiable urge to acquire more and more, making quantity choices as did William Randolph Hearst a few decades later. In twenty years of collecting, she found herself in competition with other wealthy hunters of masterpieces such as Henry Clay Frick, Archer Huntington, and J. P. Morgan.

Mary's encounter with proposed acquisitions was primarily an emotional one, with intellectual and technical focus coming from others. Livingood played a relatively small part in the acquisition process, except to concern himself with his principal's financial records or to suggest to Gest where the paintings should be hung at Edgecliffe. Livingood occasionally inspected a painting at a New York dealer's gallery before it was called to Mary's attention, and visits of this sort increased the dealer's confidence in selling.

In February 1909, Charles F. Fowles, a partner in Scott & Fowles, the firm that sold most of the paintings acquired by Mrs. Emery, asked Gest about the status of the "charming Constable which you saw here and liked so much to show to Mrs. Emery. I hope she has seen it, that she likes it as well as I understood from Mr. Bartow that Mr. Livingood did. Do you know how the matter is progressing?"[2] This is one that got away, for no painting by the English landscapist, John Constable, entered the Edgecliffe Collection. Not dismayed by this failure, Scott & Fowles sold Mary another Barbizon School painting later in the spring, *Evening on the Oise*, by Charles F. Daubigny (1817–1878). Mrs. Emery heard from many art dealers once her aspirations became known, but Scott & Fowles of New York dominated her attention.

On occasion, Mary was duped by dealers who were either ignorant or unscrupulous. So-called experts even misattributed paintings when they visited the collector in Cincinnati. In the spring of 1909, Mary was introduced by a friend and dealer, Mary Morgan Newport, to Mrs. James Creelman, and through them she purchased from Creelman what some thought was one of the collection's greatest treasures, *Portrait of the Countess of Quinto*, by Francisco Goya (1746–1828). Gest and Duveneck both were convinced of its authenticity. Gest wrote to Mary: "I am very glad indeed that you concluded to keep the picture. It is really a remarkable canvas, as Mr. Duveneck told you."[3] As Duveneck had studied in Spain and was familiar with the Goya holdings of the Museo del Prado in Madrid, his knowledge was unquestioned. His assessment was poor, however, as was Gest's, and no research apparently was undertaken by Mrs. Emery's advisors to ascertain the portrait's place in Goya's oeuvre. Within a few years of Mary's death, the attribution was downgraded, correctly determining that the Countess of Quinto was masquerading and was only a mid-nineteenth-century work by a minor, unknown Spanish artist.

By late summer of 1909, and before her return to Cincinnati from Rhode Island, Mary's collecting interest increased its tempo. The first of several British paintings she would acquire came to her attention, *Portrait of Mrs. Richard Pryce Corbet and Her Daughter* by George Romney (1734–1802), and Gest pounced. "I have just learned that Mr. Duveneck is expected to arrive next Wednesday on the Oceanic. He will remain in New York only a short time, possibly a day or two. Mr. Barnhorn goes from here to meet him, and both will stop at the Grand Union Hotel. If you are prepared to have him look at the Romney, I can arrange with him to do so if you will inform me where the canvas is. Or, if you have not time to get word through me a note direct to Frank Duveneck, Grand Union Hotel, will suffice as I shall post Mr. Barnhorn."[4] Mrs. Emery promptly wrote to Duveneck, asking him to look at the painting and give her his opinion, as "I do not know its history or whether it is a good example of his work."[5] She trusted her emotional response, but needed a degree of support from those she respected. Gest confirmed the importance of the portrait with Duveneck's endorsement, and the painting was purchased in November. "A fine example better than any other he [Duveneck] knows in this country. Only a few that are in public collections abroad are superior to it. In his opinion it is an admirable canvas to own. The same dealer showed him also a portrait of a lady by Sir Peter Lely which he likewise thought very well of."[6]

Late in 1909 and throughout 1910, Mrs. Emery added nine works to her collection of paintings, making this the busiest year of acquisitions she would experience. Three or four of the works were of international significance in their quality. Sir Anthony Van Dyck's (1599–1641) masterful *Portrait of a Man in Armor* (then titled *Portrait of John Count of Nassau*) and Frans Hals's (c.1580–1666) captivating *Portrait of a Dutch Family* were the outstanding purchases, providing the collection with premier artists and prime examples of their talents. The Van Dyck portrait set a high standard. Painted in about 1621–1627, it illustrates the virtuosity and talent of this Flemish master. Van Dyck's portraiture became the yardstick for fashionable sitters in the seventeenth century, and the Emery purchase became the first true masterpiece in her collection.

The purchases in 1910 also included paintings by Thomas Gainsborough (1727–1788), Sir Henry Raeburn (1756–1823), Jean François Millet (1814–1875), Narcisse Diaz (1808–1876), and Dirk Bouts (c. 1410–1475), this latter work now attributed to the Master of the Legend of St.

Portrait of a Man in Armor *by Anthony van Dyck (1599–1641), acquired in 1909* (*Courtesy Cincinnati Art Museum*)

Portrait of a Dutch Family by Frans Hals (c. 1580–1666), acquired in 1910 (Courtesy *Cincinnati Art Museum*)

Lucy, and Adolphe Jourdan (1825–1889). The two paintings by Diaz violated her personal prohibition against duplicating artists. But she was still enamored with the Barbizon school and would acquire more examples by their masters, including two by Corot, the most important member of the school.

Mary's collection was not as large as some in the United States, but it attracted attention in Cincinnati. Livingood wrote to Director Gest in

February 1910 to notify him that there was a possibility of showing her paintings publicly for the first time. "Mrs. Emery is seriously considering the possibility of allowing the public to see her pictures during the coming summer at the Museum, say for the months of June, July, August, September, and October. Mrs. Emery would, of course, much prefer that no special mention be made of her action, but I presume it will be impossible to avoid the publicity that will follow the transfer of all her pictures to the Museum for the summer."[7]

It could be questioned if eleven or twelve paintings constituted a true collection, but, knowing that the young Cincinnati Art Museum's permanent holdings were slim and not blessed with masterpieces at that date, Mary's group certainly elevated the quality of works exhibited in the galleries. The works were lent, and visitors relished this special treat, as newspapers reported.[8]

As spring approached, Livingood found himself dealing with Lela Emery, Mary's sister-in-law, regarding a possible gift of a gallery Lela would fund at the museum that would house the John J. Emery Collection acquired in 1910. Livingood clearly was at odds with her idea, told her so, and cited excessive costs for marble floors, grand fireplaces, and pilasters. The architectural ideas of Mrs. John Emery included "a grandiose hall of Caen stone or some similarly colored stone . . . and an elaborate frieze and beamed ceiling finished in reddish gold, such as we see in the more elaborate galleries in Europe. I believe she has in mind a room here in New York done by Stanford White."[9]

Lela Emery wanted a New York architect, not Garber & Woodward of Cincinnati as proposed by Livingood. Gest was to contact her as quickly as possible, Livingood pleaded in concluding his letter, as she was sailing for Europe for five weeks before returning to her summer home at Bar Harbor, Maine. "As a Trustee, and interested also on behalf of my principal [Mary M. Emery], I am wondering whether it would not be wise for you to consider seeing her with Mr. Garber before she sails. She is most anxious to have you see the simplicity of the exterior of J. P. Morgan's Gallery here. I should not feel this matter so urgent except that I believe she is thoroughly in earnest, and as you know that my principal is ready to cooperate financially, provided a proper plan can be worked out." Livingood noted that Lela Emery was setting aside $250,000 for the new gallery or wing, adding that Mary Emery was prepared to contribute to it with the hope that the building be dignified in every way. This interesting scheme, apparently creating a structure to house the John J. Emery Collection primarily, enlisted Mary's support either to help honor her brother-in-law or to join in creating a facility to house her collection as well. The project never was consummated.

In June 1910, Mary began correspondence negotiating with Scott & Fowles for one of the finest pictures she would acquire. "I have just sent you from Scott and Fowles a group of Frans Hals for your approval. It pleases me and if you, Mr. Duveneck, and Mr. Meakin approve you may hang it in the room [the gallery in the museum where her paintings were shown for the summer] with the other pictures from Edgecliffe. If I buy it, the firm will send you a glass for it and a tablet as a signature. It comes from the 'Secretin' Collection 1889 and was hung in the Paris Exposition of 'Cent Chef-d'Oeuvres' in 1883. I shall be greatly interested to know how it strikes you at the Museum."[10]

In the artist's lifetime, as in Mrs. Emery's, Hals was considered the equal of Rembrandt and Vermeer. His renderings of rich burghers or jolly families were painted with a loaded brush, briskly stroked. Mrs. Emery's portrait appealed, no doubt, for its subject along with its artistry. Although it appears that Mary agreed to buy the Hals even before she heard from Gest, Duveneck, or Meakin with their recommendations, she repeated her interest in obtaining their opinions before finalizing the purchase. Gest's comments were most welcome; she was pleased with his "acceptance" of the painting, writing him that "[I] felt it was wiser to continue the standpoint I had taken previously that I preferred having your opinion on any canvas before accepting it. I had it here [at Mariemont, Rhode Island] a day before sending it to you."[11]

The price paid for the Hals, $120,000, was exceeded by the payments for two pictures by Van Dyck and one by Raeburn, each costing $140,000. These three paintings were the most expensive additions to her collection by that date, but, in another year, even these amounts would pale. One of the Van Dyck paintings, *Portrait of Mlle. Gottinges*, was acquired for questionable reasons, such as its attractive pairing with her other Van Dyck and its resemblance to a painting by Rubens.

> This new portrait is certainly very pleasing and might do as a companion picture to the "John" though I think the canvas a little short. When it reaches you will you bear in mind that, if bought, it is to go in the atrium at Edgecliffe, to hang where the Sir Joshua hung, that is on the other side of the entrance into the picture gallery, as a companion piece to the other Van Dyck. Mrs. Emery favors it because it looks, to her mind, more like a Rubens which she says will give her variety; and I say Why not get a Rubens then?
>
> Mrs. Emery has told Mr. Labey that after this picture has been submitted to you for judgment, and the price made to correspond to the Sir John [the other Van Dyck, apparently] we will consider taking it (if it meets with your and Mr. Duveneck's approval) provided they can show a satisfactory pedigree. All they are willing to say is that it comes to them through Mr. Sulley who does not wish to disclose its source because they don't want other dealers to hear that a certain group of pictures can be had.[12]

With the purchase of the large-scale canvas of the *Elphinston Children* by Sir Henry Raeburn, her fourth British purchase, Mary closed her acquisitions for 1910. The Raeburn portrait was the largest canvas she had acquired to this date, and it had an impressive appearance on the walls of Edgecliffe with its vivid coloring and compelling subject. Raeburn was Scotland's greatest painter, and his portraits commanded especially high prices in the early twentieth century. She declined interest that same year in a landscape by the noted Dutch artist, Aelbert Cuyp. Gest studied the painting for her, rendering a report, but Scott & Fowles soon was asked to remove the picture from her house, according to Livingood. The latter's influence on his employer in her various philanthropic enterprises, as well as on the installation of the art collection, is clear even at this early period of accumulating paintings. Livingood writes, "Mrs. Emery is very much interested in what I have to say about the disposition of her pictures and about the very attractive room you have made with the J. J. Emery pictures."[13]

Mrs. Emery's involvement with the Cincinnati Art Museum grew when she and Livingood were elected shareholders of that institution in

1911.[14] This body elected all trustees except for three appointed by the mayor of Cincinnati. Her election as shareholder did not suggest a future trusteeship, nor did she show any interest in this post, for women were not considered in those days to be eligible as trustees. She joined many other Cincinnati patricians in the group elected with her: Frank Suire, A. B. Meader, Robert Resor, Lucien Wulsin, John L. Stettinius, Frederick A. Geier, R. M. Burton, Ralph Kellogg, Frederick W. Hinkle, and George W. Warrington. Mrs. Emery clearly was the museum's most important patron, yet gratitude for her generosity as donor and her potential service and fiduciary responsibility as trustee were kept separate. As Director Gest wrote her in acknowledging her acceptance as shareholder, the shares were offered to "those who are most interested in what the Museum stands for in Cincinnati."[15]

Up to this point, Mrs. Emery was in the hands of Scott & Fowles for all but a few purchases. She turned to them again in 1911 for two of her most notable treasures. The first was a monumental canvas with an impressive history by the Spanish artist, Bartolomé Esteban Murillo (1617–1682), *St. Thomas of Villanueva Dividing His Clothes Among Beggar Boys*. The purchase price paid to Scott & Fowles, $215,000, dwarfed amounts paid previously, but it garnered for her one of the masterpieces she so avidly sought. The painting's subject, a compassionate act of a child, found a sympathetic buyer, whose interest in children's welfare was significant. In this painting, Murillo's usual religious subject matter is nearly transformed into a genre scene of street life.

In that year, she also bought from the same dealer what is considered to be one of the finest paintings ever executed by Thomas Gainsborough (1727–1788), *Portrait of Mrs. Philip Thicknesse*. This was Mary's second Gainsborough. The significance of this portrait in Gainsborough's career and its ravishing beauty rank it as one of her most important acquisitions. Gainsborough and Sir Joshua Reynolds were the leaders of Britain's Golden Age of painting, and the master's virtuoso brushwork in this dramatic portrait of his friend support this laurel.

Mary's expenditures for paintings in 1911–1912, including a Hoppner and a portrait by Nattier, totaled $489,500, an awesome investment for its day.[16] Other dealers soon heard of her acquisitions, as word travels fast in the art dealers' arena, and they were alert to newspaper coverage of her loans to the Cincinnati Art Museum. From time to time, art museum directors descended on Gest, or wrote first to Mrs. Emery, hoping to visit Edgecliffe to see what this retiring lady of great wealth was acquiring. She encouraged their calls, for they did not require the tactful decline of offered purchases, and their opinions could fortify her taste. "I have just heard that Dr. Bode [Wilhelm von Bode, director of the Kaiser Friedrich Museum, Berlin] is to be in Cincinnati on Thursday next or very soon

St. Thomas of Villanueva Dividing His Clothes Among Beggar Boys *by Bartolomé Esteban Murillo* (1617–1682), *acquired in 1911* (Courtesy Cincinnati Art Museum)

Portrait of Ann
Ford, Mrs. Philip
Thicknesse *by
Thomas Gainsbor-
ough (1727– 1788),
acquired in 1911*

after. Of course you will meet him and if you find it will give him any
pleasure to see the pictures at Edgecliffe, I hope you will take him there. I
regret exceedingly that I cannot be at home but Miss Hopkins is there and
will be very glad to receive you."[17]

Mary's knowledge of art history and artists has never been fathomed, as
she left little trace of this in her letters. Once a purported work by J. M. W.
Turner (1775–1851) was brought for her consideration, and her reaction
to its appraisal surely influenced her.

I have asked Mr. Meakin and Mr. Grover to carefully look over the Turner with me and find that they agree that the canvas is very far from being in good condition, having scaled in a good many places. This would need to be repaired rather thoroughly, the paint perhaps being transferred to another canvas, all of which would involve certain risks. Nor do we think that the picture itself is quite up to the standard of those you have been collecting as representative examples of various painters. One is always reluctant to reach this conclusion in connection with the work of a man of Turner's importance, but when we have before us the unusually high quality of the other canvases in your collection and also bear in mind that you do not care to go beyond a certain limited number of examples, we feel that we cannot heartily recommend to you this canvas.[18]

In the winter of 1912, the New York dealer Walter L. Ehrich attempted to gain her interest in his offerings, especially with several paintings by Tintoretto, Zurburán, Goya, and Bordon that Gest had seen in his gallery.[19] Mary expressed interest in the Ehrich offerings, noting that she also had in hand a photograph of a "Velasquez" that was sent to her "by the friend of whom I got my Goya." That person was Mary Morgan Newport, the lady who engineered with Mrs. James Creelman the purchase of the "Goya," a painting with a dubious provenance and an even shakier attribution. Mrs. Emery decided to investigate the Velázquez and asked that it be sent out to Edgecliffe.[20] Her involvement with Newport and Ehrich as dealers, however, was fruitless for them, and she never seriously considered their proposals again.

News from New York and London in December 1913 astonished the art world, revealing that Mrs. Emery had acquired an outstanding masterpiece for her collection, a portrait by the Venetian master, Titian (c. 1490–1576), for an astronomical sum. The *Cincinnati Enquirer* broke the story to Cincinnatians as a major news item, greatly impressed with the supposed purchase price "in the neighborhood of $400,000," although the actual price was $315,000.[21] Titian's *Portrait of Philip II*, painted in Augsburg in 1550–1551, has a lengthy record of past owners and an air of mystery due to its radical change in appearance in the nineteenth century.[22] The painting remained in Titian's studio during his lifetime as a *modello* or "master" from which other court portraits might be derived. After the artist's death the portrait passed to his son and to the noble Barbarigo fam-

Portrait of Philip II *by Titian (c. 1490–1576), acquired in 1914 (Courtesy Cincinnati Art Museum)*

ily, eventually making its way about 1880 into the collection of the German artist, Franz von Lenbach (1836–1904). His widow sold the portrait to the London dealer, Thomas Agnew and Sons in 1911, who resold it to Sir Hugh Lane, another London dealer in 1913. Mary Emery bought it from Lane that same year, but paid for it in February 1914. How the painting became Lenbach's property is perhaps the most interesting saga in the provenance of this Renaissance masterpiece.

Lenbach's ownership of the paintings, after nearly three centuries of Barbarigo possession, resulted from a misunderstood agreement with Dr. Wilhelm Bode according to a recently discovered letter from Sir Hugh Lane's agent to Cincinnati Art Museum Director, J. H. Gest: "Perhaps it will interest you as a director of a museum to know why the picture did not pass into the Berlin gallery on the death of Lenbach. Dr. Bode himself told the story to Sir Hugh Lane in Paris last week. Dr. Bode said he found the Titians, Philip II and Francis [the latter now at Harewood House, Leeds] with a Giorgione in the Giustiniani palace, and had paid a deposit on them but could not get together a sufficient sum of money to get all three away, and that he was fearful that someone else would find them and offer the family more money. This he told Lenbach, who at that time was a great friend. Lenbach offered him the money if he would let him have the Titians for one year to study. Bode agreed, took the Giorgione now in Berlin and turned the Titians over to Lenbach till he could collect the money. When he had collected it he went to Lenbach who refused to give the pictures up and said, 'No, I bought them for myself.' Bode said, 'But you promised.' Lenbach replied, 'You did not really believe that did you?' Dr. Bode said he had never spoken to Lenbach since nor could he bear to even think of the Titians and his loss."[23]

The English press berated the National Gallery, London, for not acquiring the Titian portrait owned by Mrs. Emery. Cincinnati's newspapers gleefully reported this coup by repeating the comments from abroad. "Had it been possible to secure Sir Hugh Lane's picture for our national collections it would have been a valuable acquisition on historical as well as aesthetic grounds. . . . [It is,] as The Times remarks, by far the most interesting example of Titian's work, for it represents the husband of one of our Queens and the suitor of another."[24] Other London writers summarized in the same Cincinnati article praised the ability of American collectors, like Mrs. Emery, to act quickly in making a purchase. They also hoped Cincinnatians would be properly grateful to Mrs. Emery, "a generous lady." The painting was exhibited for a short period in New York and then shown in the museum's galleries before moving to Edgecliffe.

Two other paintings were acquired by Mary Emery in 1913, a work she considered a particular favorite by Rembrandt, and a *Madonna and Child* by Lorenzo di Credi (c. 1458–1537). Her favorite dealer, Scott & Fowles, supplied both of them. Rembrandt (1606–1669) was considered the author of *Young Girl Holding a Medal*, but scholarship in the 1970s and 1980s downgraded it decades after Mary's death to a follower or someone working in the Dutch master's circle. The expertise of the dealer, Gest, and Mary Emery was in tune with that of renowned experts of her day, however, such as Adolf Rosenberg, Wilhelm Valentiner, Wilhelm von Bode, Emile Michel, and Cornelis Hofstede de Groot. Each of them considered the canvas to be an authentic work by Rembrandt. Even their connoisseur's eyes and scholarship were not infallible.

As Europe disintegrated into war in 1914, Mary's generous giving continued intensely while her collection expanded by only two canvases. One Venetian master, Titian, was joined by another, Tintoretto (1518–1594), when she added to the collection's strength with the *Portrait of the Doge Marino Grimani*. Mary's artistic advisor, Frank Duveneck, rightly surmised that the head and hands in the Doge's portrait are by this master, while the robe, cap, and other elements probably from the hand of an assistant, such as the artist's son, Domenico.[25] A landscape by Corot, an artist she long coveted for the Edgecliffe collection, was the second purchase from Scott & Fowles in October of that year. Unfortunately, the Corot attribution was bogus.

Throughout the years of her collecting energies, Mary received many offers for truly spectacular catches, assuming the attributions were correct. Her collection when concluded was blessed with many masterpieces and was regarded as one of the nation's outstanding private holdings. If she had acquired all of the proposals, and if they were by the artists as suggested, she would have had an index of painting history from the Renaissance to the twentieth century. An amazing offer came in the winter of 1915, when a Boston dealer, H. B. Eaton, dangled a purported Michelangelo before Director Gest.

> Every artist who has seen it, or a photograph, is immediately convinced that no one but Michael Angelo [*sic*] could have painted it. [The price] is not high, when one considers that it was painted by the greatest artist the world has ever known, and not one cent is to be paid until Berenson, of Florence, has substantiated my claims that the painting is a Michael Angelo. Furthermore, if desired by the purchaser, I am willing to have Dr. Laurie, of Edin-

burgh, examine the canvas, testing the pigments, and microphotographing a section of the painting in order to compare with other works of Michael Angelo already examined by him.[26]

Gest immediately followed this intriguing lead, warning his patron to be cautious and showing some awareness that the painting was not likely to be authentic. "I have just read the remarkable letter from Mr. Eaton regarding the supposed Michael Angelo. I must say that I would require the strongest kind of intrinsic evidence to prove this claim. Of course, a photograph of a photograph which he offers to send would mean very little. I shall talk the matter over with Mr. Duveneck, Mr. Meakin, and Mr. Barnhorn and ask Miss Kellogg to look through the Library for any references to the existence of such a picture."[27]

The anxious Eaton persisted in correspondence with the museum, sending different dimensions and an asking price of $500,000. He alluded to a recent cause célèbre in the art world. "The bringing of this painting to the United States will cause as big a stir in the newspapers of the civilized world as did the theft of the Giaconda [the so-called *Mona Lisa*] from the Louvre."[28] Apparently, Mrs. Emery and Gest never considered Eaton's "Michelangelo" very seriously, for in February Gest thought the whole episode had a "sensational look," and by March all interest faded.

Mrs. Emery made no acquisitions in 1915, yet the offer of the Michelangelo and two portraits, supposedly by the American Colonial painter John Singleton Copley, came to her attention in that year. The latter works, being American in their origin, were not the usual fare for her taste. American pictures were of no interest. Nevertheless, her kindness or friendships occasionally prompted her to investigate a prospective purchase, as she did with the Goya painting and Miss Mary Morgan Newport, the liaison for the sale. In November, from the Hotel Touraine, Boston, Mary called Gest's attention to the Copleys.

"[I saw] two Copley portraits for sale in New York being restored by the Metropolitan Museum which I wish you could see if you happen to be in New York soon. They are owned by some friends of mine and are family portraits—so keep them in mind."[29]

In the early summer of 1916, Mrs. Emery joined another Cincinnati patron of the arts, Mary Hanna, along with members of the Taft family and the dealer Stevenson Scott in purchasing for the museum a handsome painting from a long-separated and dispersed cycle of religious narratives by the Spanish master, Francisco de Zurburán (1598–1664). The painting, *St. Peter Nolasco Recovering the Image of the Virgin,* was given by its donors in memory of Charles F. Fowles, Scott's partner and the other half of the team that supplied the majority of Mrs. Emery's acquisitions. The large-scale painting once was part of a series commemorating incidents in the life of a Spanish saint. Donated by 1917 to the museum, it was not part of Mary's Edgecliffe collection. Later that same year, Scott deluged his patron with tantalizing works she might consider, each with impressive provenances. Shipped to Cincinnati by Scott were portraits by Hals and Lawrence, landscapes by Ruisdael and Hobbema, two saints by Utili, and a seascape by Willem van de Velde. In the flush years of collecting in the first decades of the twentieth century, art dealers catered eagerly to their clients, shipping rare and costly paintings, sculpture, and prints on approval or with no assurance of sales, hoping to entice them and precluding the need for clients to travel to their galleries. Large and small dealers followed this practice. In Mrs. Emery's case, past purchases and the cordial dealer-collector relationship encouraged future dealings. In this case, however, only one of these offerings, the *View in Westphalia* by Meindert Hobbema (1638–1709), was acquired, and this work was not paid for until ten months later. It remained in the Edgecliffe collection until it was traded for another, more impressive painting. It was not unusual for Mrs. Emery to trade or dispose of paintings, particularly when she upgraded her holdings or tired of a work. This practice was pursued by many collectors. One such disposal from the collection was a portrait by Matsys (1466–1530), purchased from the prominent New York dealer, F. Kleinberger, in November 1916 and sold sometime before Mrs. Emery's death.

Mrs. Emery had strong opinions about the focus of her collection. She commented occasionally about this focus, but her guidelines dictated choices of distinguished European masters from the Renaissance period to the Barbizon school of the nineteenth century. Consciously or not, she collected portraits, showed considerable interest in landscapes, and had no inclination for literary or mythological subjects. It is inconsequential, perhaps, to study Mrs. Emery's acquisitions to determine their psychological relationships to her motherhood and the loss of her husband and children, but she wrote fondly in a few letters of those paintings that represented parent and child subjects. At least fourteen works in her collection depicted family-oriented subject matter or children. American artists were never bought, with the exception of the *Portrait of George Washington* purchased in 1923, then thought to be by Gilbert Stuart (1755–1828). When Mrs. James Creelman wrote to Gest, stating she had two important Whistlers with her in New York and wanting to show them to Mary Emery, the director informed Livingood of another concern, physical condition. "You can use your judgment in that they appear important but must be seen, as some Whistlers are not in good condition. Duveneck is away this week. Perhaps Mrs. Creelman could send them here next week if Mrs. Emery wishes, or Duveneck may possibly go east with me next week if necessary."[30]

Livingood quickly squelched further contact with Mrs. Creelman, noting that Mrs. Emery was not interested in Whistler's work and was unable to concern herself with paintings due to her health. Writing from Newport, where Mary spent the summer of 1916, Livingood stated she was recovering from a "very sharp attack of bronchitis." Apparently irritated by the ever-aggressive dealers who descended on her or wrote incessantly to her, he added that he had encountered James Labey, a dealer's representative. "By now, however, you will probably have received at the Museum a painting by Quentin Matsys which Labey brought here without any forewarning, and to get rid of him Mrs. Emery said that if he were going to Chicago anyway with it she knew you and Mr. Duveneck would be glad to look at it. The price is not exorbitant. What do you think of it?"[31] In spite of Livingood's opinion that his patron could not consider any acquisitions because of her health, Mary succumbed to Gest's enthusiasm for the Matsys. Livingood wrote a few days later that the decision was almost assured. "She thought it a delightful subject, well handled but of course wanted your judgment and especially to know if you think it genuine. If there is no doubt about this we are inclined to take up its purchase with Kleinberger when I get to New York which will be about the end of this month.

I assume that Labey has left the picture with you until he hears from either you or us. If he writes, Mrs. Emery is considering it."[32]

Labey and Kleinberger continued to dangle important painting prospects before Mary Emery in 1917, tempting her with works by Rubens, Piero di Cosimo, Pinturicchio, Gerard David, and others, but they were all returned.[33] By April of that year, she again purchased from Kleinberger, adding the *Portrait of Queen Eleanor of Portugal and France* by Jan Mabuse (c. 1478–1532). Two other notable paintings joined the Edgecliffe collection that year, a long-sought Rubens (1577–1640) and a swagger portrait by Sir Thomas Lawrence (1769–1830). As a curious reflection of the times, when British eighteenth-century portraits were as costly as canvases by Renaissance and Baroque masters, Mary paid the dealer the same amount for each: $40,000.

The collector of the Edgecliffe pictures rejected offered works from time to time if they had no emotional appeal to her, even if they were by well-known masters and were approved by Gest and Duveneck. And occasionally she sought a particular artist to fill an imagined gap.

> Mrs. Emery is being tempted to buy (entre nous) a very fine Rousseau from a private collection in Chicago which means that you would have to make a trip there to see it before she commits herself. Will you kindly advise me at once whether it would be convenient for you to go and whether the trip could be made without attracting attention to her purchase, for frankly I think this is a bad time to be known to be negotiating for important canvases.
>
> We have of course seen a photograph and know something about the value placed upon it but would do nothing until we had your approval. Mrs. Emery has always wanted a Rousseau. And by the way, in this connection would you have made for us a photograph of her Israels, something large enough to submit to the dealer in the above transaction, who thinks he may be able to dispose of it?
>
> We may be leaving here the middle of next week so would appreciate a prompt answer, although we cannot say just when you should go to Chicago. Mrs. Emery may not reach Cincinnati until the 6th or 8th of November, when she may want to take up the matter vigorously.[34]

Livingood wrote again to Gest regarding the Théodore Rousseau landscape after hearing that the museum's director was willing to travel to Chicago to view the painting.

Enclosed is the only photo that has been submitted. It is a lovely subject though rather general and to our minds the composition is perfect, but wait until you hear the price! I shall not know when you must make the trip until I hear from Mr. Sedgwick [the dealer G. Stanley Sedgwick, from whom Mrs. Emery had made purchases in the past] who must be away for he has not answered my letter. I know that he intends to pass through Cincinnati on his way to St. Louis about the 15th of November when his firm, Lewis and Simmons, intend to show their Van Dycks and Rembrandts.[35]

That example by Rousseau was declined, for the first of two paintings by this artist was not acquired for the Edgecliffe collection until 1922. Mrs. Emery's interest in the Barbizon school and its focus on the woods and pastures of France did not wane, apparently, between 1907 (the first year of a Barbizon school purchase) and 1917. An interesting postscript added to the first letter about the Rousseau records Livingood's admiration of Duveneck, a respect felt by hundreds of students who studied with this Cincinnatian and by collectors who admired him as adoringly as Whistler had done when first encountering Duveneck's virtuoso etchings. "Again entre nous, do you think Heerman's 'Life of Duveneck' does justice to that great man, and has his publication as well as the use of his pictures in it the full approval of Mr. D.? Mrs. Emery is thinking of 'staking' Heerman. Please write about this with your own hand." Impatient for an answer, Livingood reminded Gest that he would reach Cincinnati soon, although Mrs. Emery was stopping at the Hotel Aldine, Philadelphia, before returning to her Ohio home. She would wait there for an answer about the Duveneck publication. In the years before his death in 1919, Duveneck continued in the select group that dealt with authenticating and commenting on prospective acquisitions. He sometimes returned to his earlier opinions, as he did with the Tintoretto portrait, passing them on to the owner.

As I once told you, it seems to me that in your portrait of a Doge of Venice the head and hands are unmistakably by Jacopo Tintoretto. I have been for many years familiar with his work and know no other painter who could have painted those portions of this portrait—certainly not his son Domenico. You may recall my saying, however, that Jacopo Tintoretto would hardly at this time of life have had the patience to paint the detail of the robe and the other accessories, fine as they are, but followed the usual custom of the period in leaving these to some competent assistant in his studio.[36]

Mary's art collection expanded almost every year between the time of her husband's death and World War I. Displayed on Edgecliffe's walls, the collection was her ever-present companion, demonstrating her own accomplishment. She was usually parted from her pictures only in the summer months, but the paintings remained hers, unlike her many monetary gifts for buildings and programs she seldom encountered after a contribution was made.

CHAPTER 9

The Edgecliffe Collection of Paintings
World War I to 1927

LIFE PATTERNS in Mary Emery's later years seldom changed. Purchasing pictures, spending summers in Newport, enjoying Cincinnati the rest of the year, donating to charitable causes—these filled a schedule that varied little. Only her frail health dictated responses to demands, either for time or money. World War I and the end of that conflict had a negligible effect on her lifestyle. In the remaining years before her death, the Edgecliffe collection expanded by twenty-one paintings.

In 1919 and 1920, two dealers emerged as the primary contacts for new acquisitions, the eminent New York firms of Duveen and Knoedler. Each had far-reaching connections and offices in Paris and London. From Duveen in 1919, Mary acquired the majestic *Portrait of Eleonora di Toledo and Her Son, Francesco de'Medici*, by Bronzino (1503–1572), and paid for Corot's *Don Quixote* from Knoedler in that same year.

In January 1920, an illness distracted Mary from confronting dealers, such as Duveen's agent Jarman who was called off by Livingood. Writing to Gest, he felt "compelled to reply that Mrs. Emery's health is such that she cannot consider pictures at this time."[1] But Jarman was not to be deterred, and he again pursued his client in April. "I simply called to tell you that I left the fine Velasquez [sic] head with Mr. Gest and sincerely hope that it will be appreciated as much in Cincinnati as it apparently was in New York. I am sorry that I could not bring the Luini or the Mainardi, but those two pictures in company with the Francia, which I think you also admired, were sold at the beginning of the month in confidence to Mr. Clarence M. [McKay?]. I hope the Velasquez [*sic*] may find favor. It is a superb work and one which I should imagine should find a ready place in Mrs. Emery's collection."[2] Mrs. Emery's interest in acquiring a work by Spain's great Baroque master was not tempted by this example, for she sought a work of higher quality, as Livingood conveyed to the dealer. This was one of the occasions when she returned a painting that failed to sustain her interest or fell short because she felt she could acquire a better example than the one at hand. How she defined "more important" is unknown, nor do we know the identity of the Velázquez portrait offered by Duveen's gallery. Clearly, she was unimpressed by it. "The picture is at Mrs. Emery's residence and has already given her much pleasure, but I regret to say that the conclusion reached is that she had better reserve the space for a more important portrait, although by this I do not wish in the least to minimize the value and beauty of execution which is very apparent in the subject presented."[3]

By the summer of 1920, with Mary ensconced in Rhode Island, the dealer of dubious professional abilities, Mrs. James Creelman, again approached her client with a purported Rembrandt, *Saskia as Flora*. During the first two days of July, correspondence between Mrs. Emery and Gest led her to reject the painting because it duplicated an artist.[4] This guideline was an excuse used often with dealers, but Mary broke it several times. Corot, Diaz, Gainsborough, Reynolds, Rousseau, and Troyon eventually were represented in the Edgecliffe collection by more than one example. As the summer wore on, Mary's health improved as she relaxed at her estate. She considered several major acquisitions by Moroni, Moro, Reynolds, and Luini. Knoedler offered a portrait by Reynolds, but she felt overcommitted financially at that moment. "[I am] anxious for a fine picture by Sir Joshua so sent to Knoedler for a photograph of the one you saw. It is charming, but the price soars away beyond me at present with all the obligations I have on hand. It is almost as great as the wonderful portrait I declined of a Lady and her two children—and which I have always wished I had bought."[5] Knowing his opinion was sought as her consultant and advisor, Gest coached his patron's knowledge of art history. He said little about the painting's past but praised its technique. "The two pictures at Knoedler's are totally different in character. The Moro is a very unusual piece of realistic portraiture. The drawing is masterly and the composition and the presentation of the subject are large in scale, being in that respect like many of your pictures. The Reynolds is simply lovely in its decorative quality and its style and the ease of its masterly painting. The photograph I saw in New York by no means does it justice. I often think of the pleasant day I had with you in Newport and of your beautiful garden and lovely home."[6]

As Mary considered Knoedler's offerings, she contemplated from Duveen a religious subject by Bernardino Luini (c. 1480–1532), *Madonna and Child with St. Catherine of Alexandria*. Mrs. Emery sought more than the dealer's word on the painting's authenticity, seeking confirmation from art historian Bernard Berenson. She also expressed regret that Gest had "some uncomfortable times with Mr. Jarman about the Luini picture." Nothing is known about this "uncomfortable" episode, yet Mary's letter underscores her persistent request that a painting's history be provided to her by the dealer, as well as some expert opinion, before she bought it. "I am enclosing the only letter I have received concerning the picture and I have been waiting for further account from Berenson—about the 'provenance,' etc. which has not come to me. Charley [Charles J. Livingood] is to be in New York sometime this week and I will write him to see Jarman if possible. Of course, I would like to have the picture, but would also like a little history."[7] While the Luini painting was tested on Edgecliffe's walls, Livingood added his thoughts on its frame and its location in Mrs. Emery's house. While his advice may not have been as foundational as Gest's in approving proposed acquisitions, Livingood's opinion on the Edgecliffe setting was certain to weigh importantly with his patron. "They [Duveen] have good judgment, and by so doing may open the way for other 'primitives' which in my opinion this room should be devoted to. I wish it might go in the middle of the East wall, with perhaps the Credi and Matsys on either side, but I fear the Dirk Bouts is too long. I thought for the price that a Moroni is not important enough. I am so glad she did not add another small Rembrandt to her collection."[8]

By August, Mrs. Emery agreed to buy the Luini, although its price of $180,000 was not paid until January 1921. Her acceptance was conditional on being charged no tax, that the painting was described on the bill of sale as by Luini, and that Joseph Duveen and his librarian would furnish the painting's provenance.[9] Her nature was to trust her dealers, relying on their reputations and expected honesty. After agreeing to acquire this work that once belonged to Pope Pius VI and was attributed to Leonardo da Vinci in the eighteenth century, Mary engaged in a lengthy discussion of frame style and placement of pictures with Gest. As the collection was housed at Edgecliffe, she expected an attractive appearance in its display. Gest obliged her. "Mr. Jarman brought the Luini yesterday with the frame in which you saw it in Newport, and also the top and bottom sections which belong with it as complete architectural frame of the Florentine type of that period. He also brought several old frames of a simpler, square shape and a lot of photographs besides. The Luini looks extremely well over the cabinet in the reception room, even in its complete architectural frame, though I feel the frame to be rather out of scale with the other frames in the room."[10]

Mrs. Emery responded a few days later to Gest from Mariemont, writing in her own hand an unusually lengthy commentary on frames, spacing of pictures, and wall coverings. That she cared about these matters, although she deferred to both Gest and Jarman, is suggested by very specific instructions.

> I have your very interesting letter of 31st August before me, and thoroughly appreciate your kind efforts to place the pictures most advantageously. I am glad the Dirck Bouts can hang in the Hall, and of course you can have the upper corners of the frame cut off but I shall keep them to be replaced when it is hung somewhere else. Lange, the carpenter in the house can do that and also the necessary change in the mantle of the dining room to put the Bronzino into the frame over mantle just as you describe. Of course the picture must be tilted to avoid reflections on the glass. Lange can arrange with our electrician Harry Kaiser to put up the wiring for lighting the D. Bouts in the Hall. The Luini will have to have a reflector if you have used the one on the Bouts

for it in the Hall. I leave it entirely to you and Mr. Jarman to frame the Luini.
As the space is ample, perhaps the informal architectural frame will not be out
of place when it hangs alone on the space? I like the old Florentine frames a
thousand times better than any made at the present day! As I failed to get the
wall covering I wanted before leaving home, the walls will remain as they are
now in the Reception Room for this winter and the Luini can be hung perma-
nently there in the middle of the space that was formerly occupied by the
Bouts. You have made everything so clear that I am hoping I have been equally clear in writing, but if not please let me know and send me a typed letter.[11]

The troublesome framing of the Luini was completed by Jarman, who provided a service to clients quite customary in the 1920s. Jarman even suggested suitable wall coverings for the Reception Room at Edgecliffe,
knowing Mrs. Emery's interest. In an age of major collectors with fortunes
to spend, careful cultivation was expected and freely given.[12]

Correspondence in the summer and autumn of 1920 between dealers
and Mrs. Emery's representatives offered several works of art tantalizing in
their attributions. Livingood heard of a remarkable portrait of poet Alfred
Lord Tennyson by Sir John Everett Millais, the Pre-Raphaelite painter,
and Jarman had in hand a terracotta bust of the Medici duke, Lorenzo the
Magnificent, by the Italian Renaissance master Pollaiuolo. In addition,
the nefarious Mrs. Creelman reappeared, as Livingood wrote to Gest.
"Mrs. Creelman is after us again, first to purchase for the Museum some
tapestries and then to take up those other pictures that she had to offer. I
have just wired her that the Museum has no money for tapestries, that
Mrs. Emery is not interested in them, but I say nothing about the paintings. I hope she won't think I am a brute, but really Mrs. Emery has her
hands full."[13] Livingood wrote earlier, tempting Gest with the Millais
painting and making a halfhearted case for its acquisition.

> Now here is another "job." Under separate cover I am sending you a photo-
> graph of a portrait by Millais of Tennyson. Do you think it is worth $15,000,
> and is it good enough for Mrs. Emery? Was Millais of sufficient importance?
> Depending of course upon its size, the picture appeals to me as being by at
> least a well-known painter of our own times of a man who will always be
> remembered. Who can forget the portraits of Castiglione? How we wish we
> might have an authenticated portrait (as this certainly is) of say Ariosto?

Won't you and some of your friends study the photograph and let me know
whether it looks worthwhile and of sufficient importance. I appeal to you first
because if your decision is favorable I will stop at Quebec and bring also to
Mrs. Emery an enlarged photograph of the head only which will show her and
then you a little more as to the quality of the painting.[14]

Mrs. Emery did not acquire the Millais, apparently showing no interest in
the Pre-Raphaelite's work, nor did she purchase the bust of the Medici
prince, Lorenzo the Magnificent.[15] That the Millais was not acquired
seems in keeping with her focus on acknowledged masters and the very
popular Barbizon painters of her own time. However, as the British School
was well represented in her collection, inclusion of the highly regarded
Millais as a nineteenth-century figure would have lent depth to this focus.

Duveen's agent, Jarman, kept alive Mary's interest in new art purchases
with persistent letters and advice to Gest throughout 1921. For his part,
the art museum director relished the role of intermediary and consultant,
one day urging his patron to get more information on the "Goya" portrait
from its dealer, Mrs. Creelman, and the next day responding to Jarman
about tantalizing works of art Mary was considering.[16] Photographs of
paintings by Daddi, Borgognone, Filippino Lippi, and Lorenzo di Credi,
"together with a photograph of each of two fine marbles and the Pollaiuolo terra cotta," were dispatched to Gest. A photograph of the Luini painting recently acquired for the Edgecliffe collection was sent directly to the
collector in her Rhode Island home, "which I gather with much joy that
she has sufficiently recovered to go there."[17] In these closing years of Mrs.
Emery's collecting, Duveen provided major paintings to his client, but his
firm also vied with Knoedler and Labey, especially, for her purchases.

In 1922, Mary Emery was seventy-eight years of age and not in robust
health. Her paintings and her summer home and gardens in Rhode Island
were her special pleasures. Mary Emery's most unusual painting purchase,
and certainly the rarest, occurred that same year when Duveen supplied
her with a masterpiece, a grisaille painting by the Italian Renaissance
master Andrea Mantegna (c. 1431–1506). Its purchase price, $163,800,
was amazingly low, considering its rarity and comparing it with prices
fetched by British portraits or Barbizon school paintings. In the United

States at this time, there were only two or three works by this painter from the second half of the fifteenth century, now considered one of the giants of Renaissance art. Although Mantegna's place in the history of art was known when Mrs. Emery purchased the painting, his significance and the full recognition of his oeuvre were not ranked as highly as they are today. The grisaille technique intended the figures to appear as bronze sculpture, dramatically modelled. Mantegna's curious subject, no doubt dictated by his noble patron who commissioned the work, has been debated for centuries. Acquiring this painting was perhaps her greatest coup, yet the price of the painting and acclaim by the public did not coincide with later recognition granted Mantegna. The Emery Mantegna may be defended easily as the rarest and best painting in the Edgecliffe collection.

By February, she negotiated with another dealer, Labey of New York, and bought her first work, *Road in the Forest*, by the well-known Barbizon school artist, Théodore Rousseau (1812–1867). This painter was one Mary had sought since at least 1916, hoping to add an example to her rich holdings of art from that favored French school.[18] In the summer, she remembered her old friend and advisor, Frank Duveneck, who died in 1919, with a major donation to a Cincinnati Museum Association endowment in his name.[19] Income from the endowment supported students at the Art Academy of Cincinnati, the institution headed by Duveneck for many years, and it memorialized one of America's greatest teachers of painting. In 1922, Mary purchased her second work by the Barbizon master, Constant Troyon (1810–1865), *Autumn Morning*, declined "the little Memling" that was with her on approval, and showed no interest in photographs of paintings by Turner, Goya, and El Greco.[20] In the summer, Gest carefully interceded with dealers in her behalf. "[Mrs. Emery] has disposed of the canvas by Israels that was in her collection [and that] would indicate that she would not be interested in another canvas by that painter. The Signorelli would be more likely to appeal to her. I do not know at this moment how inclined she is to make further investments in her collection of paintings. She has recently taken up quite a large and important suburban building project that may absorb her for a while."[21] Gest correctly assessed the situation, for he reported to his collector that

A Queen Disputing with A Philosopher *by Andrea Mantegna (c. 1431–1506),* *acquired in 1922 (Courtesy Cincinnati Art Museum)*

an important painting by Signorelli was available, although "rather mud-dy" in the illustration he sent her. He compared it to others by the same artist he saw in the Sistine Chapel, "great favorites of mine among the recollections of Rome." Mary was always satisfied with her dealings with Mr. Sedgwick, she stated to Gest, but the Signorelli was not to be hers. "It is not worthwhile to send me the magazine as I am not spending for pictures at present but saving for 'Mariemont #2!' You are quite right in telling Mr. Sedgwick that I am 'absorbed in that project.' I can give you no idea how intensively CJL is working to get it started."[22]

Gest was not easily deterred, however, and he encouraged dealers to continue to propose important works for Mrs. Emery's consideration. The highly regarded New York dealer, Knoedler, established a significant foothold with her in the 1920s, beginning with the Troyon acquisition. Recognizing her ability to purchase paintings of great value, Knoedler offered a tempting Rembrandt to Gest for his patron. "Your letter of the twenty-eighth instant is at hand. I'll be glad to talk over with you the Rembrandt 'Portrait of a Man' when I get to New York. It is hard to say just how far Mrs. Emery's absorption in her real estate venture, the model town of Mariemont, just outside of the confines of Cincinnati, may keep her attention away from the purchase of paintings. However, there is no reason for not bringing before her anything of importance of painting."[23]

As the year closed, Mary Emery's extensive collection of paintings was featured in the *New York Times Magazine* and applauded above the rather meager holdings of the Cincinnati Art Museum at that time.

> For the old masters of Italy, Flanders, Holland, England, France, it is necessary to go to the rich private collections where brilliant authentic works are amazingly numerous. You will find Italian art dominant in Mrs. Emery's collection, and absent from that of Mr. and Mrs. Taft. Mrs. Emery's pictures, which are catalogued as the Edgecliffe collection of paintings, also are on a plane of highest importance. The collection has been assembled, and goes on being assembled, with the definite idea of an ultimate placing in the museum. No pains have been spared to maintain a museum standard of quality, and the range is through half a dozen centuries and as many countries.[24]

Although the "ultimate placing in the museum" would not occur for five more years, sometime during 1922 either Mary Emery or Livingood commissioned the artist, Vernon Howe Bailey (1874–1953), to record the collection's setting in Edgecliffe. His two glowing watercolors, one of the music room and the other showing the atrium, illustrate nearly a dozen paintings on the walls of the Emery home. They are the only known depictions of any part of the collection in its original setting.

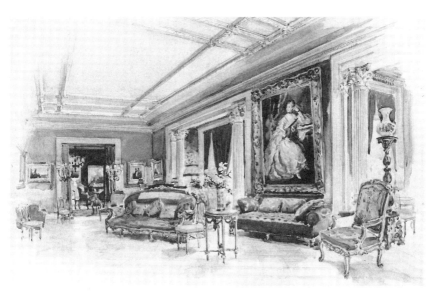

Music Room at Edgecliffe, *watercolor by Vernon H. Bailey, illustrating paintings as shown in home of Mary M. Emery, 1922 (Courtesy Cincinnati Art Museum)*

Hall and Atrium at Edgecliffe, *watercolor by Vernon H. Bailey, illustrating paintings as shown in home of Mary M. Emery, 1922 (Courtesy Cincinnati Art Museum)*

With Gest continuing to advise Mary and act as intercessor with dealers, Livingood's absence was not a factor as she considered future acquisitions. Her acquisitiveness added eight paintings in 1923 to the Edgecliffe collection, while a number were declined for various reasons, as noted in a typical letter from Gest to a Knoedler's representative, returning a portrait by Sir Joshua Reynolds.

> Too late Saturday for shipment and too late even for me to write to you [that] Mrs. Emery returned the Reynolds portrait. She was greatly interested in it and kept it in her house throughout the week. The very beautiful profile and the painting of the white dress attracted her very strongly but she could not feel quite sure of continuing to like some of the things in the left hand part of the canvas. The canvas looked very well in her house, even better than it did in the Museum, and seemed to hold up well with her other things. It seemed to be merely a question as to whether she could become accustomed to the positive oval form of the drawing board and the faintly suggested area and hand against it. It is a pity that should stand in the way because the rest of the canvas is so very beautiful.[25]

Knoedler's gallery in New York enjoyed a prosperous 1923 in supplying Mrs. Emery three paintings selected from those shipped to Cincinnati on approval. In February, she turned down another Rubens, this time a portrait. Gest remained hopeful, however, even as his collector showed little interest in Knoedler's proposal.

> The photograph of Rubens portrait of Francesco IV of Mantua I left with Mrs. Emery for a while, and later had a chance to talk with her about it. It seemed to interest her not a little, but she finally sent it back to me. Whether the canvas itself would make a sufficiently strong impression to warrant your sending it out I hardly know. There is always the difficulty that she is not inclined to duplicate. A certain comparison between the painting of this and her Van Dyck might be impressive. Is the price particularly high? Perhaps the canvas has already been disposed of. If not, and it remains in your possession when I come to New York next time you can show it to me then.[26]

Gest's two letters confirm Mary's earliest practices as collector. She reacted emotionally to paintings. Did the work appeal to her? Would it fit into her house along with the other pictures? Did it duplicate an artist? For Gest's part, it appears that he was not aware of purchase prices, as this was left to Mrs. Emery and Livingood to handle. Strangely, throughout the years Gest advised her, he offered little art historical research in support of the dealer's attributions and history for the paintings she considered and acquired. Sometimes information from the dealer came even after a purchase was made, as when Gest confirmed the importance of the *Portrait of Luigi Cherubini* by J. A. D. Ingres (1780–1867) that she bought from Knoedler Gallery, writing her one month after its purchase in March 1923 that her portrait ante-dates the version in the Louvre by one year.[27]

During the summer of 1923, Duveen and his agent, J. Jarman, pursued Mary Emery with other tempting acquisitions. To her Newport estate in May, he sent photographs of paintings by Rembrandt and Bellini, works she agreed were interesting; but, in returning them, she noted for Gest, "the Rembrandt may be very fine but I am satisfied with my canvas."[28] She confided to Gest that she was communicating with Miss Helen Frick, daughter of the New York collector Henry Clay Frick, who volunteered her staff at the Frick Library to produce a catalogue of the Edgecliffe collection. Mrs. Emery naturally sought a scholarly appraisal of her collection. Turning to one of the nation's best research centers, the Frick Library, when the Cincinnati Art Museum could not provide the curatorial expertise needed, she was disappointed. The assigned researcher, Lavinia Buckler, never saw the actual paintings, and she was an inexperienced art historian. However, in response to Miss Frick's offer, Mary sent as much information on her paintings as she could find in her records.

At about the same time, Mrs. Emery and Gest encountered Major Arthur de Bles, a shadowy character intent on selling subscriptions for an art history outline while promoting himself as an expert in preparing catalogues of private collections. Mary first heard from Gest about the mysterious Major de Bles in June, when she returned to the director "enlightening" information he had sent her.[29] Gest soon reported on what he knew about the purported British major who served in World War I. "Instead of practicing art as a profession, a restless enthusiasm for innumerable forms of art expression seems to have led him far and wide all over the field with what seemed to be an almost uncanny insight into the most varied qualities. That one with this temperament should gather himself together and systematize his experience in a series of tabulated blueprints and written outlines is remarkable."[30]

Gest subscribed $30 to de Bles's program, "a helpful skeleton to work in a pinch even though all of it does not prove completely trustworthy," he added in the same letter. Some months after this initial contact, Gest explained how de Bles entered the Cincinnati scene, performing as a speaker for the American Legion.

> His visit to Mrs. Emery's house was most interesting and his appreciation of her paintings was entirely to the point. Undoubtedly he did wish to make a study of her collection and through the unfortunate and entirely unauthorized statement of a third party he assumed for a time that Mrs. Emery wished him to make research and there was some correspondence between him and her and myself before we realized that he was working on that supposition. The matter was then immediately cleared up and stopped. Please understand that this was not authorized by Mrs. Emery who was quite unconscious of any work being done upon her catalogue other than what you have undertaken to do.[31]

Throughout the summer of 1923, Major de Bles studied the photographs of Mrs. Emery's Edgecliffe collection that were given to him by Gest, who was charmed by the suave British officer. Mary wrote Gest that she was "a bit overwhelmed over Mr. de Bles' work as I had no idea of suggesting he should 'expert' the pictures!" and Gest soon discovered that he was not hired to undertake any catalogue research.

> I too have my correspondence with Major de Bles. From the start he has puzzled me, partly by what I mentioned to you as a remarkable artistic insight that fitted curiously into many of our own observations here at the Museum, and, as you know, accorded with some of Duveneck's judgement from the painter's standpoint. Regarding the amount of time he is devoting to a study of your pictures I cautioned him the other day that he perhaps was letting his interest as an artist and his possible friendliness toward our Museum lead him to a lot of work not warranted by the circumstances and I warned him that he had as yet no authority to do it on your account. This caution seemed to me necessary in order to avoid any misunderstanding.[32]

When Mary had enough of de Bles's assuming a commission he did not receive from her, she instructed Thomas Hogan, who was with her in

Newport, to enter the fray and conclude further contacts with him. The matter was left with Gest and Hogan. "[Gest will see with Hogan] as to the best way of dealing with the gentleman as I do not like his attitude in taking for granted I was giving him an order for investigation after I had told him explicitly that Miss Frick was making my catalogue."[33]

By August, after Hogan discovered that a third party, a Mr. Campbell (who may have been a dealer's representative) had misled Major de Bles in a letter stating that Mrs. Emery wanted him to catalogue her collection, he ended any further contacts with the would-be researcher. "We consider the incident closed," he wrote to Gest.[34] This episode must have been similar to many encounters Mrs. Emery experienced with individuals wanting to curry favor or to be retained for unrequested, but costly, services.

An assistant in the Frick Art Reference Library, Lavinia Buckler, labored that summer to produce a detailed catalogue of Mrs. Emery's paintings, the first such undertaking. During this period, the Edgecliffe collection acquired its only American work, *Portrait of George Washington*, by Gilbert Stuart (1755–1828) one of six paintings Mrs. Emery bought from Knoedler's. Scanty information on this and other pictures came from Mary to Mrs. Buckler. As a collector, she kept no track of provenances and invoices, leaving this to Livingood. And, as she was in Newport and away from any records, it is not surprising that she frustrated the researcher, who could get little response to her queries.

> It was a new venture for this Library to undertake the making of a catalogue of a private collection and, the work being entrusted to me, I can personally testify how much time and effort has gone into Mrs. Emery's catalogue. Every picture has been looked up in every conceivable sort of reference book in our own Library, Knoedler's, Duveen's, etc. The history of previous collections, through which the pictures have passed have been made really unusually complete, through correspondence with former owners, or their heirs, or representatives. . . . The dealers have given splendid cooperation, and there has only been one difficulty. The majority of Mrs. Emery's pictures have been acquired, as you know, from Scott and Fowles, and Scott and Fowles, being unwilling to cooperate with the regular work of this Library in which all other dealers take such a generous and active interest, and we, consequently, not having anything to do with them in the course of our regular work, could not go to them about Mrs. Emery's pictures.[35]

Buckler then complained to Gest about the failure of Mary Emery to answer her questions about signatures on the paintings, colors, measurements, and other points essential to an art historian. She added that Mrs. Emery responded only briefly, saying she could not check anything until she returned to Cincinnati in the autumn. Buckler wrote in late June to Mrs. Emery but had no answer. To add to the researcher's concern, Buckler encountered Major de Bles one day in the New York Public Library surrounded by photographs of works in the Edgecliffe Collection. "Mrs. Emery had written to me that she had met him and that he knew a great deal about art and that she had suggested that he come and see me about her catalogue. She referred to him as 'Major.' In the Public Library register he has signed himself everything from General to Lieutenant Colonel, at different times, and my curiosity being aroused, I made inquiries."[36]

She concluded correctly that de Bles was assuming too much and was posing as the author of a catalogue of the Emery paintings. By mid-August, Major de Bles disappeared from Mary Emery's life.

Gest attempted to ease Buckler's concerns in a letter to Helen Frick, explaining the apparent disinterest of Mrs. Emery and offering to help by contacting various dealers. "I have spent my life in museum work and know from experience that there never is such a thing as a finished catalogue. Mrs. Emery is no longer young and for some years has been in bad health, and has also been greatly absorbed this season by responsibilities connected with the building of a model community, Mariemont, on the outskirts of Cincinnati. I venture a guess that the development of the catalogue under Mrs. Buckler's patient research has raised questions that Mrs. Emery did not anticipate and which she finds it hard to answer."[37] Throughout 1923 and into the next year, research continued on the catalogue, with information for the entries flowing between Gest and Buckler. Other problems surfaced, including Lavinia Buckler's illness and eventual resignation from the Frick Library staff. Finally, the catalogue was completed but never published. It was filed with the Cincinnati Art Museum as a forlorn typescript in a loose-leaf binder, lacking critical analysis or serious attempts at attribution.

The year 1923 ended with significant additions to the Edgecliffe collection, only one less than the banner year of 1910 when eight works were acquired. In November, four portraits of Burgundian dukes thought to be by Simon Marmion (active 1450–1489) were bought. By December, she purchased the charming *Boy with Grapes* by Sir Joshua Reynolds (1723–1792) for $25,000 and Théodore Rousseau's (1812–1867) *Summer Sunset* for $22,500. The prices illustrate the relative market value of a British genre subject against the then very popular Barbizon school landscape. Enclosed with a letter from Director Gest was the invoice for the Reynolds painting and his newsy observations on a visit of two noted art historians, Dr. Abraham Bredius and the director of the Haarlem Museum. "It happens that when Dr. Bredius, the Dutch expert, and his friend Kronig of Haarlem (Director of the Gallery) were here, your canvas of Philip II was standing in the trustees' room at the Museum. Their enthusiasm was remarkable. Dr. Bredius recalled having seen the canvas in Lenbach's possession in London, thus double identification was complete. During the little luncheon I gave them there in the room they commented on the rare privilege of such company as Titian's portrait of Philip."[38]

Mrs. Emery prepared in May to leave for Newport, closed Edgecliffe, and covered the paintings for the summer months. Gest deferred visits from dealers when she was away, but Mary welcomed visits from friends, showing her collection up to the date of her departure. A prospective acquisition from Duveen hung on her walls, *The Music Party* by Gerard Terborch (1617–1681), when the librarian of the Cincinnati Art Museum, Elizabeth Kellogg, sent her some information on the "Terbourg" under consideration. This painting was her only acquisition in 1924, an exquisite work by one of Holland's immortals. The music lesson theme was a popular subject with Dutch painters in the seventeenth century. Terborch's scintillating colors, exquisite rendering of fabrics, and crisp details all contributed to the fame he enjoyed with collectors.

Trouble was brewing in 1924 with the Frick's researcher for the catalogue of the Emery paintings. Mary wrote to Gest to comment on her displeasure at some of the research interpretations and asked Gest for advice. Seeing that Mrs. Emery was "greatly troubled at the whole performance," Gest wrote her about the many problems he encountered in dealings with

The Music Party by Gerard Terborch (1617–1681), acquired in 1924 (Courtesy Cincinnati Art Museum)

Mrs. Buckler. "You will remember that I was greatly disappointed in the matter submitted to you by the Frick Library. Mrs. Buckler seemed to be doing the best she could under the circumstances and appears to have worn herself out in attempting more than the organization back of her is equipped to do. Manifestly it is out of their province to attempt to expertise, and surprise has been expressed to me that they should assume to do so."[39] In August, after Gest waded through all of the correspondence with the Frick Library, he again wrote Mary of the regrets he shared with her. After this date, the abandoned catalogue never was revived. Gest wrote to Mary that

> [The catalogue was] an unfortunate venture into expertising with a staff so little experienced outside of library records pure and simple. How is it possible to attach equal importance to a vague unverified "say so" concerning the claim set up by somebody for another canvas? Must we refuse a fact to chase a shadow cast by we know not what? By the way, I have just heard that our "friend" Berenson, whose contradictory and unexplained opinion re the Tintoretto puzzles us—is no longer in high favor as a critic in the leading circles at Cambridge, the Fogg Museum and the art teachers at Harvard. So don't worry over possible controversies.[40]

Gest tried his best to extend Mrs. Emery's art holdings, but he never overstepped his position as advisor, realizing that the final word was hers. He was discreet in responding to dealers but persistent in suggesting possible acquisitions to his patron. Anthonis Mor (c. 1517–c. 1576), frequently called Antonio Moro, was an outstanding Netherlandish portrait painter of the sixteenth century and an artist Gest first proposed in 1920 for Mrs. Emery's consideration. Turned down then, the New York dealer, Knoedler, through his representative, Gerrity, suggested another Moro portrait to Gest in January 1925. Mary was not well, and Gest delayed in presenting it to her. "This brings me to the Moro portrait. I found Mrs. Emery well enough on Monday to see it and therefore took it over there. She was interested, but not sufficiently to want to buy it. She appeared to have a pleasanter recollection of the large full-length that you brought out some time ago. Consequently we shipped the Moro back to you yesterday."[41]

Other paintings that failed to interest Mrs. Emery in February 1925 included works by Nicolas Poussin (1594–1665) and Colijn de Coter (c. 1455–c. 1540). Dealers were willing to ship works on approval, and seldom was a picture turned down without her seeing it. Gest showed only mild disappointment on the many occasions when a work was packed and returned. "Your letter of the sixteenth of February is at hand. The Poussin was shipped to you yesterday. Before sending it back I was fortunate enough to find Mrs. Emery in better health and, therefore, willing to let me show her the canvas. She was greatly charmed with it and appreciated the opportunity given her by you of seeing it. She recognizes the great importance of it as a Museum picture, but I judge from her remarks that she feels hardly like placing it in her gallery at home."[42]

That spring, Gest wrote Mrs. Emery about two great works, paintings by Rogier van der Weyden (c. 1400–1464) and Johannes (or Jan) Vermeer (1632–1675) that slipped away. "From Labey I learned the other day that the Van Der Weyden picture was sold to Mortimer Schiff. He told me also that the Ver Meer [sic] which Jonas wrote me from Paris is the one showed you here a while ago. I recall it quite clearly and our discussions of it."[43] But Mary did not miss acquiring any painting she truly wanted, such as the *Portrait of Francis I* by Joos van Cleve (ca. 1485–1540), bought from the New York dealer Jacques Seligman, in May 1925. Fortified by statements from noted art historians Wilhelm Valentiner and Max Friedlander that authenticated the picture, Mrs. Emery paid $17,000 for it. She was impressed that the portrait depicted a great noble, a king of France. The aristocratic portrait was a subtheme in her collection, whether she acknowledged this or not. "[The] beautiful Portrait of Francis I, which is undoubtedly one of the best portraits done from the life of this king shows an artist of remarkable draftsmanship and a fine color scheme. It is, at the same time, a work of much decorative quality and in very good condition. When you showed me the picture in Paris, you will remember that I said it undoubtedly belonged to a group of portraits which Dr. Friedlander has recently attributed to Joos van Cleve, the elder, who as we know from documents, worked on the French court, about 1530, for some time, although he was a Flemish painter from Antwerp."[44]

Mary Emery renewed her interest in her collection of paintings later in the spring, declining three works from the dealer Kleinberger by Gentile Bellini (c. 1429–1507) or Giovanni Bellini (c. 1430–1516), Sandro Botticelli (1445–1510), and Francois Clouet (c. 1516–1572). She also refused a portrait by Lorenzo Lotto (c. 1480–1556) from Wildenstein. Writing to Gest she showed her willingness to exchange paintings to improve her holdings, but apparently did not consult Gest before making her decision, an unusual move for her. "Having it [the painting by Lorenzo Lotto] beside the Perugino does not work for its attractiveness! Do you know I am letting Jarman take the Hobbema in part payment for the Perugino—which pleases me greatly. I hope you will approve."[45]

The New York and London dealer, Wildenstein, was a relative late-comer in seeking Mrs. Emery as a client. Contacts from Felix Wildenstein, a partner in the firm, all occurred in 1925 or later. But to the dealer Klein-berger she turned for one of her strangest acquisitions, ultimately deter-mined to be by the infamous counterfeiter, the so-called Spanish Forger. The picture, a three-panel painting or triptych, was ascribed to the French master, Jean Fouquet (c. 1420–c. 1480), and supposedly depicted the *Pre-sentation of an Illuminated Missal to Anne de Beaujeu, Regent for Charles VIII*. Mrs. Emery's purchase price, $25,000, was wasted. It is remarkable that the painting's crude handling and amateurish technique fooled any-one, for the painting has little resemblance to Fouquet's authentic work. Perhaps Mary was intrigued by its aristocratic subject and the story it told, suggesting an historical relationship with her portraits of the Dukes of Bur-gundy purchased in 1923. Art collectors sometimes make poor choices, and dealers may be ignorant or intend to deceive their clients, but the Spanish Forger's panels join a few other paintings in the Edgecliffe collec-tion with original attributions that are indefensible today.

By 1925, Mary Emery recognized that she should provide funds for a new wing with galleries to house the Edgecliffe collection she would even-tually bequeath to the Cincinnati Art Museum. Her representative con-veyed the good news to the trustees of the museum. "As President of the Thomas J. Emery Memorial it gives me great pleasure to advise you that Mrs. Emery, having long wished to see provided at the Museum a special and suitable building for the display and care of such of her pictures as she may give to it, has requested us to notify you that it is our intention, pro-vided the building will be acceptable, to pay for the erection of a structure to be known as 'The Emery Wing'."[46] Livingood's letter noted his close work with Gest in developing plans for the new wing that would be designed by Cincinnati architects Garber & Woodward. Construction cost was estimated at $240,000, exclusive of interior decoration. Expecting that Mrs. Emery's latest gift to the public was newsworthy, Livingood prepared a press release outlining the proposed wing's layout of galleries, rotunda, and entrance that would form a handsome addition in classical style to the main building.[47] By the end of May, Livingood again used the Commercial Club of Cincinnati as the forum for announcing Mrs. Emery's intended gift, now grown to $300,000.[48]

Summering in Newport, Mary Emery prepared a statement, apparently in response to an unknown letter writer, clarifying her intentions regarding the future of her collection of old master paintings. Addressed in her own hand to "My dear [left blank in the letter]" and signed "Yours very sincerely, M. M. Emery," the letter's body formed a ready response to inquiries that she or the museum might receive. It is not known if it was ever sent to anyone.

> Your letter of the [left blank] was very sincerely appreciated by me and I would like to tell you how it all came about at this time. When I decided to leave the pictures to our Museum, I asked for the expert advice of the directors in buying, both for authenticity and usefulness of subjects to help the Art Students. This advice was given me generously by Mr. Gest, Mr. Duveneck, Mr. Meakin, Mr. Barnhorn and others and thus I was enabled to secure specimens of value always.
>
> Some years ago the drawing was made of an addition to the Museum— about the time that Mrs. Alms' will gave a large donation for a building. This sum has not yet been made available and it was holding in abeyance any work. My two recent illnesses of 1923 and 1924 have made me solicitous that what I had arranged to do in my "will" should be done now, as I could see no place for my pictures to be put in the present building.
>
> One of the letters I received during the controversy about the School Building [Art Academy of Cincinnati, a sister institution of the Art Museum and governed by the same trustees] advised me to take a large view of the situation for the future, intimating that with my pictures in Edgecliffe the benefit to the School would be much enhanced. I felt an explanation should be given publicity that I did not intend leaving the pictures in Edgecliffe and that was another of the reasons for building the Wing in the Museum now. You are at liberty to give these reasons to anyone interested, without newspaper publicity.[49]

The trustees of the art museum reviewed Garber & Woodward's drawings at their meeting on June 9, 1925, and recorded their pride in the double promise of a new wing and a collection. They also sounded the alarm for future funding of operations, a never-ending crusade for the Cincinnati Art Museum. "The importance of the erection of this Emery Wing and its contributions towards the completing of our central court and the even greater importance of the wonderful collection of paintings being formed by Mrs. Emery, together mark an epoch in the history of the museum of the greatest possible consequence in its future development, for which adequate support becomes a pressing necessity."[50]

By August, Gest sent the plans for the new wing to its benefactor so she could review them at leisure in Newport. He also passed them by Duveen's agent, Jarman, during one of his visits to Cincinnati, and he was "thoroughly enthusiastic."[51] The two men then spent an hour mentally arranging the Edgecliffe collection in the future galleries while discussing lighting and spatial relationships for pictures on the walls. Sketches for the new wing reached Livingood at his Canadian summer home by late September, and he urged Gest to form a small building committee to supervise the project, "probably yourself, myself, and one other who we can count on as to experience, judgment, and attendance to duties. Frankly, I cannot do it all, though I do claim the right to build according to your and my ideas, guided by the architects and aided by such men as Jarman."[52] As President of the Emery Memorial, Livingood controlled the funds for the new wing. "My plan would be, and I am sure this will meet the approval of both Mrs. Emery and its board of trustees, that the Thomas J. Emery Memorial should simply supply funds en bloc as needed, say $25,000 at a time. This is the way Mrs. Emery paid for the erection of the Medical School Building [at the University of Cincinnati]. The Memorial is already a going concern and has monies at its command, only I must be given a little time as President to turn around and secure from its Board of Directors authority to undertake the carrying out of Mrs. Emery's wishes. They were very explicit in that letter to me."

Mrs. Emery's fascination for portraits of kings and nobles prompted her to exchange the landscape by Meindert Hobbema, *View in Westphalia*, acquired in 1910, for a sombre *Portrait of Philip IV* by Diego Velázquez (1599–1660). It is tempting to believe that Mary's interest in the portrait was partly prompted by the sitter's relationship to his grandfather, Philip

Portrait of Philip IV *by Diego Velázquez (1599–1660), acquired in 1925–1927 (Courtesy Cincinnati Art Museum)*

II, depicted in the portrait by Titian that she owned. Additionally, she must have admired the glazes and brushwork in this perceptive portrayal of Philip IV. "I was sorry to lose the Perugino," Mary wrote to Gest concerning the Italian Renaissance painting she had on approval since May, "but the other was too tempting to refuse."[53] Duveen, the New York dealer, gave her $85,000 credit (the amount paid for the Hobbema) towards the Velázquez's purchase price of $254,625. This was a hefty price, exceeding all others with the exception of the Titian's cost. Gest was impressed with the portrait's acquisition, writing Mrs. Emery, "Your feeling that Perugino had to give way before Velasquez [sic] is easily understood."[54]

Among the artists who failed to attract her was the Spaniard, Mariano Fortuny (1838–1874), for as Mary explained to Gest: "I am not inserting a picture of his date and character."[55] The Fortuny picture joined the Millais refused earlier in her collecting years, thus reinforcing her focus on major old master paintings. Mary Emery's last acquisitions in 1925 were not auspicious. The first, *Portrait of the Prince de Polignac* by Marie-Louise Vigée-Lebrun (1755–1842), purchased in November, was determined sixty years later to be incorrectly attributed. Her second purchase, *A Knight in Armor*, was thought by its dealer, Duveen, to be by the great German master, Albrecht Dürer (1471–1528) when sold to Mrs. Emery in December. It was published as a Dürer in the distinguished Ashburton and Rothschild collections, but by 1930 scholarly opinion assigned it to an anonymous German painter of the mid-sixteenth century. These two misattributions attest to the inability of dealer, curator, or collector in those days to determine authenticity. Art history was a somewhat primitive scholarly discipline in 1925 in the United States, although Europe had a number of well-trained historians. Mrs. Emery seldom reached beyond the words of dealers and the recommendations of the Cincinnati Art Museum director, except when she occasionally sought an expert's opinion in a letter that may have been bought by the selling dealer. The few mistakes she made can be forgiven. Most collectors of art have not been infallible in the authenticity of their acquisitions. Mary Emery acquired a notable collection filled with many masterpieces—a quest difficult to achieve today.

In 1926, Mary Emery made her last acquisition for the Edgecliffe collection. Paintings, summers in Rhode Island, and infrequent contacts with a few individuals and organizations she had benefited occupied her time when she was not recovering from illness. She added the third codicil to her will, providing an annuity of $5,000 per year to Theodora Mary Williams, a relative of her father.[56] Gest continued to intervene with dealers, such as Jacques Seligman's representative, who proposed a portrait by Anthony van Dyck. Her collection had its limits, and she was well aware of the holdings of other Cincinnati collectors. "Mr. Taft has a full-length

portrait of this Genoese period, as you may remember. Mrs. Emery has her
fine 'John of Nassau.' So I am quite sure neither of them would be interested."[57] But in January and February, Duveen's agent presented two sculptures purportedly by the Italian Renaissance masters, Leonardo da Vinci
(1452–1519) and Antonio Rossellino (1427–1479). Gest responded
excitedly to the dealer that he met with Mrs. Emery about these remarkable opportunities. "Yesterday morning on receiving your letter and also
the book on Leonardo I took Mr. Barnhorn [Clement Barnhorn, sculpture
instructor at the Art Academy of Cincinnati] over to Mrs. Emery's where
we had an interesting talk with her. She could not fail to be deeply
impressed by what you were offering, but she said that she could not very
well change her decision to keep her collection within the limits of painting only, which she has established."[58] Gest's postscript, "The possibility of
a Leonardo da Vinci of this supreme scarcity and amazingly beautiful quality being within grasp seems a fairy tale indeed," closed consideration of
this sculpture but did not deter Jarman from offering another only one
month later. "Mrs. Emery called me up last evening to see if you were in
town as she wished to tell you that she had decided not to keep the little
Rossellino bust. So it falls to me to give you this disappointing news. I told
her that you might be back shortly, and with that she let the bust remain
in her house, though I rather expected at one moment that she was about
to ask me to send for it, fearing possibly the risk of anything happening by
accident to it."[59] True to the focus she determined for her collection shortly after her husband's death, Mary refused both sculptures but negotiated
with Knoedler & Company, New York, for the last painting she would
acquire. *St. Helena, Mother of Constantine the Great*, by the German master Lucas Cranach (1472–1553), a panel painting once in Europe's prestigious Liechtenstein Collection, was purchased for a trifling $6,000.

Following her purchase of the Cranach painting, Mary Emery showed
little interest in acquiring additional pictures. Health worries, expanding
cash needs for Mariemont, and the projected new wing for the Cincinnati
Art Museum were quite enough to occupy her time. A query from a New
York dealer, offering a portrait of a gentleman by "Bellini," either Gentile
or Giovanni, brought a quick response from Gest. "I have your letter and

also the photograph of the 'Portrait of a Gentleman' by Bellini. The last suggestion of another purchase brought from Mrs. Emery and Mr. Livingood a frank declination on account, I believe, of their deep absorption in the development of their real estate project at Mariemont. From the Museum standpoint, we should like, naturally, to have a Bellini in the collection."[60]

Gest had a little more control with plans for the museum's new wing, for he acted not only as liaison between the museum's board of trustees and Mrs. Emery, but he was that institution's longtime director and the individual most involved as her collection's advisor. In the spring of 1926, discussion of plans for the wing suggest that some disagreement over the wing's location occurred. Mrs. Emery and Livingood were already at Newport. Gest wrote to Livingood concerning his patron's desires for the addition she was providing for the museum, stating that the building committee would "restudy the program with a view to bringing it entirely into accord with Mrs. Emery's wishes."[61] Eventually, the wing was designed and built to harmonize with the Classic Revival style imposed on the museum in 1907 by Daniel Burnham, architect of the Schmidlapp Wing.

Mary Emery's art collecting was over by 1927 except for two payments she concluded in an unknown month of that year. Livingood cabled Gest that "We have bought the two Dukes,"[62] and asked that the carpenter at Edgecliffe be instructed to "take down the two earlier Dukes from the corner of dining room and complete the group which you might display when Mrs. Alexander's [art critic for the *Cincinnati Enquirer*] article is sure to appear." Art dealers continued to entice Mary to purchase paintings in spite of her reluctance to add to the Edgecliffe collection. Wildenstein's New York office sent her photographs of works by Titian, Velázquez, Bellini, El Greco, and Jan Provost, and all were returned by the art museum's director.[63] Kleinberger Galleries in New York offered her a work by Rogier van der Weyden, but she was "not inclined to buy anything just now."[64] The door was closed for acquisitions.

The Edgecliffe collection was bequeathed to the Cincinnati Art Museum at Mary Emery's death in 1927. The man who assisted the collection's growth, Director Joseph H. Gest, retired in 1929 after forty-three years on the museum staff. Mary's collection was not seen by the public until 1930, when its installation in the Mary M. Emery Wing heralded the completion of the building its donor never saw.

Mary's purchases began with a few Barbizon school pictures she bought in the first years of her inheritance. From this beginning, she was purposeful in her goal of amassing a world-class group of old master paintings. The collection expanded in twenty years into a rich assembly. The collection formed by Mary Muhlenberg Emery remains the renowned core of old master paintings in the museum she loved and supported.

CHAPTER 10

Death Ends a Selfless Embrace

Mary emery's tenuous health in her last year drew her attention away from art collecting, her many philanthropies, and her new town in Ohio, even preventing her from being present at the dedication of the Mariemont Community Church.[1] That event heralded another progressive step for the town she founded and its families, now numbering 320, who were living in some of the 750 completed homes, according to a full-page newspaper advertisement placed by the Mariemont Company.[2]

In the spring of 1927, Mary Emery was stricken with gallstones and underwent an operation at Cincinnati's Jewish Hospital. On April 19, a second operation was performed to relieve adhesions.[3] She recovered in the same hospital during May. Her faithful nurse, Helen Baird (1885–1963), pictured at her side in the frequently reproduced photograph of Mrs. Emery at the Mariemont groundbreaking in 1923, attended her. She was an important member of Mary's retinue in her mistress's last years.[4] Baird and Thomas Hogan accompanied Mary to Newport in the summer so that her recovery might continue away from Cincinnati's heat. A Newport newspaper commented on the area's well-known resident. "She was seriously ill in the spring, and there was some question as to whether she would be able to come to Newport during the summer, but her love for the place was so intense that she insisted upon undertaking the trip. During the summer she seemed to gain a little, but it was felt advisable to curtail her stay here, and she returned to Cincinnati in late August."[5]

When her health failed to improve during July and August, Mary longed to return to the Cincinnati home she once shared with her husband and sons. Probably she wished to consult her regular physicians. For whatever reasons, she returned to Edgecliffe in late August, or "about September 1," as a newspaper reported. This was earlier than usual. She was accompanied by Livingood, Hogan, Baird, and various servants. About October 6, she contracted a cold that developed into bronchial pneumonia. She remained at Edgecliffe and was placed under the care of her Cincinnati physicians, Drs. Roger S. Morris and Mark A. Brown. On Tuesday, October 11, 1927, at ten o'clock in the evening, Mary Muhlenberg Emery "closed her eyes peacefully" at her Cincinnati home, Edgecliffe, and "slipped off into eternal sleep."[6]

The death of Cincinnati's greatest benefactor was announced in front page stories in the city's newspapers on October 12, with headlines citing her as "Cincinnati's Most Revered Philanthropist" and "Noted Woman Benefactor." The obituary in the *New York Times* correctly described her as "one of America's richest women, founder of the model city of Mariemont."[7] Lengthy accounts of her generous benefactions and biographical facts, occasionally inaccurate, filled the columns as newspapers vied in their editorials to memorialize the eighty-two-year-old lady who had touched so many lives. "This gentle patroness used her great wealth wisely, unostentatiously—giving where, in her judgment, the greater good might result. Her gifts were purposefully made. They blessed the community of her heart, Cincinnati, beyond estimation. Her choice was to go her way extending benefactions that should serve to stay the tide of human tears— to lift the mortal soul to higher levels of appreciation of the values of life."[8]

Within a tiny envelope in Livingood's files, marked "Chas. J. Livingood, a Last Request," Mary gave her handwritten instructions for her funeral. On two sheets, the first one headed "For C. J. Livingood," she detailed specific requests. "If Chalmers [Chalmers Clifton, pianist and an Emery protégé] is in this country, he will arrange for the aria in Bach's Suite in D Major to be played at the funeral. If he is not available I would

like to have Ferundelier arrange it—*no one else*. At the commitment service have the first and last verses of Hymn 242 in the Prayer Book *read*. If
Mr. Nelson is not in the city I would like Dr. Guthrie to officiate."[9]

In a separate note in Mary's hand and enclosed in the same envelope,
she listed her preferred honorary pallbearers: "Dr. [Robert] Sattler, W. S.
Ludlow, Dr. [B. K.] Rachford, G. H. H. Wiggers, President [Frederick C.]
Hicks, Dr. Roger Morris, Prof. H. M. Benedict, Nettleton Neff, Albert
Halstead, Edgar S. Kelly, Charles P. Taft, Emery D. Potter of Toledo, Mor-
rison R. Waite, J. H. Gest, Richard F. Wright, Judge W. Worthington, and
R. Schneider." Next to the seventeen names, Livingood wrote that
Wright was away, Worthington was dead, and Schneider was sick. Neff's
name was marked with a question mark and Morris and Wiggers with an
"x." Apart from these six men who did not serve, the remaining eleven
were honorary pallbearers, with Charles B. Wilby added to their number.

All work was cancelled at Mariemont on Friday, October 14, the day of
the funeral. A stream of visitors was received that morning at Edgecliffe
by Mary's sister, Isabella Hopkins. The funeral service, orchestrated by
Mary herself, began shortly before 2:30 P.M. as active pallbearers carried
the casket from the hearse, up the short flight of steps from Fourth Street,
and into the Gothic Revival interior of Christ Church, Mary's beloved
religious home. Acknowledging their affection for the widow of their late
employer, the active pallbearers were employees of Thomas Emery's Sons
and The Mariemont Company: Charles L. Burgoyne, Henry Gruesser, W.
W. Everett, Thomas Hogan, Jr., John H. Hall, Louis T. Kaiser, Robert
Mecke, and F. J. Schlanser. Banks of flowers overflowed the nave in the
crowded church. The Episcopal service, conducted by the Reverend Frank
Nelson and assisted by Bishop Boyd Vincent, included songs and hymns
sung by the thirty-member choir and a solo performed by Dan Beddoe,
"Be Thou Faithful Unto Death." Another piece was played by Cincinnati
Symphony Orchestra cellist, Walter Heerman. "Only one departure from
the set ritual of the church—and this at Mrs. Emery's own request. The
Bach Air in G was played on the church organ by Parvin Titus, the organ-
ist, after Rev. Frank H. Nelson, rector of the church, announced this was
to be done by Mrs. Emery's request."[10]

Following the service, a long train of friends, servants, and business associates accompanied the hearse to Spring Grove Cemetery for Mary's interment in the family burial plot alongside her husband and two sons. A longtime friend in attendance that October day wrote her sentiments to Isabella Hopkins, expressing what many citizens knew in their hearts. "It seemed to me that the services held at Christ Church on the day of her burial were the most beautiful and impressive I had ever witnessed, with the exquisite music and masses of lovely flowers, and as we turned away from the grave at Spring Grove, with Mr. Nelson's solemn words still lingering in our ears—'Father in thy loving keeping, Leave we here thy servant sleeping,' I felt that indeed all was well with her, but that the world was poorer by the loss of a very noble and lovely character."[11]

Two days after the funeral, on October 16, the Lady Bountiful (as she was often titled by the *Mariemont Messenger* and other newspapers) was eulogized in a memorial service embracing the founder of Mariemont. Held appropriately at the Mariemont Community Church, Pastor Paul Hoppe recounted Mary Emery's many benefactions, correctly stating that Mariemont "was her especial pet project, which she followed in detail up to the very last. It is the culmination of her life-long dream to improve the housing conditions of Cincinnati."[12] His eulogy, "She Went About Doing Good," assessed her life since her husband's death as devoted to philanthropy, a life that surely "felt the Divine approval guiding her in her ways of loving service."

In the days following the funeral, the public's speculation about Mrs. Emery's wealth and the value of her estate was answered when terms of the "Last Will and Testament of Mary M. Emery"[13] were released to the Cincinnati press. This was front-page news, of course, in a city long accustomed to frequent announcements of her beneficence. "An unofficial estimate of $25,000,000 was made as to the probable total of her estate, with the statement that this was an undervaluation, rather than an overvaluation. If this is true, then the amount going to the Thomas J. Emery Memorial for public beneficial purposes forever, is not less than $20,000,000."[14] By Monday, October 17, only six days after Mrs. Emery's death, the executor of her estate, Charles J. Livingood, was in Newport, Rhode Island,

Family burial plot of Mary M. and Thomas J. Emery, Spring Grove Cemetery, Cincinnati (Author's collection)

where he appeared at the Probate Court of Middletown, site of her legal residence, to initiate probate proceedings. Mary Emery's fifteen-page, printed will was accepted by the clerk of court, Albert L. Chase, the same official who certified her husband's will in 1906.[15]

Mary's will indicated her wish "to dispose of her entire estate, including that which I received under the Will of my beloved husband, the late Thomas J. Emery." In the first paragraphs she ordered the payment of debts, provision of funds for perpetual care of the Emery plot in Spring

Grove Cemetery, followed by several outright bequests. The first named bequest, awarding her portrait by John Elliot of Julia Ward Howe (1819–1910), the noted social reformer, went to the Cincinnati Woman's Club. Her richly colored painting, *The Holy Family*, bequeathed to her church and thought to be by the Flemish master, Peter Paul Rubens (1577–1640), is now regarded by art historians as a work of Rubens's studio.

Most significant in value was the collection of paintings willed to the Cincinnati Museum Association. Mrs. Emery generously offered them those works "said Museum may care to accept." By Livingood's calculations, Mrs. Emery expended over $3,000,000 for the paintings she collected.[16] Since the Edgecliffe collection's importance was known, and Mrs. Emery had announced the destination for the old master paintings years before her death, Gest and his trustees were surprised at the modest wording of the bequest.

Mary's sister, Isabella, was to receive all her personal effects and the use of Edgecliffe and the Mariemont estate in Rhode Island during her lifetime, in addition to a lump sum of $500,000. Both properties reverted to the residuary estate of Mrs. Emery after her sister's death. The will's provision for sixteen individuals, including her sister ($500,000), Livingood ($500,000), her five nephews and nieces ($100,000 each), and various relatives and friends totaled $2,135,000. The most compassionate section of Mary's will set aside $2,500,000 in trust to provide for annuitants, each to receive $200 to $4,000 or more per year for life. These annuitants included men and women (the latter far outnumbering the male recipients) who were artist friends, the three children of Livingood, the noted author Dorothy Canfield Fisher, Chalmers Clifton and his wife, and others living across the country and in Europe. Although sixty-nine individuals were listed by name as annuitants in the will, a provision requested ongoing payments to others known to the executor and who depended on regular support from Mary. For most of the annuitants, their friendship or relationship to Mary Emery is unknown.

Each servant employed at either the Cincinnati or Rhode Island estates was given fifty dollars for each year of service.[17] A group of social welfare agencies, many of them supported in her lifetime or her husband's, were awarded $870,000.[18] That portion of her Mariemont estate known as Seacroft, she bequeathed to Chalmers D. Clifton and his wife Wanda Baur Clifton, both distinguished musicians and frequent summer guests. The remainder of her wealth she willed to the Thomas J. Emery Memorial, her residuary legatee, a provision modified only slightly by the second codicil that recognized the Memorial's incorporation. This amount, thought to be between $20,000,000 and $30,000,000, fired the speculation of the press.[19]

Conjectures on the estate's value and residuary benefits were far from the facts. Mary's federal estate tax return recorded her worth in excess of $14,000,000, with bequests and gifts reducing the estate's net value to slightly more than $3,000,000. An undated appraisal of Mary Emery's estate, probably prepared no later than October 1928, listed the estate's assets and commitments, providing a detailed chronicle of its worth at the time of death. In 1927–1928, the federal tax laws required "an itemized inventory by schedule of the gross estate of the decedent with legal deductions to be filed in duplicate." Therefore, the inventory for Mrs. Emery's estate was prepared and submitted by her attorney, Robert A. Taft, partner in the prestigious Cincinnati law firm of Taft, Stettinius, & Hollister.[20] Listed on the first pages of the report were twenty-one heirs and legatees and seventy-one annuitants, this latter group to receive regular payments of varying amount during their lifetimes. Following this portion, Mrs. Emery's assets and deductions were divided among fifteen "Schedules," each listing specific holdings and an assigned dollar value by the appraiser. From these records, a fuller picture of Mary's financial worth may be gained.

The gross value of the estate was recorded as $14,419,837.97, with deductions of $11,345,123.19, leaving a net value for tax purposes, the estate submitted, of $3,074,714.78.

Real estate ownership included thirty-seven properties in Cincinnati; thirty in the Indianview subdivision of Mariemont, Ohio; homes in Middletown and Cincinnati; and other holdings including an especially valuable building at Broadway and 54th Street in New York City. Mrs. Emery's cash evaluation of stocks and bonds deriving from her ownership of the

Mariemont Company, was valued at $2,398,458.51, far exceeding her largest single holding, 1,515 shares in United States Fidelity and Guaranty Company, appraised at $514,721.25. The worth of the Edgecliffe collection of paintings was estimated conservatively at $4,000,000 within "Miscellaneous Property," while one of the lowest values, $100, was placed on Mary's 1920 Packard touring car housed in Middletown, Rhode Island. This same schedule itemized every piece of furniture and decoration, books, and clothing in the thirty-one rooms of Edgecliffe, twenty-six rooms at Mariemont, and sixteen rooms at Seacroft. A remarkable library of over fifteen hundred books was housed at Edgecliffe, spread throughout the residence, mostly in matched volumes of famous authors ("32 Vols. Kipling, 15 Vols. Hawthorne, 22 Vols. George Eliot, 12 Vols. Irving"). This collection was appraised modestly at $2,567. Interestingly, the property and equipment owned by Mrs. Emery at Resthaven, the farm located in the new town of Mariemont, included a Guernsey bull and several cows.

Beginning with Schedule H, the tax report focused on deductions claimed by the estate. As executor, Livingood received $200,000; lawyers' fees accounted for $100,000; $12,000 was owed for "Two Dukes of Burgundy" to James Labey and $207,125 to Duveen for the Velázquez portrait; and pledges ranged from $10 to the Newport Permanent Firemen Pension Association to $50,000 to Kenyon College. Two disabled employees of Thomas Emery's Sons were owed modest sums totaling $1,026.36. The most significant amount in bequests to charitable institutions was registered with the paintings received by the Cincinnati Art Museum, valued at $3,974,000.

Court opinions in suits brought by Ohio and Rhode Island during the settlement of the estate differed widely in their readings of the estate's true value for probate purposes. Rhode Island finally agreed to an established taxable value, in 1929, at $4,996,747.51.[21] The residuary estate of Mary Emery, bequeathed to the Thomas J. Emery Memorial after all bequests and gifts were concluded, finally was resolved in 1930 in a suit before the Ohio Supreme Court. By this action, the taxable estate was valued at $3,039,652.43.[22]

Two codicils added to the will in 1927 reflected Mary's compassionate nature. The first of March 30, forgave a loan of $4,000 owed to her by Alexander J. Dorward and he was to be retained as estate caretaker for one year after her death. Two other individuals, in addition to those already named, were to receive bequests of $1,000 each. The second codicil of May 2, recognized her "faithful butler," John Rodger Jackson, and her "faithful housemaid," Margaret Delahanty [Dolanty?], bequeathing each of them $1,000. Although many of the bequests and annuities in Mrs. Emery's will may be reckoned as mere remembrances or tokens of appreciation rather than retirement maintenance, the scale of her thoughtfulness and the value of the dollar in 1927 provided welcome assistance to many whom she named in her will.

Unfortunately, the first meeting of the Thomas J. Emery Memorial held after Mrs. Emery's death did not record her demise nor did the trustees offer a resolution in memory of their founder.[23] An organization that did remember Mrs. Emery shortly after her death, the Ohio Mechanics Institute, ended the sad year with their annual program for Founders Day, honoring her and acknowledging her gifts of $1,500,000, made during her lifetime.[24]

The distribution of Mary Emery's wealth prescribed in her will concluded her personal participation in her estate. She had not exhausted her husband's fortune. Through her foresight, she used her estate's remaining dollars to provide support for future causes. Her provision for the Thomas J. Emery Memorial insured a continuation of her philanthropies through grants determined by a group of trustees.

In addition to her will's provisions, Mary gave instructions for the dispersal of her personal effects, primarily her jewelry, books, and furniture.[25] Buried in an undated three-page list in Mary's handwriting and in a confirming, typed account by Livingood prepared one month after his patron's death (but also listed in the estate's assets for the Internal Revenue Service) was the assignment of a remarkable marble sculpture to her nephew, Thomas, son of her brother-in-law John J. Emery. Decades earlier, J. Howard Emery, the younger of the Emery brothers, had ordered in Rome a marble replica of *Nydia, the Blind Flower Girl of Pompeii* from its sculptor, Randolph Rogers (1825–1892). After its completion and installation in Cincinnati, it decorated the Emery homes on West Fourth Street and at

Edgecliffe. When Mary's brother-in-law commissioned the sculpture, Randolph Rogers was one of America's most renowned artists, and his *Nydia* was one of the most popular nineteenth-century images.[26] At least fifty-seven replicas of both versions of *Nydia* were commissioned by visitors to Rogers's Rome studio. Mary's brother-in-law was but one of the many tourists and expatriates awed by the sculpture's translation of the famous character in Bulwer-Lytton's novel, *The Last Days of Pompeii*. Since its acquisition in 1868, *Nydia* remained in Cincinnati, residing with the Emery family in their downtown home until it was moved to Mary and Thomas's residence, Edgecliffe, sometime after Howard's death. There it was exhibited in the reception room adjacent to the main floor hall. It was valued at $500 in the appraisal of Mary Emery's estate. Mary intended the famous sculpture "that belonged to his grandmother Emery" to go to her husband's nephew, also named Thomas. Probably the most important work of art in the collection of Thomas J. and Mary Emery prior to her purchases of paintings for her collection, this Victorian sculpture by one of America's "white, marmorean flock" disappeared and is now lost.

Mary's provisions in her will for the Cincinnati Art Museum were impressive. Specifically, the bequest of the Edgecliffe collection elicited much local interest due to its value and the realization that Mrs. Emery's magnificent group of old master paintings would remain in Cincinnati. Director Gest and the art dealers who joined with Mary to build the collection were honored to see the paintings enrich their intended home, but they were distressed at the loss of a major American collector. "Mrs. Emery's death is a very serious loss indeed to this community. It was her practice constantly to use the resources of her fortune with the utmost benevolence in public service. Few know how widespread this was or how generous. Her collection which she formed for the Museum is one of the few things that will carry her name as she refused ordinarily to have it appear."[27] As executor of Mrs. Emery's estate, Livingood wasted no time in removing the paintings from the walls of the Emery mansion in East Walnut Hills. On October 26, 1927, with Isabella Hopkins's cooperation, as she still resided in the house, the collection was brought by trucks through Eden Park to the museum, where Gest acknowledged receipt of forty-seven paintings that included the Rubens intended for Christ Church.

Only a few months after Mary's death, Emery Industries was incorporated under the leadership of Mary's young nephew, John J. Emery, a talented and thoughtful businessman. The Emery Candle Company, the initial basis of the Emery family fortune, was absorbed in the spring of 1928 into a diversified manufacturing and holding organization. Closing Mrs. Emery's financial involvement with many arms of the Emery enterprises while dealing with the complex settling of her estate involved much of Livingood's time and energy. Distinguished lawyers advised him, including Robert A. Taft and John Hollister, two of Cincinnati's lawyer-notables, but the need for cash to pay annuitants and other claims on the estate required constant shuffling of the estate's assets by Livingood and his colleagues on the board of the Emery Memorial. Real estate holdings not surprisingly comprised much of Mrs. Emery's wealth; consequently, cash fluidity was lacking.

Mary's sister, Isabella, felt no cash pinch, however, as a primary beneficiary in Mary's will. On April 21, 1928, she offered $100,000 to the Emery Memorial to erect in Mariemont "a tower and carillon of bells, in loving memory of my only sister, Mary M. Emery" and for a swimming pool to be constructed at the Girls' Friendly Vacation House, one of Mary's charities east of Cincinnati.[28] Just one month after the shock of the stock market crash of October 1929 was felt by millions across the nation, the Bell Tower was completed, memorializing Mary's love of music in the village she founded. Her collection of paintings was installed that autumn in the new wing she financed for the Cincinnati Art Museum. Seldom seen by the public during Mary's lifetime, but now to be viewed in its permanent home, her acclaimed collection highlighted the reopening of the museum on January 14, 1930, and the recently completed Emery, Mary Hanna, and Herbert Greer French Wings.

The crushing blow of the American stock market collapse in 1929 ushered in economic disaster replete with bank failures, factory closings, and high unemployment. Sometime in 1930, the Thomas J. Emery Memorial offered for sale the Mariemont, Rhode Island, estate of Mary Emery. It was a poor time to expect the sale of a large tract of sixty acres with extensive

Mary M. Emery Wing (left), Cincinnati Art Museum, begun 1928 (Courtesy Cincinnati Art Museum)

gardens and expensive maintenance, but Isabella Hopkins, who had a life interest in the property, had little affection for it now that her sister was gone. Mary's summer home that she loved and developed into one of America's premier garden spots was sold by Livingood for only $43,970.87 and reported to the Emery Memorial trustees.[29] The proceeds were invested to provide income for Miss Hopkins, who died in 1935.

The Mariemont Company explored ways of dissolving its organization in the autumn of 1931, and Livingood met with a bank official in Cincinnati to discuss loans affecting the estate of Mary Emery. Two memoranda record the value on that date of her estate as requested by the bank. "Mr. Charles J. Livingood came in to see Mr. Davis. Mr. Davis asked him for a statement of the resources of the income for the preceding year. He told

Mr. Davis that the Estate had thirty or forty pieces of property in Cincinnati, and also owned all of the shares of the Mariemont Corporation, which he regarded worth nine million dollars. They get total rentals out of the Mariemont property of about $230,000."[30]

The second memorandum records a discussion with her attorney, Robert A. Taft, who was asked for "approximate figures of the Estate, of which he is connected as attorney." Taft's response elucidated the extensive real estate holdings and the estate's need to borrow funds to provide cash bequests before sales of property could be concluded. Total income expected each year from the extensive properties of the Emery estate was about $600,000.

> They had to use the income to clean up some things, amongst which was $200,000 which Mrs. Emery had paid for a picture just before she died, and the balance was government taxes, etc. As matters now stand, the only indebtedness he [Robert A. Taft] says the Estate has is what they owe us, and a contested claim with the Government for taxes, which Mr. Taft thinks undoubtedly the Estate will win. He especially asked us to treat the attached statement confidentially, because they do not want the public to be talking about the Emery Estate—how much it is worth, or how little. Mr. Davis thinks that Mr. Livingood regards the Estate worth about fifteen million dollars, all told. He says they only have about forty vacant apartments in the various apartment buildings in Mariemont, and no vacant houses. They do not expect to ask us for any money to pay taxes this year.[31]

The Depression and its financial pressures caused the Emery Memorial and Livingood to seek a better organization to administer Mrs. Emery's estate and the village of Mariemont. On December 8, 1931, the stock holders of the Mariemont Company (with Livingood voting the shares in Mary Emery's name) passed a resolution to dissolve the company and transfer its assets to the Emery Memorial.[32] Thus, the organization designed to create and administer Nolen's planned community fulfilled its original purpose and merged its operations into a foundation that would have a dual assignment: administering Mrs. Emery's estate and the village of Mariemont, still essentially a private town. It would remain so until its incorporation in 1941 under Ohio law as a village with elected mayor and council.

Mary Emery's advisor, manager, and surrogate son, Charles J. Livingood, continued his active role in Cincinnati long after his patron's death, serving as president of the Cincinnati Art Museum until 1955 and in the same office for the Thomas J. Emery Memorial, among many other positions and memberships he enjoyed. His home in Quebec lured him in the summer months, but he kept his Baker Place residence in Cincinnati long after his wife died and his children moved away. He died at Holmes Hospital, Cincinnati, on February 26, 1952. His demise concluded the career of the man most responsible for guiding a remarkable lady in her life's activities from 1906 to 1927.

Afterword

A Philanthropist's Commitment

THE LIFE STORY of Mary Emery is a tale of simple beginnings and rich endings. Her middle-class rearing in New York and Brooklyn contrasted dramatically with her life as the wife of a rich industrialist landowner in Cincinnati, providing her with city mansion and country estate, extensive travels abroad, and a happy family life. She moved gracefully through marriage, child rearing, and into matronhood. Her years were free from financial worries after her marriage, and she had the finest comforts that one could have at that time. Mary had no direct heirs. This fact encouraged a philanthropic course of action. She could have lived well and done nothing to divest herself of her great wealth, but she chose instead an enlightened commitment.

Her last twenty-one years might have been radically different if her children and husband had not predeceased her, or if the friend of her oldest son had not entered her life when he did. Beginning with her first year of widowhood, she began an impressive and selfless philanthropic program. Her sharing of wealth elevated her in Cincinnati's estimation, but she remained relatively unknown outside of that city, as most of her benefactions were directed to its agencies. Large gifts of money, land, or art to cultural, educational, and various causes were newsworthy in the early twentieth century, when such giving was uncommon. Astounding to the average wage earner was the magnitude of Mrs. Emery's generosity. The clerk in a Cincinnati department store or an automobile assembler earning $100 per month in a six-day week in one of Henry Ford's factories hardly could conceive of such wealth as made her gifts possible.

Mary Emery had few role models among women as philanthropists. Mary Emery expanded the traditional role allotted to women, contrasting sharply with one historian's view that "Biographers often find little overtly triumphant in the late years of a subject's life, once she has moved beyond the categories our available narratives have provided for women."[1] Philanthropy was a man's job, or, if gifts were made in a wife's name, the money was the husband's. It is more common today than it was in Mrs. Emery's lifetime for wealthy individuals to contribute to worthy causes and institutions. There were very few charitable foundations in existence in the late nineteenth and early twentieth centuries, and most of these were initiated and governed by men. Mary Emery was one of very few women to establish a foundation to continue her charitable giving, but the Thomas J. Emery Memorial was not an active force in the philanthropic picture until after its founder's death.

Mary was committed to the generous dispensing of her wealth for reasons beyond her lack of direct heirs. She was part of Cincinnati's upper class, a group of men and women of means who felt obliged, because of their leadership in society and their ability to give, to assist their city in its cultural and educational endeavors. Another influence was her church. She supported her religion and its teachings of Christian brotherhood and almsgiving. But more importantly, Mary Emery was innately unselfish in the aid she provided. Her "feminine largesse" had a common denominator with the interests of other women philanthropists, few as they were. They seemed to share "an abiding interest in helping women and children; a tendency to move into gaps overlooked by government and male donors and volunteers; and a desire to exercise power."[2] Mary's shyness, however, precluded any interest in personal power.

The Cincinnati coterie that included Mary Emery offered inspirational leadership as well as financial benefits to the city's various institutions. These select citizens admired their hometown and served it, integrating themselves into the boards and leaders' posts in Cincinnati's commercial, educational, and cultural activities. Mary was not prone to accept a leadership role in any agency, however. She was a patron on the sidelines. Her commitment emanated from the "vital American tradition of voluntary association,"[3] yet she refrained from an active participation in operations and leadership in any of the causes she supported.

Mary never expected to serve on any governing board of trustees; in an age when women could not vote, and in some states could not own property, this was not unusual. This duty she left to Charles J. Livingood. As her representative and the man who helped loose the purse strings of a generous donor, he served on many boards associated with her bounty.

The holders of America's nineteenth-century fortunes often formed art collections, and a few wives of the fortune builders established themselves quite independently as collectors, notably Isabella Stewart Gardner of Boston and Mrs. Potter Palmer of Chicago. Mary Emery gained status as one of the nation's important collectors of art only after her husband's death, when her inherited fortune was hers to spend. Thomas Emery was not particularly interested in cultural affairs, preferring children's causes and those helping the unfortunate, although he made modest contributions to the Cincinnati Art Museum, the Symphony Orchestra, and the May Festival. Instead, his wife gave her name, some relatively modest gifts, and her membership in several shareholder organizations that supported the financial well-being of these cultural mainstays. Mr. Emery and his businessmen contemporaries probably ascribed to the statement attributed to Chicago's meat packing magnate, P. D. Armour, that defined the sponsors and supporters of major educational and cultural organizations: "My culture is mostly in my wife's name."[4]

During Mrs. Emery's maturity, Cincinnati brimmed with female-led cultural programs. The city differed noticeably from New York, Boston, and Chicago in this respect. Women were vital to Cincinnati's fostering of art.[5] The Cincinnati Academy of Fine Arts was formed in 1854 by a group of ladies determined to influence public taste. Under the indomitable Sarah Worthington King Peter, this group purchased copies of old master paintings and casts of classical sculpture, such as the *Apollo Belvedere* and the *Venus de Milo*. The Women's Centennial Executive Committee, formed in 1874, presented a display at the Centennial Exhibition in Philadelphia two years later. In 1877, these ladies created the Women's Art Museum Association in Cincinnati as they sought to build a museum. They enlisted Mary Emery in their membership.[6] Although the Cincinnati Art Museum was initiated by the ladies, the incorporators were men, who then assumed control of the vision.[7] Before the incorporation, however, Cincinnati women aggressively pursued an art museum (albeit one following industrial or applied art models), and they were its staunch supporters after it was established. Their willingness to drop their leading part in this undertaking may be due to the limits of custom, or perhaps they felt unqualified in any managerial role, so the field was left to men.[8]

Another example of female entrepreneurship was the Rookwood Pottery Company, a commercial venture started by Maria Longworth Nichols in Cincinnati in 1880, one year before the founding of the Cincinnati Art Museum. This company had its roots in porcelain painting undertaken by lady volunteers to promote the Centennial Exhibition of 1876. The Rookwood Company prospered well into the twentieth century as America's leading manufacturer of decorative arts in clay.

Many women in Mrs. Emery's Cincinnati practiced a volunteerism that focused primarily on organizational efforts without necessarily contributing large financial gifts to favorite causes. There were, of course, always a few ladies like Maria Longworth Nichols, Anna Sinton Taft, and ladies from the Fleischmann, Anderson, Ault, and Kilgour clans who gave both time and funds. Mary Emery's monetary giving, after 1906, however, greatly overshadowed theirs.

Today's volunteerism for women has few of the limitations that women encountered in the nineteenth and early twentieth centuries. Much practical volunteer work can be undertaken without criticism by women acting as docents in museums, or mentors for school children, serving meals for the elderly, or staffing a free food store. Battalions of volunteers, a "mostly female array of virtually full-time, unpaid labor," stage benefits today to raise money for charities.[9] And if this volunteerism embraces financial giving, either by itself or in league with the gift of time and talent, so much the better.

Mary was neither the organizational leader nor the worker type of volunteer. She was prominent because of the magnitude of her gifts, not because of her personal involvement. Although she is credited as founder of Mariemont, her role in that enterprise and with her other benefactions was as giver, not as participant in the activities of the organizations she supported, with the exception of Christ Church.

Mary Muhlenberg Hopkins Emery lived throughout the reign of Queen Victoria, during America's Gilded Age, and well beyond World War I. Her generous giving and retiring nature set her apart from many of the very wealthy in America, who gratified themselves, primarily. Her compassionate interest in humanity dictated her use of her fortune. This Lady Bountiful's life was one of devotion and dedication, affluence without ostentation, investment in art and culture, creation of a new town, and warm affection towards children. She selflessly embraced humanity.

The Families of Mary M. Hopkins and Thomas J. Emery

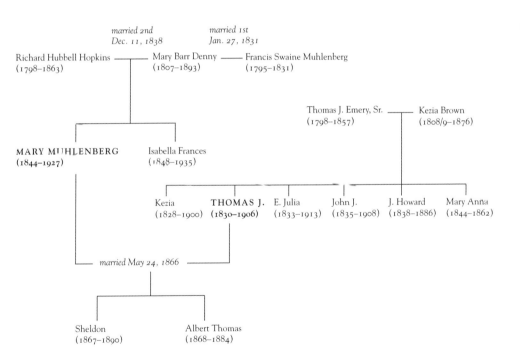

married 2nd
Dec. 11, 1838

married 1st
Jan. 27, 1831

Richard Hubbell Hopkins
(1798–1863)

Mary Barr Denny
(1807–1893)

Francis Swaine Muhlenberg
(1795–1831)

Thomas J. Emery, Sr.
(1798–1857)

Kezia Brown
(1808/9–1876)

MARY MUHLENBERG
(1844–1927)

Isabella Frances
(1848–1935)

Kezia
(1828–1900)

THOMAS J.
(1830–1906)

E. Julia
(1833–1913)

John J.
(1835–1908)

J. Howard
(1838–1886)

Mary Anna
(1844–1862)

married May 24, 1866

Sheldon
(1867–1890)

Albert Thomas
(1868–1884)

The Philanthropies of Mary M. Emery

$\mathcal{M}$ARY EMERY's philanthropies and gifts date primarily from the period following her husband's death in 1906 until her own demise in 1927. Her last will and testament recorded bequests as indicated in Chapter 10 of this biography. The provisions of her will were her last generous acts that involved her personally. Before her husband's death, a few gifts may have been made in both her name and his. At least one gift was made jointly with her husband, such as the Fresh Air Farm they donated in memory of their two sons, Sheldon and Albert. For at least two of the Cincinnati agencies listed, the Babies Milk Fund and the Council of Social Agencies, Mary Emery was the founder as well as the principal and initial donor. She and Anna Sinton Taft became the sole owners of the Cincinnati Zoo when they each contributed $125,000 to save it. In this compilation, some gifts are recorded with unknown dates and unknown amounts. These were taken from often scanty records, and, although incomplete, this information offers the fullest picture of her generosity during her lifetime. Due to incomplete records, the listed dollar amount for some recipients only reflects Mrs. Emery's support in part.

Army-Navy YMCA, Newport, Rhode Island	1910–1911	$250,000
Babies Milk Fund Association, Cincinnati, Ohio	1909 and later	$75,000
Berea College Library Endowment and Domestic Science Building, Berea, Kentucky	1907, 1914, 1916	$50,000
Miss Berry's Schools, Rome, Georgia, two farms and dormitory	1915–1927	$26,000

Cathedral Shelter Houses for Children:
  Salt Lake City; Phoenix; Sacramento;
  Circleville, Ohio

Cercle Concordia, Paris, France	1907	$250,000
Children's Hospital Free Bed, Denver, Colorado		
Children's Home, Central Building, Cincinnati	1915–1916	
Christ Church, Land for Centennial Chapel, Cincinnati	1917	
Christ Church, Parish House, Cincinnati	1909	
Cincinnati Art Museum Free Day Endowment	1907	$100,000
Cincinnati Art Museum, Mary M. Emery Wing	1927	$300,000
Cincinnati Museum Association, Frank Duveneck Endowment	1922	
Cincinnati Zoological Park	1916	$125,000
Council of Social Agencies (Community Chest), Cincinnati		
Edgecliffe Collection, Cincinnati Art Museum	1927	$3,500,000
The Thomas J. Emery Memorial, Cincinnati	1925–1927	
Esmaralda Hospital Free Bed, Sewanee, Tennessee		
Federated Charities, Cincinnati	1915	$5,000
Fresh Air Farm, Terrace Park, Ohio	1898	
Girls' Friendly Society Vacation House (Christ Church), New Richmond, Ohio	1902	
Good Samaritan Hospital Free Beds, Cincinnati		
Hobart College, Geneva, New York, Gymnasium	1907	
Holmes Hospital, University of Cincinnati	1915, 1918	$300,000
Home for Colored Girls, Cincinnati	1914	$3,000
Hospital of the Protestant Episcopal Church, Diocese of Southern Ohio, Park Avenue, Cincinnati	1884	
Hospital of the Protestant Episcopal Church, Diocese of Southern Ohio, Mt. Auburn, Cincinnati	1887	
Jewish Relief in Europe, Rockdale Temple, Cincinnati	1922	$3,000
Kessler Park (formerly Tuchfarber's Botanical Garden), Cincinnati	1912	

Last Will and Testament of Mary M. Emery, bequests for individuals, annuitants, agencies and others	1927	$5,505,000
Lincoln Institute (Kentucky?)		
Mariemont Company and Village of Mariemont	1910–1927	$7,000,000
Model Homes Company, Cincinnati		
Colored Orphans Asylum, Cincinnati	1925–1926	$25,000
Ohio Institute for Public Housing, Cincinnati		
Ohio Mechanics Institute and Emery Auditorium, Cincinnati	1908–1912	$1,500,000
Packer Collegiate Institute, Brooklyn, New York, Teachers' Pension Fund	1914	$50,000
Pine Mountain School Water Works (Kentucky?)		
Rescue Home for Colored, Cincinnati	1916	$12,000
St. Luke's Hospital Free Beds, Denver and McAlister, Oklahoma		
St. Margaret's Hospital Free Bed, Boise, Idaho		
St. Philip's Church Parish House, Circleville, Ohio	1918	$10,000
Trudeau Sanatarium (Sheldon and Albert Emery Medical Building), Saranac Lake, New York	1907–1908	$25,000
Tuskegee Institute Memorial Building, Alabama		
University of Cincinnati Bird Preserve	1911–1912	
University of Cincinnati General Hospital, Department of Pathology	1913	$125,000
University of Cincinnati Endowment Fund Association	1915	$250,000
University of Cincinnati Medical School, Department of Pediatrics	1920	$250,000
University of the South Nurses' Home, Sewanee, Tennessee	1916	$50,000
YMCA Central, Cincinnati	1917–1918	$565,000
YMCA (Negroes), Cincinnnati		
	total	$20,354,000

Art Dealers, References, and Acquisition Notes

MARY EMERY'S inherited wealth and emergence as a collector in the first quarter of the twentieth century placed her in competition with some of America's renowned collectors, Henry Clay Frick, Isabella Stewart Gardner, Henry Huntington, George Widener, and Cincinnati's own Anna and Charles P. Taft. Unfortunately, dealers' invoices for Mrs. Emery's purchases are lost, but lists kept by her agent, Charles J. Livingood, and the Cincinnati Art Museum indicate that she spent $3,425,750 for paintings. This figure does not include unknown prices paid for the Calame and four paintings not included in the bequest to the museum, perhaps works purchased by Thomas J. Emery: *Portrait of a French Girl* by Adolphe Jourdan, *The Signal* by H. Leister, *German Soldier* by an unknown painter, and *Marine* by M. H. F. de Haas. These four works were housed on the second floor of Edgecliffe and were valued modestly at $675 for the lot in the estate appraisal. Mary Emery engaged at least fourteen different dealers or sellers for her acquisitions: Andrew Burt, Frederick A. Chapman, Mrs. James Creelman, Duveen & Co. (through J. Jarman, representative), F. Kleinberger, Knoedler & Co. (through T. Gerrity, representative), Sir Hugh Lane, John Levy, Julius Oehme, Scott & Fowles (through James Labey, representative, who may have acted sometimes on his own behalf), G. Stanley Sedgwick, Jacques Seligmann, and Arthur Tooth & Son. Among these dealers, Mrs. Emery patronized Scott & Fowles more than any other, acquiring twenty-one of her paintings from this New York firm.

Mary Emery rarely searched for specific artists, yet once she eagerly sought a painting by Théodore Rousseau, the Barbizon school master. Dealers pursued her and actively engaged the director of the Cincinnati Art Museum, Joseph Henry Gest, to assist them. Paintings submitted to Mrs. Emery for her consideration were studied first through photographs sent directly to her or via Gest. If interest was expressed, the canvas or panel picture, handsomely framed, was shipped to Cincinnati, where Emery servants or art museum staff installed it on the walls of Edgecliffe. There the painting remained "on approval" as a loan until a decision was made to purchase or to decline. The dean of Cincinnati painters, Frank Duveneck, and his colleague, Lewis H. Meakin, often were consulted on the proposed painting's authenticity, condition, etc. Little research was conducted, however, by Mrs. Emery's advisors. Usually the dealer provided whatever information he or she possessed, such as published references, past owners, biographical facts about the sitters, or attribution statements from various experts. During the years of Mrs. Emery's collecting, little art historical expertise was available in the United States (the Cincinnati Art Museum had no professionally trained curators during Mary Emery's lifetime), so that the art dealers and a few European scholars (such as Berenson, Bode, Friedlander, and Valentiner, for example) reigned supreme in bestowing attributions and confirming authenticity.

The Emerys travelled widely in Europe and the United States, and presumably Mrs. Emery was familiar with the great museums and their collections, yet her knowledge of art and artists was limited. She was no connoisseur of art, if we rely on her correspondence with Gest and dealers, and she readily admitted this shortcoming. She placed little reliance on her own "eye" in determining a picture's quality, but her emotional reaction to a particular work usually was decisive. Mary's collecting goal was to acquire works by major European masters. She bought only one painting by an American artist. Her fondness for portraits is obvious. Landscapes were secondary to the human form in her choices, while literary subjects interested her not at all. She had a few religious subjects, but no martyrdoms nor depictions from mythology. It is risky, perhaps, to read psychological implications into any of Mrs. Emery's selections, but the loss of her two sons may have influenced, however subtly, the choice of fourteen paintings depicting family-oriented subjects or children. Although Mrs. Emery lived through some of the greatest movements in art (Impressionism, Post-Impressionism, Cubism) as well as the revolutionary Armory Show held in New York City in 1913, her taste did not flirt with any modern expression. Her earliest purchases were tentative, conservative, and focused on Barbizon school and English painters. Such choices were typical for their times with many collectors. A number of tantalizing paintings were offered to Mary, but declined, works thought to be by Vermeer, Lotto, Moro, Clouet, El Greco, Memling, and Leonardo da Vinci. One of her most quoted requirements for the Edgecliffe collection was the nonduplication of artists, although she violated this prohibition several times. Also, she made it clear that the collection was formed with the Cincinnati Art Museum in mind as its ultimate home.

Of the fifty-four paintings purchased by Mary Emery during her lifetime, seven of these were sold or traded before her death. Forty-five works were bequeathed to the Cincinnati Art Museum in 1927, and one went to Christ Church, Cincinnati. Research by scholars, museum personnel, and other experts reattributed fifteen paintings in the bequest, making more plausible assignments to painters, usually those of lesser importance than the dealers and Mrs. Emery accepted.

Since receiving Mrs. Emery's magnificent bequest in 1927 and installing it for the first public viewing in the Mary M. Emery Wing in 1930, the Cincinnati Art Museum in the decades since then has integrated her collection with other works, grouping them by national schools. Several well-researched catalogues of paintings have been published by the museum, and these provide full information and documentation on Mrs. Emery's Spanish, Italian, Dutch, Flemish, German, and British paintings. The following synopsis lists the fifty-four paintings acquired by Mrs. Emery in order of their acquisition and notes the artist and title when acquired, Cincinnati Art Museum accession number, present artist attribution and title (if different), dealer source and price paid, and reference (if existing) to appropriate permanent collection catalogue of the Cincinnati Art Museum.

CATALOGUE REFERENCES

Hayes, John. *British Paintings in the Cincinnati Art Museum*. Cincinnati: Cincinnati Art Museum (forthcoming).

Rogers, Millard F., Jr. *Spanish Paintings in the Cincinnati Art Museum*. Cincinnati: Cincinnati Art Museum, 1978.

Scott, Mary Ann. *Dutch, Flemish, and German Paintings in the Cincinnati Art Museum*. Cincinnati: Cincinnati Art Museum, 1987.

Spangenberg, Kristin L. *French Drawings, Watercolors, and Pastels, 1800–1950*. Cincinnati: Cincinnati Art Museum, 1978.

Spike, John T. *Italian Paintings in the Cincinnati Art Museum*. Cincinnati: Cincinnati Art Museum, 1993.

THE PAINTINGS

Example:
　　Date acquired
　　Artist and title (originally as acquired), accession number
　　Artist and title (current or if different from above)
　　Dealer source and price paid
　　Catalogue reference

　　May 1870
　　Alexandre Calame, *The Sycamores*, 1927.383
　　Andrew Burt

February 1907
Constant Troyon, *Landscape with Goats*, 1927.423
Frederick A. Chapman, $15,000

March 1907
Jules Dupré, *Plateau de Belle-Croix, Fontainebleau Forest*, 1927.391
Frederick A. Chapman, $16,000

May 1907
Leon-Augustin Lhermitte, *Departure of the Flock*, 1927.400
Arthur Tooth & Son, $7,000
Spangenberg, 84–85

May 1907
Jozef Israëls, *Flitting* [Sold to John Levy Galleries, January 1922]
Julius Oehme, $17,500

1907
Emil Fuchs, *Portrait of Thomas J. Emery*, 1927.395
Unknown source (the artist?) and price

May 1909
Charles François Daubigny, *Evening on the Oise*, 1927.389
Scott & Fowles, $27,000

June 1909
Francisco Goya y Lucientes, *Portrait of the Countess de Quinto*, 1927.398
    [Deaccessioned 1988]
Unidentified Spanish Artist, *Portrait of the Countess de Quinto* ?
Mrs. James Creelman, $25,000
Rogers, 25–26

November 1909
George Romney, *Portrait of Mrs. Richard Pryce Corbet and Her Daughter*,
    1927.417
Scott & Fowles, $105,000
Hayes

November 1909
Sir Joshua Reynolds, *Portrait of Captain Peter Porter* [Sold to G. Stanley
    Sedgwick, 1917]
Scott & Fowles, $20,000

December 1909
Sir Anthony van Dyck, *Portrait of John, Count of Nassau*, 1927.393
Sir Anthony van Dyck, *Portrait of a Man in Armor (Member of the Spinola
 Family?)*
Scott & Fowles, $140,000
Scott, 54–56

January 1910
Thomas Gainsborough, *Portrait of Viscount Downe*, 1927.397
Thomas Gainsborough, *Portrait of John, 5th Viscount Downe*
Scott & Fowles, $60,000
Hayes

January 1910
Narcisse Diaz, *Edge of the Forest* [Traded for Hobbema, *View in Westphalia,*
 December 1916]
Scott & Fowles, $36,000

February 1910
Jean François Millet, *Going to Work—Dawn of Day*, 1927.411
H. S. Henry Sale, Philadelphia, $53,100

April 1910
Narcisse Diaz, *Gathering Fagot*, 1927.390 [Deaccessioned March 1956]
Scott & Fowles, $36,000

May 1910
Dirck Bouts, *The Adoration of the Magi*, 1927.380
Master of the Legend of St. Lucy, *The Adoration of the Magi*
Scott & Fowles, $5,000
Scott, 84–87

June 1910
Frans Hals, *Dutch Family*, 1927.399
Frans Hals and Studio, *Portrait of a Dutch Family*
Scott & Fowles, $120,000
Scott, 59–61

September 1910
Sir Anthony van Dyck, *Portrait of Mlle. Gottinges* [Traded to Scott & Fowles,
 November 21, 1911, for $140,000 credit]
Scott & Fowles, $24,800

December 1910
Sir Henry Raeburn, *The Elphinston Children*, 1927.414
Scott & Fowles, $140,000
Hayes

February 1911
Bartolomé Esteban Murillo, *St. Thomas of Villanueva Dividing His Clothes Among Beggar Boys*, 1927.412
Scott & Fowles, $215,000
Rogers, 19–21

November 1911
John Hoppner, *Portrait of Lady Herbert as a Little Girl*, 1927.401
John Hoppner, *Portrait of the Hon. Augusta Herbert (later Lady Vincent) as a Child*
Scott & Fowles, $48,000
Hayes

November 1911
Thomas Gainsborough, *Portrait of Mrs. Thicknesse*, 1927.396
Thomas Gainsborough, *Portrait of Ann Ford, Mrs. Philip Thicknesse*
Scott & Fowles, $186,000
Hayes

October 1912
Jean-Marc Nattier, *Portrait of Mme. Therese de la Martiniere*, 1927.413
Scott & Fowles, $40,500

February 1913
Lorenzo di Credi, *Madonna and Child*, 1927.388
Scott & Fowles, $35,000
Spike, 38–39

July 1913
Rembrandt van Rijn, *Young Girl Holding a Medal*, 1927.415
Circle or Follower of Rembrandt, *Young Girl Holding a Medal*
Scott & Fowles, $80,000
Scott, 110–113

February 1914
Titian (Tiziano Vecellio), *Portrait of Philip II*, 1927.402
Sir Hugh Lane, $315,000
Spike, 90–97

March 1914

Tintoretto (Jacopo Robusti), *Portrait of the Venetian Doge Marino Grimani*,
   1927.422

Domenico Tintoretto and Collaborator, *Portrait of the Doge Marino Grimani*

Scott & Fowles, $75,000 [On January 15, 1917, Scott & Fowles allowed a
   deduction of $37,500]

Spike, 86–89

October 1914

Jean Baptiste Camille Corot, *La Lac,* 1927.385 [Deaccessioned February 1981]

Scott & Fowles, $40,000

November 1916

Quentin Matsys, *Portrait* [Not in 1927 Bequest]

F. Kleinberger, $21,340

January 1917

Sir Thomas Lawrence, *Portrait of Mrs. Francis Gregg and Master George Gregg,*
   1927.403

Sir Thomas Lawrence, *Portrait of Mrs. Francis Gregg and Her Son, George*

G. Stanley Sedgwick, $40,000

Hayes

January 1917

Sir Peter Paul Rubens, *The Holy Family* [Bequeathed to Christ Church, Cincinnati, 1927]

G. Stanley Sedgwick, $40,000

April 1917

Jan Mabuse, *Portrait of Queen Eleanor,* 1927.405

Studio of Joos van Cleve, *Portrait of Queen Eleanor of Portugal and France*

F. Kleinberger, $8,000

Scott, 41

October 1917

Meindert Hobbema, *View in Westphalia* [Exchanged for credit with Duveen,
   October 1925]

Scott & Fowles, $85,000

January 1919

Jean Baptiste Camille Corot, *Don Quixote,* 1919.1

Knoedler, $52,500

April 1919
Agnolo di Cosimo Bronzino, *Portrait of Eleonora di Toledo and Her Son, Francesco de'Medici*, 1927.381
Duveen, $85,000
Spike, 22–25

January 1921
Bernardino Luini, *Madonna and Child with St. Catherine of Alexandria*, 1927.404
Copy after Bernardino Luini, *Madonna and Child with St. Catherine of Alexandria*
Duveen, $180,000
Spike, 40–41

January 1922
Andrea Mantegna, *Tarquin and the Cumaen Sibyl*, 1927.406
Andrea Mantegna, *A Queen Disputing with a Philosopher*
Duveen, $163,800
Spike, 46–49

February 1922
Théodore Rousseau, *Road in the Forest*, 1927.419
Labey, $35,000

May 1922
Constant Troyon, *Autumn Morning*, 1927.424 [Deaccessioned March 1956]
Knoedler, $50,000

March 1923
Jean Auguste Dominique Ingres, *Portrait of Luigi Cherubini*, 1927.386
Knoedler, $22,000

June 1923
Gilbert Stuart, *Portrait of George Washington*, 1927.420 [Deaccessioned February 1988]
Knoedler, $29,925

November 1923
Simon Marmion, *Philip the Bold, Duke of Burgundy*, 1927.407
Flemish, late 16th century, *Philip the Bold, Duke of Burgundy*
Labey, $24,000 for 1927.407–1927.410

November 1923
Simon Marmion, *Charles the Bold, Duke of Burgundy*, 1927.408
Flemish, late 16th century, *Charles the Bold, Duke of Burgundy*
Labey, $24,000 for 1927.407–1927.410

November 1923
Simon Marmion, *Philip the Good, Duke of Burgundy*, 1927.409
Flemish, late 16th century, *Philip the Good, Duke of Burgundy*
Labey, $24,000 for 1927.407–1927.410

November 1923
Simon Marmion, *John the Fearless, Duke of Burgundy*, 1927.410
Flemish, late 16th century, *John the Fearless, Duke of Burgundy*
Labey, $24,000 for 1927.407–1927.410

December 1923
Sir Joshua Reynolds, *Boy with Grapes*, 1927.416
Knoedler, $25,000
Hayes

December 1923
Théodore Rousseau, *Summer Sunset*, 1927.418
John Levy, $22,500

September 1924
Gerard Terborch, *The Music Party*, 1927.421
Duveen, $130,200
Scott, 24–27

May 1925
Joos van Cleve, *Portrait of Francis I*, 1927.384
Studio of Joos van Cleve, *Portrait of Francis I*
J. Seligmann, $17,000
Scott, 43–44

May 1925
Jean Fouquet, *Presentation of an Illuminated Missal to Anne Beaujeu, Regent for Charles VIII*, 1927.394
"The Spanish Forger," *Presentation of an Illuminated Missal to Anne Beaujeu, Regent for Charles VIII*
F. Kleinberger, $25,000

July 1925? July 1927?
Diego de Silva y Velázquez, *Portrait of Philip IV*, 1927.425
Diego de Silva y Velázquez and Assistants, *Portrait of Philip IV*
Duveen, $254,625 [Final payment made after MME's death]
Rogers, 26–28

November 1925
Marie-Louise Vigée-Lebrun, *Portrait of the Prince de Polignac*, 1927.382
    [Deaccessioned June 1987]
Scott & Fowles, $49,500

December 1925
Albrecht Dürer, *Knight in Armor*, 1927.392
Anonymous German, *Portrait of a Man in Armor*
Duveen, $99,960
Scott, 159–161

February 1926
Lucas Cranach, *St. Helena, Mother of Constantine the Great*, 1927.387
Lucas Cranach, *St. Helena with the Cross*
Duveen, $6,000
Scott, 45–46

NOTES

A number of sources, quoted frequently in the notes, use the following abbreviations:

CAM   Cincinnati Art Museum
CAMA   Cincinnati Art Museum Archives
CAMRO   Cincinnati Art Museum Registration Office
CHS   Cincinnati Historical Society
CJL   Charles J. Livingood
Gest   Joseph Henry Gest
JN   John Nolen
MFR   Millard F. Rogers, Jr.
MME   Mary Muhlenberg Emery
MPF   Mariemont Preservation Foundation
NCU   John Nolen Papers, Carl A. Kroch Library, Cornell University
Steele Papers Lela Emery Steele
Taft Papers   Library of Congress, William Howard Taft Papers
TJE   Thomas J. Emery
UCA   University of Cincinnati Archives

CHAPTER I

1. *Cincinnati Daily Gazette*, December 31, 1857.

2. Emery's office was on Gano Street, between Sixth and Seventh Streets. This is the first known address for Emery's business in Cincinnati. Emery does not appear in the *Cincinnati Directory*, 1831, published by Robinson and Fairbank.

3. "Conteur," *Cincinnati Enquirer*, March 21, 1921. This reference suggests a birth date of 1799 for Emery, but interment records at Spring Grove Cemetery, Cincinnati, list the earlier date.

4. *Cincinnati Enquirer*, April 24, 1949. The article states that Emery settled in

New England, then moved west to Kentucky, where he tried his hand at raising silkworms. The reporter verified Emery's presence in Cincinnati through an advertisement placed in the *Philanthropist*, April 21, 1840, but this date is some eight years following the first known listing of Emery as land agent.

5. *Cincinnati Daily Gazette*, September 30, 1833. His English heritage was a positive recommendation, he felt, for his services. He advertised himself, by October 2, as "from England", and claimed he would provide a conduit for "cash remitted to and received from England, Ireland, and other parts of Europe."

6. Cist, *Cincinnati in 1841*, n.p.

7. *Cincinnati Commercial Tribune*, January 17, 1906.

8. Ford and Ford, *History*, 82.

9. Ibid., 83.

10. J. H. Woodruff, the *Cincinnati Directory*, 1836. The grocery was located on Main Street between Fifth and Sixth Streets.

11. The article in the *Cincinnati Daily Gazette*, December 31, 1857, concluded by noting that Emery had a wife and six children and was a member of the Baptist Church.

12. Cist, *Cincinnati in 1851*, 284.

13. Cincinnati directories list Emery's residence in 1850–1851 as Sycamore Street, between Webster and Liberty. By 1851–1852 the lard oil factory listed the same address, perhaps in error, but the residence was located at 131 West Ninth Street.

14. The lard oil factory continued operations on Water Street throughout the Civil War, with the Emery family moving its residences to 131 West Seventh Street by 1856 and to 301 West Fourth Street by 1857. At this latter address, the family lived together until Thomas J. Emery married Mary Muhlenberg Hopkins in 1866.

15. *Chamber of Commerce Memorial*, 1906, Steele Papers.

16. In addition to the two oldest children, Kezia and Thomas J., four were born in Cincinnati: E. Julia (1833–1913), John J. (1835–1908), J. Howard (1838–1886), and Mary Anna (1844–1862).

17. Maxwell, *Saxby's Magazine*, 51.

18. Agreement between Kezia Emery, Thomas J. Emery, and John J. Emery, with J. Howard Emery, witness, September 28, 1859, Steele Papers. The two sons provided no capital, and Mrs. Emery provided the building and lot (value $32,255.18), machinery and fixtures (value $46,212), and cash notes and manufacturing stock (value $102,869.97).

19. Richard H. Hopkins to Mary D. Muhlenberg, April 2, 1838, Steele Papers. The miniaturist mentioned by Hopkins is Edward Dalton Marchant (1806–1887), who exhibited regularly at the National Academy of Design, New York, between

1832 and 1852 and was an associate of that institution after 1853. The Hopkins portrait noted in the letter is in the collection of the Cincinnati Art Museum (accession no. 1937.4). A miniature of Mary Denny Muhlenberg, also in the museum's collection (accession no. 1937.5), may have resulted from Hopkins's request and may also be a work by Marchant.

20. Clipping [unknown newspaper], April 24, 1863, Albert Emery Scrapbook, and typed list (pre-1927), Steele Papers. The clipping notes that Hopkins worked in Dunkirk, New York, and in Circleville, Ohio, before New York City. In Circleville, Hopkins was senior warden of St. Philip's Episcopal Church. In New York, he continued his Episcopal membership by joining first the Church of the Ascension, New York, and later Christ Church, Brooklyn, after moving to that city. Hopkins was born to Hezekiah Hopkins and Eunice Hubbell, September 5, 1798, in Harwinton, Connecticut. The record of Mayflower passengers and descendants, however (see McAuslan, *Mayflower Index*, no. 18571) lists Richard Hubbell Hopkins as the son of Hezekiah Hopkins and Sarah Davis. He married Theodora Phelps (d. 1833) in 1822. He had one child, Theodora Amelia (1827–1887), by his first wife.

21. Clipping [unknown newspaper], Albert Emery Scrapbook, Steele Papers. The clipping, dated "Dec. 1838" in ink, states that Hopkins was with "Williams, White & Co." and that vows were exchanged on the 11th.

22. *Cincinnati Enquirer*, October 12, 1927; Spring Grove Cemetery, Cincinnati, interment records; and certificate of death, No. 824, Board of Health, Cincinnati, Ohio, October 15, 1927. Although the *Cincinnati Enquirer* article states that MME was born on Bond Street, New York City, this is not confirmed by any other record. Birth records do not exist for 1844 in the municipal archives of New York City. Bond Street was "once the headquarters of fashionable society," only one block from Amity Street. As MME lived at three different addresses in New York and Brooklyn from 1844 to 1862, she may not have recalled the correct one for her birth location, which appears to be 15 Amity Street.

23. *John Doggett's New York City Directory for 1844 and 1845*, *New York City Directory for 1849–1859*, and the *New York City Directory for 1851–1852* are the sources for this information. Hopkins does not appear in the *New York City Directory for 1860–1861* for either a business or home address.

24. *Catalogue of the Packer Institute*, 9. Mary was enrolled in 1861, according to the Packer Institute catalogue of that year, but there is no existing record of the graduating class of 1862 that would confirm her commencement.

25. Notebook of Mary Muhlenberg Hopkins, Steele Papers. The notebook is inscribed in Mary's hand: Mary Muhlenberg Hopkins/Nov. 1861. A pension fund to benefit Packer Institute faculty was established by Mary M. Hopkins (as Mrs. Thomas J. Emery), according to the *Cincinnati Enquirer*, April 8, 1914. Mrs.

Emery's gift of $50,000 was made in honor of one of Mary's teachers at Packer, Adeline L. Jones, who died in 1912.

26. Richard H. Hopkins is listed in *Williams Cincinnati Directory*, 1863, at the dry goods company and at the Mount Auburn residence of Lewis Hopkins. "Deceased" is added for Richard at the Lewis Hopkins residence. An undated newspaper clipping in the Albert Emery Scrapbook, Steele Papers, stated that Hopkins came to Cincinnati about a year [1862] before his death. He joined St. John's Church, Seventh and Plum Streets, where his daughter Mary would be married in 1866.

27. Maxwell, *Suburbs*, 125.

28. Aaron, 266.

CHAPTER 2

1. Marriage Register of St. John's Church, Archives of the Diocese of Southern Ohio, Cincinnati. The marriage was performed by the Rev. J. E. Homans, rector of the church, and the Rev. E. H. Canfield, of Brooklyn, New York. The Albert Emery Scrapbook contains an undated clipping from an unknown newspaper noting the wedding. St. John's Church is now demolished.

2. The wedding dress by an unknown designer is in the collection of the Cincinnati Art Museum (accession no. 1935.116, 117).

3. The entire Emery family, including the widow, Kezia Emery, lived at this address, according to the *Williams Cincinnati Directory*, from at least 1857. This was the home of Mary and Thomas J. Emery until 1874, when the couple moved to their own residence at 357 West Fourth Street.

4. J. Howard Emery to Thomas J. Emery, June 17, 1866, Steele Papers.

5. Baptism Certificate, Christ Church, Albert Emery Scrapbook, Steele Papers and Parish Record, 1852–1870, No. 2, 173.

6. Clipping [unknown, undated newspaper, 1886?], Steele Papers. The article states that Howard Emery concluded the purchase on July 8, 1871 and that $1,000,000 worth of lots had been sold to individual buyers by 1886.

7. Agreement, January 11, 1873, Steele Papers. The partnership papers were signed by Thomas J., John J., and J. Howard Emery in Cincinnati. The agreement stated that their partnership would operate for five years from September 11, 1872, for the "purpose of carrying on the candle and oil manufacturing business. The style of the firm is to be Thomas Emery's Sons." Each partner was to receive 12 percent interest on his capital, decisions would be made jointly, and no private investments would be made by a partner without first offering it to the firm.

8. Kezia Emery to Thomas J. Emery, May 11, 1877, Steele Papers. The letter was written from Rome, where Kezia was staying with her sister, Julia.

9. Albert Emery Scrapbook, Steele Papers, includes clippings from mostly unknown, undated newspapers, with dates occasionally added in margins. Some

clippings date as early as 1838 and as late as 1884. Thus, the scrapbook may have been compiled by Albert from clippings collected by his mother and father, with the last entries made after Albert's death.

10. Albert Emery Scrapbook, Steele Papers. Also starring in the cast of the play were Sheldon Emery, A. Halstead, and J. F. Kerr.

11. Perry, 5–6.

12. Clipping [unknown newspaper], erroneously dated in margin March 2, 1878, Cincinnati Art Museum Scrapbook, CAMA. The exhibition was held in May 1878 at Cochnower's house. Loans to the exhibition from "Mrs. T. J. Emery" included a Japanese cloisonné plaque (no. 442), a Limoges vase (no. 448), a Winged Victory bronze (no. 805), "The Dawn," a bronze by Polet, a pedestal carved by William Fry (no. 923), and a "fine porcelain vase" (no. 141, p. 80). These loans of decorative arts and sculpture do not foretell the greatness of Mrs. Emery's collection of paintings, formed after 1906.

13. Venable, 440.

14. Isabella Hopkins, Mary Emery's sister, lived in this venerable building after Mary Emery's death until 1935. Edgecliffe was subsequently sold by the Thomas J. Emery Memorial to Our Lady of Cincinnati College, serving as administration building, dormitory, and art department over the years. Sold to a developer, Edge-cliffe was demolished in 1987. The site is now occupied by Edgecliff [*sic*] Point, a condominium building near Kemper Lane and Columbia Parkway.

15. Each of the Hannaford structures, the Brittany at Ninth and Race Streets, the Saxony at 105 West Ninth Street, and the Steinkamps' Norfolk (sometimes called the Waldo or Talbot) at Eighth and Elm Streets, is a melange of architectural styles. The Steinkamps also designed or superintended construction of many apartment buildings for the Emerys, including the San Rafael, Somerset, Cumberland, Roanoke, and Warwick.

16. Minutes of Annual Meeting, April 18, 1881, Christ Church, note that Emery served until 1886 as trustee of the new endowment fund.

17. *Cincinnati Enquirer*, April 10, 1882. The musicale was held at the home of Dr. and Mrs. N. Foster to benefit church work in Mexico. Mary Emery sang in a quartet along with William N. King, Joseph Wilby, and William Ridgway. Two hundred guests attended.

18. Children's Hospital Medical Center, *Centennial Annual Report, 1883–1993*, 3.

19. Ibid., 6.

20. The *Daily Monitor*, Concord, New Hampshire, February 4, 1884.

21. Ibid., February 12, 1884.

CHAPTER 3

1. Leonard, 176.

2. *Cincinnati Enquirer*, January 18, 1906. The article quotes an "old Cincinnatian" who knew Howard well and admired his land-purchase skills. He noted that Thomas and John employed a man to accompany Howard on his travels after his mental condition became acute, so that the company would not be committed to more real estate purchases without their authorization. The "old Cincinnatian" stated that Howard died in an English sanatorium [probably to be under the eye of his sister Julia, who lived in London]. J. Howard Emery died on August 14, 1886, at Southend-on-Sea, England, a popular seaside resort, and his burial service was conducted at Christ Church, Cincinnati, on September 29 before interment in Spring Grove Cemetery.

3. Biographical folder, Harvard University Archives (HUG 300).

4. Sheldon Emery presented a widely praised paper on "Finance Ministers of Louis XVI," February 16, 1889, at the Literary Club in its Federal-style building, a former residence, on East Fourth Street.

5. *Cincinnati Enquirer* October 27, 1890.

6. Ibid., October 30, 1890.

7. CJL to MME, November 11, 1890, Steele Papers.

8. Biographical folder, Harvard University Archives (HUG 300). See also typescript biography, c. 1922 [by CJL?], NCU.

9. CJL, "Did Harvard College Prepare Me Properly for My Life Work? An Autobiography by Charles J. Livingood," March 1918, Virginius Hall, Jr., Papers.

10. CJL, "Business Aside, An Anecdotal Autobiography of a Businessman," Paper for the Literary Club, Cincinnati, January 7, 1935.

11. *Harvard College Class of 1888 Second Anniversary Report*, Cambridge, Massachusetts, 1890, 45.

12. *Cincinnati Times Star*, November 26, 1940.

13. CJL, "Autobiography," 1918. Livingood's entry in *Harvard College Class of 1888 Second Anniversary Report* states: "In June returned home to Reading, Pa., where for next six months served an apprenticeship under a practical electrician with a view to engaging eventually in the manufacture of electrical supplies."

14. *Cincinnati Times Star*, November 26, 1940.

15. George R. Denise to Whom It May Concern, July 5, 1890, Virginius Hall, Jr. Papers. The engineer's letter was posted from Catlin, Colorado, and praised Livingood's abilities and character, recommending him "for favorable consideration to anyone in need of a gentlemanly, conscientious workman of good ability and willing mind."

16. *Williams Cincinnati Directory*, 1891, 1892, 1893.

17. Photograph, Livingood File, Cincinnati Historical Society.

18. Morris, 63. Mary Emery accepted rather humble committee assignments in

the 1890s, serving as registrar for the "new envelope system" and as secretary-treasurer of the church's hospital committee, then called the Christ Church Branch of the Cooperative Society of the Children's Hospital, Cincinnati.

19. Morris, 68.

20. Minus its baptismal bowl, the font was placed in the Christ Church plot at Spring Grove Cemetery in 1955, following the demolition of the 1835 building.

21. Herrick, 105.

22. Gest to MME, November 22, 1892, CAMA.

23. Gest to MME, January 5, 1898, CAMA.

24. *Cincinnati Commercial Tribune*, October 4, 1896.

25. Agreement, signed by Thomas J. and Mary M. Emery, John J. and Lela A. Emery, May 20, 1895, Steele Papers. Also noted in the agreement were procedures for dividing the properties and the ability to appoint a commission to resolve any disputes.

26. Maxwell, 53.

27. *Cincinnati Enquirer*, November 25, 1900.

28. Richards, 1.

29. Ibid., 2. The farm served long after Mary Emery's death, becoming a Community Chest organization. In 1962, its mission changed to support handicapped individuals. The farm was renamed Stepping Stones the following year.

30. *The Christian*, n.d. [September, 1900?], Steele Papers. Kezia Emery died unmarried at Gavinana, near Florence. She was especially dedicated to the poor, aiding Dr. Giuseppe Comandi's Industrial School for Boys in Florence, while also funding various Protestant causes in Italy. The obituary in *The Christian* stated: "She lived and dressed in the simplest manner, regarding her large income as 'not her own.'"

31. Genealogical chart, Virginius Hall, Jr., Papers. Lily Livingood (1872–1936) was the daughter of Dr. Nathaniel Foster and Josephine Lytle. Lily and Charles Livingood had four children: Nathaniel (1897–1898), Josephine (1900–1991), John Jacob (1903–1986), and Elizabeth (born 1907). From 1894 to 1896, Livingood lived at Flat 5, 45 Southern Avenue, and from 1897 to 1901, he and his family resided at 2718 Reading Road.

CHAPTER 4

1. *Cincinnati Enquirer*, [January?], 1901, Steele Papers.

2. *Cincinnati Commercial Gazette*, [undated], Steele Papers.

3. TJE to MME, February 16, 1902, Steele Papers.

4. Memorandum, Thomas Hogan, Jr., November 12, 1974, Warren Parks Papers, CHS, states that TJE came upon an estate in rural England named Mariemont and adopted this name in tribute to his wife. No English estate is

known to bear this title, and TJE's Francophile inclinations point to a French connection.

5. Property records in the Town Hall, Middletown, Rhode Island, indicate that TJE purchased the property, in 1901, from the Silas H. Witherbee estate. However, the *Providence Sunday Journal*, March 4, 1906, reported that TJE purchased 18 6/10 acres and its buildings from Bradley and Currier, New York City. The present address of the original land purchase is 386 Green End Avenue.

6. "The News of Newport," *New York Times*, May 27 [1902?], Steele Papers.

7. *Atlas of Newport, R.I. and Environs*, Sanborn Map Co., New York, 1921, 28. At its peak, MME's property extended along both sides of Green End Avenue between Valley Road and Aquidneck Road. This included the separate estate of Seacroft, the house and grounds for the Livingood family and various guests. The six parcels of land, comprising the sixty acres, are recorded in Tax Commissioners' Report, Rhode Island, Estate No. 23205, September 24, 1929, Middletown Town Hall.

8. Frederick Law Olmsted National Historic Site, Brookline, Massachusetts, Olmsted Client Job #337. The Olmsted archives include eighteen drawings and plans for the Emery estate, planting lists, and a photograph album, dating between 1902 and 1908. Olmsted staff involved with the Emery estate included: J. C. Olmsted, Frederick L. Olmsted, Jr., Henry V. Hubbard, and J. Dawson, all well-known landscape architects.

9. Morris, 80.

10. *Cincinnati Enquirer*, May 4, 1903.

11. Washington, 190.

12. E. L. Douglass, Jr., Ohio Mechanics Institute File, April 20, 1960, University of Cincinnati Archives. Emery was approached by Walter Maxwell on behalf of OMI, an agency that MME would support generously.

13. Dabney, 96.

14. CJL to Jacob S. Livingood, July 19, 1903, Virginius Hall, Jr. Papers.

15. CJL to MME, March 8, 1905, Virginius Hall, Jr. Papers.

16. Interview, Elizabeth Livingood McGuire with the author, April 12, 1995.

17. *Cincinnati Enquirer*, [February?], 1905, Steele Papers.

18. CJL to MME, March 19, 1905, Virginius Hall, Jr. Papers.

19. CJL to Isabella F. Hopkins, May 3, 1905, Virginius Hall, Jr. Papers.

20. *Cincinnati Times-Star*, December 2, 1905.

21. Ibid., January 17, 1906. According to the *Cincinnati Enquirer*, January 16, 1906, TJE sailed on the Orient.

22. *Cincinnati Enquirer,* January 19, 1906.

23. Affidavit of Alphonse P. Ruick, February 13, 1906, given in New York City, and recorded in Hamilton County, Ohio, Probate Court, Will Record #98,

226–239. Alphonse P. Ruick's affidavit was filed in the Town Clerk's office, Middletown, Rhode Island, February 20,1906. The Hamilton County Probate Court records indicate that Emery died in "Deaconesses Hospital," Cairo, of "Pulmonary Oedema." Emery's occupation is listed as "Capitalist."

24. *Cincinnati Commercial Tribune* and *Cincinnati Times-Star*, January 18, 1906.

25. Dozens of newspapers in the United States and Europe carried the obituary of Thomas J. Emery in their editions between January 17 and 19, including the *New York Sun*, *Chicago Tribune*, *Detroit News*, and *San Francisco Chronicle*, among others. *New York Times*, January 17, 1906, recorded Thomas' s death, noting that his wife, "who was a Miss Perkins of Baltimore," [*sic*] did not accompany him on his trip.

26. *Cincinnati Times-Star*, February 14, 1906. Lodwick's business was located at 128 West Ninth Street, Cincinnati.

27. *Cincinnati Enquirer*, February 14, 1906. The casket was thought to be zinc. Representatives of Emery's Sons at the opening of the casket included John H. Hall, Charles L. Burgoyne, Henry Gruesser, and Robert Mecke.

28. *Cincinnati Commercial Tribune*, February 17, 1906.

29. *Louisville Courier Journal*, February 11, 1906.

CHAPTER 5

1. *Cincinnati Enquirer*, January 17, 1906. The house on the grounds of Mariemont, the Emerys' Rhode Island estate, already existed when they acquired the property.

2. *Providence Sunday Journal*, March 4, 1906. This article considered Thomas Emery to be the owner with his brother of "one of the largest holders of paying real estate in the country."

3. Myers, 503.

4. MME followed Mrs. Russell Sage's activities in the press, collecting clippings (now in the Steele Papers) that discussed the establishment of the Russell Sage Foundation. MME formed her own foundation, The Thomas J. Emery Memorial, in 1925.

5. Glenn and Brandt, 3–4.

6. Carnegie, 207.

7. Galbraith, 69.

8. *Cincinnati Enquirer*, January 19, 1906. The reporter noted: "Some great surprise is expected, as Mr. Emery once said that he would leave half of his estate to the city of Paris for municipal improvements. His love for the French capitol was almost a passion with him, and he made frequent trips there, where the estate has large real estate holdings."

9. *Cincinnati Enquirer*, March 1, 17, 1906. The newspapers valued the estate at $20,000,000, stating: "The deceased had 1600 tenants alone, income from his

properties, and the profits of his candle company in Ivorydale, as well as properties in seven other states." *New York World,* March 3,1906, estimated the same value: "According to the probate officers of Middletown, Mr. Emery was one of the wealthiest men in the United States."

10. Hamilton County (Ohio) Probate Court, Will Record 98, 226–39. The witnesses were John D. Johnston and Joseph P. Cotton, both of Newport, Rhode Island. Also on February 21, 1906, MME filed her Acceptance of Executrix with the Probate Court, Middletown. She posted bond of $300,000 as executrix and appointed Alexander Anderson of Middletown as her agent in probate matters, February 26, 1906. Perhaps this is the same Alexander Anderson who leaped to his death on July 16, 1907, according to the *Newport Herald,* July 17,1907. Anderson had been a gardener at the Emery estate until a week before his suicide.

11. *Cincinnati Times-Star,* February 21, 1906. This statement in TJE's will is the third of listed items.

12. Among the named individuals in Ivorydale and the Thomas Emery's Sons office given shares of stock were Charles L. Burgoyne, John H. Hall, Robert Mecke, and Ernest Twitchell. Ten shares of Emery Candle Company stock were awarded to CJL and others named in the will. But perhaps the most touching remembrances were the bequests of $30 for each year of service for "all the men, boys, and girls at the factory" and "all the younger stenographers and all the boys in office at Ivorydale the sum of forty dollars each for every year of service."

13. The agreement, signed May 20, 1895, was endorsed by MME, on February 3, 1906, as follows: "As the will of my husband Thomas J. Emery does not refer specifically to the foregoing agreement, in order that there may be no question as to its existence and binding force, I, as his widow and as residuary legatee and devisee of his estate, do hereby ratify and confirm said agreement in every respect." The ratification was witnessed by attorney Drausin Wulsin and Isabella Hopkins. After the death of John J. Emery in 1908, the agreement ceased and the two estates were managed separately: MME's by CJL and John's by the Girard Trust, Philadelphia.

14. MME to Dorothy Canfield Fisher, January 2, 1923, Virginius Hall, Jr., Papers. A popular writer in the first decades of the twentieth century, Fisher is best known for her book, *The Deepening Stream.* This letter thanks Mrs. Fisher for a photograph of "Jimmie and his mother" (perhaps the author and her son, James) and notes that she is pasting it in her copy of Fisher's book, *Rough Heron* [sic].

15. CJL, "Did Harvard Prepare Me Properly For My Life Work? An Autobiography by Charles J. Livingood," March 1918, Virginius Hall, Jr., Papers. CJL notes in this autobiographical account that his responsibilities with MME did not begin until TJE's death in 1906.

16. It is ironic that Mary's generous offer was accepted readily, when a proposal in June 1888, to remodel the church and make needed repairs, was refused by the

Vestry of Christ Church, according to Christ Church, *Wardens and Vestry Records,*
1878–1901, 150–51.

17. MME to Gest, December 27,1906, CAMA. The Board of Trustees accepted
MME's gift at their meeting, December 28, 1906.

18. *Cincinnati Enquirer,* July 2, 1907. MME's offer was made in a letter to the
city, March 30, 1907. On July 1 city council voted to raze the historic house and
convert the site into a park.

19. Adirondack Cottage Sanatarium, *Twenty-Third Annual Report,* 1907. Additional information on the facility and its later history appears in Elizabeth Cole,
Fifty Years at Trudeau Sanatorium (Saranac Lake, 1935). The handsome two story,
shingled structure funded by MME contained waiting rooms, an X-ray facility, lab-
oratories, and rooms for patients during their first two weeks at the hospital.

20. Warren H. Smith, *Hobart and William Smith Colleges: The History of Two
Colleges,* 219. The child may have been a relative of MME, perhaps Theodora
Williams or another member of the Williams family. Reverend Nelson, a close
friend of MME and her pastor for many years, graduated from Hobart College in
the Class of 1890.

21. Gest to MME, April 5, 1907, CAMA. Gest requested portraits of both TJE
and MME for the museum. CJL to Gest, April 23, 1907, CAMA. In this letter,
CJL notes that a portrait of MME's husband, TJE, is completed by Emil Fuchs: "It
is the present intention of Mrs. Emery to leave it to your Association, and further,
that Mrs. Emery will feel honored to have it occupy a place in your collection of
portraits of patrons." It is this latter letter that CJL signs himself as "Secretary" to
MME.

22. *Cincinnati Commercial Tribune,* October 12, 1927. The five-story building of
stone with mansard roof was located at 19 rue Tournefort, south of the Luxem-
bourg Gardens in the St. Medard quarter of Paris. At its opening, it housed 120
girls and was operated by the American Church in Paris. See the *Cincinnati
Enquirer,* February 23,1935, for an article recording Isabella Hopkins's gift of a
fountain in memory of MME, her sister, at Cercle Concordia. This same article
records the address as 41 rue Tournefort.

23. *Cincinnati Enquirer,* June 6, 1907.

24. Agreement, Ohio Mechanics Institute and MME, December 1, 1908,
UCA. The agreement established a building committee with CJL as one of its
members. MME also required that a suitable tablet be inscribed to indicate that
the building was a memorial to her husband and that rent for various concerts
should be as low as possible. MME's offer was accepted by resolution of the Institute on October 15, 1908.

25. Clubbe, 227.

26. *Annual Report of the Cincinnati Orchestra Association Company,* 1905–1906,
and Thomas, I, 265.

27. Morris, "Recollections," September 4, 1979, Christ Church Archives.

28. CJL, "The Building of a Parish House," November 7, 1908, Literary Club of Cincinnati, described the design and construction of the building in a lengthy and dry report to the club's members. CJL served on the building committee. Morris recorded in his "Recollections" that MME wanted the original three-story parish house of 1899 given to the Church of the Nativity in Cincinnati's Price Hill. Brick by brick, the building was dismantled and reassembled on its new site.

29. *The Church Chronicle,* [New York?], February 1909, 1, Steele Papers.

30. CJL to Dr. B. K. Rachford, December 20, 1909, Babies Milk Fund Archives, Cincinnati.

31. *The News-Newport,* November 9, 1910. MME's letter as published was dated November 9, 1910 as well, and written from Middletown. Accounts of the dedication of the finished building appear in the *Cincinnati Enquirer,* November 10, 1911, and *New York Times,* November 18, 1911.

32. Lyon, 36–37, quoting CJL to Dr. B. K. Rachford, November 30, 1910. Mrs. Emery's annual support of the Babies Milk Fund increased to $5,000 by 1914. From its inception in 1909 until her death, Mary remained the fund's principal donor.

33. Cook, 29. Mrs. Emery's involvement with the Berry Schools was long and generous. She provided funds in 1915–1916 for farm buildings and earlier bought land in memory of her two sons, now known as Gammon Farm. Operating support was often requested by Miss Berry in correspondence with MME, and it was usually given.

CHAPTER 6

1. CJL, "Biography," 3, NCU.

2. CJL, "Diary," August 1, 1933, Virginius Hall, Jr., Papers.

3. Survey, Thomas B. Punshon, Civil Engineer, 705 Glenn Building, Cincinnati, August 1918, NCU. The blueprint is dated in CJL's hand: "Rec'd Oct. 25, 1918."

4. Parsons, Project No. 241 (Mariemont, Ohio), NCU. JN's secretary, Charlotte Parsons, recorded each of the projects undertaken from 1913 to 1937 by JN or his associate, Philip W. Foster, in a diary-like account book. Her text was compiled from JN's and Foster's correspondence and memoranda.

5. Philip Foster, "Mr. Livingood's Visit to the Office, September 1920," NCU.

6. *Cincinnati Enquirer,* April 23, 1922, and *Cincinnati Times-Star,* April 24, 1922.

7. "Mariemont, America's Demonstration Town," *American City,* October 27, 1922, 309–10.

8. "Articles of Incorporation," The Mariemont Company, December 1, 1922, MPF.

9. Interview, MFR with Robert Britton, April 5, 1995. Britton was a school friend of Matthew Calderwood, in about 1923–1927, when the latter lived in servants' quarters above the garage with his grandfather. Britton remembers playing with his friend Matthew, on the grounds of Edgecliffe and occasionally inside the house, always cautioned to be quiet and careful. Britton also recalls frequent encounters with MME in the marble-floored atrium and the affectionate pats she gave Matthew's head.

10. CJL to JN, April 6, 1923, NCU.

11. *Cincinnati Times-Star,* April 25, 1923.

12. *Providence Journal,* May 21, 1925.

13. MME to JN, October 5, 1923, NCU. The reference to Mariemont may refer to MME's estate near Newport, but it seems likely she meant the new town near Cincinnati designed by JN.

14. "The City Set At The Crossroads," *New York Times Magazine,* August 24, 1924.

15. Parks, "Diary," December, 24, 1924, CHS.

16. "Proceedings of Incorporation," Mariemont Company, January 20, 1925, MPF.

17. Ibid., May 5, 1925.

18. CJL and JN, *Descriptive,* 13, 15.

19. Frank H. Nelson to MME, May 12, 1925, Steele Papers.

20. JN, "The Viewpoint of Town Planning," Ohio State Conference on City Planning, Dayton, Ohio, October 22, 1925, NCU.

21. CJL to JN, December 8, 1925, NCU.

CHAPTER 7

1. Interview with Elizabeth Livingood McGuire by MFR, April 12, 1995. The only surviving child of CJL at that date, Mrs. McGuire's memories of MME, her homes in Cincinnati and Middletown, and her father's management of MME's affairs were invaluable in this biography.

2. Goss, 322–23.

3. *Cincinnati Enquirer,* May 21, 1912. The area became known as Kessler Park. Before arranging the purchase, CJL studied gardens and parks in Europe, especially that at Parma, Italy, as well as the Arnold Arboretum at Harvard University and the Shaw Botanical Garden in St. Louis.

4. MME to B. K. Rachford, May 1, 1913, Steele Papers. The board of trustees accepted her offer on May 6, 1913.

5. William Howard Taft to MME, March 13, 1913, Taft Papers.

6. Anne Armour-Jones to MFR, December 20, 1995, MFR. University of the South archives indicate that the "Emery Annex" was built as a nurses' home by "T. J. Emery." The gift was MME's, given in the name of her husband, her usual

method of benevolence. The record is confused today, as the building is named in honor of Julia Chester Emery (1852–1922), perhaps a relative of TJE, but this is not the name of his sister Julia (1833–1913).

7. Transfer Deed, MME to CJL, May 26, 1913, Steele Papers. On December 1, 1919, MME amended the trust and added shares to the original amount, no doubt having acquired additional shares as a dividend. She added an interesting clause to the trust's terms, indicating that female employees who are married and leave the company shall forfeit their rights to share's income at that time and that female employees who marry after leaving service shall forfeit their rights, with the income ceasing upon marriage.

8. Elizabeth A. Sloas to MFR, December 15, 1995, Berea College Archives.

9. *Cincinnati Enquirer*, April 8, 1914.

10. Dabney, 216. With expanded services and support from the Council of Social Agencies, another agency generously supported by MME, the home's location was moved to 816 West Ninth Street in 1915.

11. Fischer, 175. The reference quotes a letter from MME to Dr. Holmes, May 24, 1915. The generous pledge was reported in the *Cincinnati Enquirer*, May 26, 1915. Subsequently her gift was increased to $300,000, July 5, 1917, (MME to Dr. Holmes).

12. Fischer, 178.

13. Lyon, 71.

14. Fischer, 176.

15. MME to Gest, December 23, 1915, CAMA.

16. *Cincinnati Times-Star*, June 3, 1915.

17. University of Cincinnati, Report of the Endowment Fund Association, January 12, 1916.

18. President W. G. Frost to MME, January 24, 1916, Berea College Archives. There is little record of MME receiving petitioners either at Edgecliffe or Mariemont, Rhode Island, but this letter substantiates at least this visit. MME paid her pledge in 1919. The gift was invested, and, by the time of the building's construction in 1924 it had grown to $63,000.

19. *Cincinnati Enquirer*, October 20, 1916. The citizens' portion was expected to be raised by January 1, 1917. Control of the zoo was vested in a board, with one vote assigned to each $1,000 contributed to the purchase price. Thus, MME and Mrs. Taft each had 125 votes, a large majority resting with them as de facto owners.

20. *Cincinnati Enquirer*, November 24, 1916. The building was located at 712 West Sixth Street. The home merged with the Catherine Booth Home in 1940, ending any discriminatory basis. Susan Mitchem, Salvation Army archivist, to MFR, December 20, 1995, MFR, stated that the home opened in November 1917 and was often called the Salvation Army Rescue Home for Colored.

21. Morris, 92–93. CJL informed the Reverend Nelson in the autumn of 1916 that MME acquired the Workum property on Sycamore Street and a shoe factory adjacent to it. She contributed this land for the chapel site.

22. Hurley, 76. The building has been remodeled extensively (1989) and retains few of the original elements.

23. Information from Rev. Steven Williamson, rector, St. Philip's Church, Circleville, Ohio, November 15, 1995.

24. Harlow, 367.

25. Kimball, 433.

26. MME to Board of Trustees, University of Cincinnati, August 24, 1920, UCA. The offer was accepted by the University's president, Frederick C. Hicks, and Dr. Kenneth D. Blackfan was appointed Rachford Professor of Pediatrics under the terms of MME's gift.

27. Interview, Elizabeth Livingood McGuire with MFR, April 12, 1995.

28. *Cincinnati Enquirer,* November 7, 1920. The award occurred on November 6, 1920.

29. Statement by Edward L. Douglass, Jr., April 20, 1960, UCA, OMI File. The letter quoted by Douglass, written in 1921, has not been found.

30. CJL to Gest, May 13, 1921, CAMA.

31. CJL to MME, July 7, 1921, Steele Papers.

32. William Howard Taft to MME, July 19, 1921, Taft Papers. MME's congratulatory telegram to Taft was sent on July 1, 1921, Taft Papers.

33. Martha Berry to MME, May 23, 1922, Berry College Archives. A check for $2,500, drawn on Chemical Bank, New York, was sent to Miss Berry as the third installment of a four-year pledge.

34. Martha Berry to MME, March 5, 1923, Berry College Archives.

35. Martha Berry to MME, March 23, 1923, Berry College Archives.

36. MME to Martha Berry, December 1, 1923, Berry College Archives.

37. Martha Berry to Fred K. Hoehler, July 8, 1924, Berry College Archives.

38. Dabney, 96. According to Dabney, the Asylum was located in Avondale on the east side of Emery Street and north of Shillito Street, but these streets do not exist today by these names.

39. "Last Will and Testament of Mary M. Emery," January 26 , 1925, CHS and MPF.

40. MME to Probate Court, Middletown, Rhode Island, January 28, 1925, Steele Papers. As this is an original letter in her own hand, the letter probably was never sent but only retained in a file by CJL for possible future use, if needed.

41. "Second Codicil," April 20, 1925. This codicil merely recognized that the Memorial was incorporated under State of Ohio laws.

42. *Cincinnati Enquirer,* April 17, 1925. The Thomas J. Emery Memorial was incorporated on April 9, 1925, by Isabella F. Hopkins, Charles J. Livingood,

Robert A. Taft, Frank H. Nelson, Thomas Hogan, Jr., and John R. Schindel. The first meeting of the Memorial incorporators was held at CJL's office, 115 East Fourth Street, Cincinnati, on May 11, 1925.

43. Interview, Elizabeth Livingood McGuire with MFR, April 12, 1995. Mrs. McGuire recalled that her husband's residency in Newport continued for the summer of 1926.

CHAPTER 8

1. Much of the information on the Edgecliffe collection formed by MME is taken from Rogers, 1986. Archival references to the Edgecliffe collection include a handwritten list by CJL, noting dates when paintings were purchased, c. 1929, CAMRO; typed lists of the collection as received by CAM and signed by Gest and Museum President Charles Phelps Taft, October 26, 1927, CAMRO; and a typed list by CJL with annotations, April 21, 1941 and January 3, 1942, CAMRO.

2. Charles F. Fowles to Gest, February 8, 1909, CAMA.

3. Gest to MME, May 24, 1909, CAMA. Gest confirmed his admiration to Mary Morgan Newport, May 25, 1909, CAMA. The latter wrote Gest, June 28, 1909, CAMA, telling how pleased she was "to know that Mrs. Emery has secured such a wonderful old master and I am delighted that you all find it so distinguished—satisfactory—as Cincinnati is my birthplace I feel too some pride that her Art Museum has the loan of such a notable picture."

4. Gest to MME, September 15, 1909, CAMA. Earlier in a letter (Gest to MME, August 16, 1909, CAMA), Gest recommended Duveneck as "an enthusiastic admirer of Romney and very familiar with his work. There is much difference in his canvases, some much better than others."

5. MME to Frank Duveneck, September 21, 1909, CAMA.

6. Gest to MME, September 27, 1909, CAMA.

7. CJL to Gest, February 28, 1910, CAMA.

8. *Cincinnati Times-Star,* May 28, 1910. The critic's review gave no anonymity to the lender, for Mrs. Thomas Emery was listed as the generous collector. Several newspapers reported on the loan exhibition during the summer of 1910, acknowledging the number of masterpieces and the rare opportunity this afforded Cincinnatians.

9. CJL to Gest, April 6, 1910, CAMA.

10. MME to Gest, June 7, 1910, CAMA. On June 8, 1910, the dealer's representative, James Labey, wrote to Gest informing him that MME purchased the Hals, that he was bringing the painting to Cincinnati, and that his visit to MME at Newport elicited her enthusiastic approval of the exhibition of Edgecliffe paintings at the museum.

11. MME to Gest, June 17, 1910, CAMA.

12. CJL to Gest, September 7, 1910, CAMA. CJL quoted a statement he

received from the noted museum director and art historian, Wilhelm von Bode, authenticating the Van Dyck. Gest offered his written advice, (September 11, 1910, CAMA), stating he preferred the other Van Dyck she owned: "If it were a choice between this and the John of Nassau I should unhesitatingly take the latter."

13. CJL to Gest, October 22, 1910, CAMA.

14. CAM Board of Trustees, Minutes, January 17, 1911. The annual meeting of shareholders was held on January 7, 1911, when CJL was elected a trustee of the Cincinnati Museum Association, the parent organization of the CAM and the Art Academy of Cincinnati. CJL served as trustee until his resignation from the board in 1945.

15. Gest to MME, January 30, 1911, CAMA.

16. MME to Gest, October 14, 1912, CAMA. The letter notes her decision to acquire the Nattier and Vigée-Lebrun works. According to CJL's annotated list of MME's collection, April 21, 1941 version and dated in CJL's hand on January 3, 1942, the dealer Scott & Fowles gave MME a credit of $24,800 for the returned Van Dyck, *Mlle. Gottinges.* She apparently tired of it and was satisfied with her other work by that master.

17. MME to Gest, November 13, 1911, CAMA. MME was then in New York, writing on Hotel St. Regis stationery, and returning from Newport.

18. Gest to MME, January 29, 1912, CAMA.

19. Walter L. Ehrich to Gest, February 9, 1912, CAMA. Ehrich intended to visit Cincinnati, on Gest's advice, and show MME a few paintings. The prices quoted for the four pictures were: Bordon, *Portrait of Lavinia, Daughter of Titian* ($12,000); Tintoretto, *Portrait of Noblewoman and Dwarf* ($45,000); Zurburán, *St. Ignatius Loyola* ($20,000); Goya [no title given] ($65,000).

20. MME to Gest, February 29, 1912, CAMA. Mrs. Newport also offered for sale in a letter to Gest, (April 3, 1911, CAMA), a flower picture by Jan van Huysum, a seventeenth-century Dutch artist. MME did not buy the Velázquez or the van Huysum.

21. *Cincinnati Enquirer*, December 20, 1913. The article quoted MME that the painting was acquired through Miss Mary Morgan Newport of New York City. Miss Newport was the liaison between MME and the dealer when the Goya painting was purchased, and she maintained a friendship with MME throughout her life. MME named her as a beneficiary in her will.

22. Rogers and Mayer, 5–10. This article is the most thorough published discussion on this important painting, and information noted in this chapter is taken from that publication.

23. Mrs. C. Lewis Hind to Gest, December 5, 1913, CAMA. Also published in Rogers and Mayer, 5. The account was corroborated in a memorandum by Gest, (December 14, 1923, CAMA).

24. *Cincinnati Enquirer*, January 4, 1914. Sir Hugh Lane was a well-known art dealer and collector. He was lost in the sinking of the *Lusitania*, torpedoed by German submarines off Ireland's coast, on May 15, 1915. The sinking of this ship was a major cause of the United States' entry into World War I.

25. Frank Duveneck to Scott & Fowles, January 31, 1914, CAMA. A letter of the same date to Scott & Fowles from Bernard Berenson confirms that the "Portrait of a Doge which I saw the other day in your place is an authentic work by Jacopo Tintoretto."

26. H. B. Eaton to Gest, January 25, 1915, CAMA. Writing from his gallery at 574 Newbury Street, Boston, Eaton described the subject as St. John the Baptist offering a cross to the Christ Child with Joseph depicted in the guise of Vittoria Colonna.

27. Gest to MME, January 29, 1915, CAMA.

28. H. B. Eaton to Gest, February 1,1915, CAMA.

29. MME to Gest, November 10, 1915, CAMA.

30. Gest to CJL, October 18, 1916, CAMA.

31. CJL to Gest, October 19, 1916, CAMA.

32. CJL to Gest, October 21, 30, 1916, CAMA. On October 30, CJL informed Gest by letter that MME bought the picture from Kleinberger and asked that it be hung at Edgecliffe, without informing anyone of its purchase except for Duveneck.

33. Gest to Kleinberger, January 9, April 4, 12, and 13, 1917, CAMA. None of the paintings are identified by title, but Gest remarked that the Rubens had "several prominent people much interested in it."

34. CJL to Gest, October 23, 1917, CAMA.

35. CJL to Gest, October 31, 1917, CAMA.

36. Frank Duveneck to MME, January 28[?] ,1917, CAMA. Duveneck's letter bears no date, but was sent to MME by Gest along with the latter's letter, dated January 29,1917.

CHAPTER 9

1. CJL to Gest, January 7, 1920, CAMA. Gest also heard of a painting by El Greco, *Portrait of St. Francis*, then in New York with the Honorable and Mrs. Alfred Anson, 5 East 68th Street. Mrs. Anson's connection with Cincinnati was through her first husband, John J. Emery, Sr., who died in 1908.

2. J. J. Jarman to CJL, April 23, 1920, CAMA.

3. CJL to J. J. Jarman, April 26, 1920, CAMA. MME's search for a painting by Velázquez was concluded in 1925 when she purchased from Duveen the *Portrait of Philip IV*.

4. MME to Gest, July 1, 1920, and Gest to MME, July 2 1920, CAMA.

5. MME to Gest, August 9, 1920, CAMA.

6. Gest to MME, August 6, 1920, CAMA. Gest wrote to CJL, July 24, 1920,

CAMA, on the same subject, wisely paving the way for his later report to MME.

7. MME to Gest, August 9, 1920, CAMA.

8. CJL to Gest, July 20, 1920, CAMA.

9. CJL to Gest, August 28, 1920, CAMA.

10. Gest to MME, August 31, 1920, CAMA.

11. MME to Gest, September 3, 1920, CAMA.

12. J. J. Jarman to Gest, September 10, 1920, CAMA. Ultimately Jarman provided samples from Schumacher's, New York, letting MME select from several damasks. MME purchased a dark green damask for the Reception Room, and it remained there until the house was demolished.

13. CJL to Gest, October 11, 1920, CAMA.

14. CJL to Gest, August 28, 1920, CAMA. CJL told Gest that the Millais painting was owned by a friend of his, Mrs. Lord of London. The painting was then on loan to the Tate Gallery, London, listed as the property of Sir James Knowles. The portrait is now in the Lady Lever Art Gallery, Port Sunlight.

15. J. J. Jarman to Gest, November 24, 1920, CAMA. Gest received three photographs of the "wonderful polychrome" bust sent to the museum's director, as Jarman knew of Gest's "interest in the Medici family."

16. Gest to MME, January 21, 1921, CAMA. Gest's request for more information on Creelman's history of the Goya painting had no results. An undated note from MME to Gest, (CAMA, found with papers dating from 1921), informed Gest that she had no interest in the Whistler painting offered to her by Mrs. Creelman. She wondered, however, if she was missing an opportunity "from ignorance."

17. J. J. Jarman to Gest, May 19, 1921, CAMA. Gest to Jarman, May 28, 1921, CAMA, indicated that there was no further comment on the Credi from CJL, but "I think they will all be settled in Newport very shortly."

18. CJL to Gest, October 21, 1916, CAMA. The museum's director was told that MME had asked Scott & Fowles to "be on the lookout for a good Rousseau" for MME's collection. This is a rare instance when MME sought a particular artist with a dealer.

19. Gest to MME, July 20, 1922, CAMA.

20. Gest to MME, April 12, 1922, CAMA, records Gest's opinion that the Troyon was "one of the richest examples of that great painter." Because MME wanted the cost of the painting to be secret, payment for the picture was made directly to Gest, who then bought it for her but in the name of the museum. Gest to J. Jarman, May 29, 1922; Gest to T. Gerrity, May 24, 1922, CAMA, refer to the declined works.

21. Gest to G. Stanley Sedgwick, July 12, 1922, CAMA.

22. Gest to MME, July 13, 1922; MME to Gest, July 20, 1922, CAMA.

23. Gest to T. Gerrity, October 30, 1922, CAMA.

24. *The New York Times Magazine*, December 24, 1922, 5.

25. Gest to T. Gerrity, January 29, 1923, CAMA.

26. Gest to T. Gerrity, February 27, 1923, CAMA.

27. Gest to MME, April 3, 1923, CAMA.

28. MME to Gest, May 29, 1923, CAMA.

29. MME to Gest, June 3, 1923, CAMA. According to a brief obituary in *Art Digest* 9, July 1935, 21, Baron Arthur de Bles was born in Manchester, England, and served with distinction in the Royal Welsh Fusiliers during World War I. A writer and lecturer, he died in Los Angeles in 1935.

30. Gest to MME, June 7, 1923, CAMA.

31. Gest to Helen C. Frick, September 10, 1923, CAMA.

32. MME to Gest, July 14, 1923, CAMA, and Gest to MME, July 19, 1923, CAMA.

33. MME to Gest, July 29, 1923, CAMA.

34. Thomas Hogan, Jr., to Gest, August 15, 1923, CAMA.

35. Lavinia Buckler to Gest, September 5, 1923, CAMA.

36. Ibid.

37. Gest to Helen C. Frick, September 10, 1923, CAMA.

38. Gest to MME, December 8, 1923, CAMA.

39. Gest to MME, July 3, 1924, CAMA.

40. Gest to MME, August 3, 1924, CAMA.

41. Gest to T. Gerrity, February 18, 1925, CAMA. A Moro portrait of Ottavio Farnese was mentioned in Gest to Gerrity, February 23, 1925, CAMA, as "too large in any space she thought she had available." This work probably is the same one offered in 1920 and still with Knoedler in 1925. A title for the Moro offered in 1920 is not known.

42. Gest to Felix Wildenstein, February 18, 1925, CAMA. The Colijn de Coter elicited little interest from MME, but between February and April, she had it on approval, according to Gest to Gerrity, February 21 and April 8, 1925, CAMA.

43. Gest to MME, March 12, 1925, CAMA. An earlier letter, MME to Gest, March 9, 1925, CAMA, records the van der Weyden as a portrait of a Burgundian duke.

44. Wilhelm Valentiner to Jacques Seligman, April 8, 1925, CAMA.

45. MME to Gest, May 1, 1925, CAMA. MME never purchased the painting by Perugino, nor did she exchange the Hobbema until she acquired the Velázquez portrait in 1925.

46. CJL to Board of Trustees, Cincinnati Art Museum, May 21, 1925, CAMA.

47. [CJL and Gest?], "Memorandum Outlining Plan for Emery Wing," [undated, but probably May 1925], CAMA.

48. *Cincinnati Enquirer*, May 30, 1925. That same newspaper, (June 2, 1925), extolled MME in an editorial for making "a dazzling contribution to the city's cul-

tural life." The reporter was unaware that MME formed the Edgecliffe collection herself, as the editorial noted that the paintings were "collected by Mrs. Emery and her late husband, Thomas Emery."

49. MME to [?],June 6, 1925, CAMA.

50. Minutes, Board of Trustees Meeting, Cincinnati Art Museum, June 9, 1925, CAMA. Formal acceptance of MME's "munificent offer" was conveyed to CJL by the board's secretary, June 12, 1925, CAMA. The Emery Wing plans were approved at the board of trustees meeting, November 10, 1925.

51. Gest to MME, August 13, 1925, CAMA.

52. CJL to Gest, September 27, 1925, CAMA.

53. MME to Gest, July 14, 1925, CAMA.

54. Gest to MME, July 17, 1925, CAMA. Behrman, 124, mentioned the Velázquez portrait in his charming biography of Lord Duveen but confused its acquisition date, stating that Duveen heard about a *Portrait of Philip IV* by Velázquez while taking the baths at Carlsbad, Germany, in 1911: "That very year, Duveen had sold one to Altman, and he had earlier sold one to Mary M. Emery of Cincinnati."

55. MME to Gest, July 17, 1925, CAMA. In the same letter, she inquired about the cost estimate for the new wing she was contributing to the art museum.

56. Codicil, January 23, 1926, to "Last Will and Testament of Mary M. Emery," CHS and MPF.

57. Gest to Clyfford Trevor, January 25, 1926, CAMA. Gest responded to a letter from Trevor, January 22, 1926, CAMA. Gest added that two other collectors in Cincinnati, Mary Hanna and E. W. Edwards, would not be interested in the Van Dyck he offered. "Mr. Taft" is Charles Phelps Taft, who created with his wife, Anna Sinton Taft, a remarkable collection of paintings, enamels, ceramics, and other objects during the same years of MME's collecting. Their collection, housed in their Federal-period residence in downtown Cincinnati, became the Taft Museum.

58. Gest to J. Jarman, January 28, 1926, CAMA. Jarman sent a biography on the great master: A.T. Cook, *Leonardo da Vinci, Sculptor* (London: Humphreys, 1923). The sculpture proposed to MME probably was the so-called Albizzi Madonna, now no longer attributed to Leonardo.

59. Gest to J. Jarman, February 20, 1926, CAMA.

60. Gest to T. Gerrity, April 6, 1926, CAMA.

61. Gest to CJL, May 12, 1926, CAMA. Gest refers to two letters he received from CJL, April 29 and May 10, 1926, concerning MME's wishes.

62. CJL to Gest, [?] 1927, CAMA. Gest to MME, July 28, 1927, CAMA, congratulated her on acquiring "the second and third Dukes of Burgundy about the same format as the first and fourth even if by another hand." Various records indicate, however, that MME purchased all four portraits of the Dukes of Burgundy in November 1923 from Labey of Scott & Fowles, New York. Payment of $12,000 for

"Two Dukes of Burgundy" to James Labey is recorded as an expense charged to MME's estate in MME's estate tax report: Return for Federal Estate Tax, form 706, Schedule I-2, Taft, Stettinius & Hollister Archives.

63. Gest to MME, February 9, 1927, CAMA. Gest to Wildenstein & Co., February 9, 1927, CAMA, noted that MME "has not been very well." Thomas Hogan, Jr., to Gest, February 10, 1927, CAMA, stated that MME's "health has not been of the best of late and just as soon as her strength will permit it is her intention to confer with you regarding the photographs in question."

64. Gest to Kleinberger Galleries, March 2, 1927, CAMA.

CHAPTER 10

1. Parks, "Diary," March 27, 1927, CHS, records the funeral of Dr. Levi Marshall, first pastor of Mariemont Community Church, held at the church that same day, when the organ was first used. The church was dedicated that evening at 7:30 P.M. MME did not attend either event.

2. *Cincinnati Enquirer*, March 30, 1927.

3. *Cincinnati Commercial Tribune*, October 12, 1927. Surgeons attending MME were Drs. George J. Heuer and J. M. Finney of Johns Hopkins University.

4. According to a handwritten note by MME, May 16, 1927, Steele Papers, witnessed by CJL at Jewish Hospital, MME conveyed to Helen Baird "my new Studebaker closed car in recognition of her devoted attendance upon me during my recent illness and operation." Baird served not only as MME's private nurse for several years, but she also functioned as housekeeper at Edgecliffe during 1927. Isabella Hopkins (letter to CJL, September 8, 1927, Steele Papers), stated that "It is Mary's wish that she shall continue to do so as long as there is need, and that she shall be paid for this extra duty at a definite price." After MME's death, Helen Baird served as superintendent of Holmes Hospital, Cincinnati, until 1955, when she retired.

5. *Newport Mercury*, October 15, 1927.

6. *Cincinnati Enquirer*, October 12, 1927. MME's Certificate of Death, Bureau of Vital Statistics, Cincinnati, Ohio, No. 824, October 15, 1927, indicates the cause as "Broncho [sic] Pneumonia" and "contributing" cause as "Carcinoma of Gall Bladder." In addition to Drs. Morris and Brown, nurses Helen B. Baird, Pauline Huffman, and Agnes Fitzgerald cared for MME in her last illness.

7. *New York Times*, October 12, 1927.

8. *Cincinnati Enquirer*, October 13, 1927.

9. MME, "Chas. J. Livingood, a Last Request," [1927?], Steele Papers.

10. *Cincinnati Times-Star*, October 14, 1927 and *Cincinnati Enquirer*, October 15, 1927. The service is recorded in Christ Church, Cincinnati, "Service Register," 6, 1920–1938.

11. Mrs. Charles Anderson to Isabella F. Hopkins, December 2, 1927, Steele Papers.

12. *Mariemont Messenger*, October 14, 21, 1927.

13. "Last Will and Testament of Mary M. Emery, dated 26 January 1925, and Codicils Thereto," CHS and MPF.

14. *Cincinnati Times-Star*, October 17, 1927. Release of the copy of MME's will and an estimate of the estate's worth must have come from CJL, the executor and only individual capable of releasing such information.

15. Bond of $1,000,000 was posted by CJL as executor, with William R. Harvey, 223 Thames Street, Newport, appointed as "local agent" for probate of the estate.

16. CJL, "List of Mary M. Emery Paintings," April 21, 1941, CAMA.

17. "Edgecliffe, Cincinnati, Ohio, Employees," July 5, 1928, and "Mariemont, Middletown, Rhode Island, Employees," July 5, 1928, MME Files, Taft, Stettinius, & Hollister Archives. Edgecliffe staff at the date of MME's death included: Sophia Rais, housekeeper (who had worked for the Emerys since 1893); Mary Agness, laundress; Margaret Dolanty, housemaid; Charles A. Singer, chauffeur; Delie Tierney, housemaid; Ben Grower, night watchman; William Mackay, [?]; Agnes Mackay, kitchen helper; John Lange, carpenter; J. R. Jackson, butler; Edward Raver, gardener; and George Powdrell [?]. The Mariemont, Rhode Island, staff included: Andrew L. Dorward, caretaker and head gardener; Charles Carr; Manuel Manise; Manuel Nunes; Joseph Lewis; Edwin L. Burdick; Manuel P. Silvia; James Mulligan; William Viera; John Rogers; Roy Underwood; Manuel Regio; Joseph Leander; John Mederios; and John Silvia. Presumably most of these men were gardeners and workers on the estate, not household servants. Named in the fourth codicil of the will is Alexander J. Dorward, a confusing reference, as the name of MME's head gardener was noted elsewhere as Andrew L. Dorward.

18. These agencies included Berkeley Memorial Church, Middletown, Rhode Island, $5,000; Cincinnati Art Museum, $10,000, as fund for care of Edgecliffe Collection; Protestant Episcopal Missionary Society, $100,000 each to its foreign and domestic missions; Women's Auxiliary of Missionary Society, $50,000; Children's Hospital of Episcopal Church, Cincinnati, $100,000, in memory of son Sheldon; Christ Church Episcopal Society, $100,000; Christ Church Maintenance Fund, $100,000, for the Parish House; Episcopal Diocese of Southern Ohio, $50,000, for upkeep of Girls' Friendly Vacation House; Fresh Air Camp and Convalescent Society, $50,000, for maintenance of Fresh Air Farm, Terrace Park, Ohio; Children's Home Endowment Fund, Cincinnati, $50,000; YWCA, Cincinnati, $25,000; Clovernook Home for the Blind, Cincinnati, $5,000; Home for Incurables, Cincinnati, $25,000; Cincinnati Bethel, $50,000; Salvation Army, Cincinnati, $25,000; Associated Charities of Cincinnati, $25,000.

19. *New York Times*, October 18, 1927.

20. Return for Federal Estate Tax, Internal Revenue Service, Form 706, Revised May 1926, Decedent: Mary M. Emery, MME Files, Taft, Stettinius, & Hollister, Cincinnati, Ohio.

Appraised Assets:	Real Estate	$4,516,272.30
	Stocks and Bonds	$5,388,043.65
	Cash, Mortgages	97,352.83
	Misc. Property	4,418,169.19
	Jointly Owned	None
	TOTAL	$14,419,837.97
Deductions:	Funeral and Administration	$351,390.46
	Decedent's Debts	843,936.07
	Unpaid Mortgages	40,000.00
	Charitable Gifts	10,009,796.66
	Exemption Permitted	100,000.00
	TOTAL	$11,345,123.19

21. Agreement, Executor CJL with State of Rhode Island Board of Tax Commissioners, August 16, 1929, MME Files, Taft, Stettinius, & Hollister, Cincinnati, Ohio.

22. Supreme Court of Ohio, Document 22866, July 23, 1930.

23. "Record of Proceedings of the Incorporators, Stockholders, and Trustees of the Thomas J. Emery Memorial," Special Meeting, October 26, 1927, MPF. An announcement was made of MME's death by CJL at the Memorial's Annual Meeting, February 6, 1928, but no resolution was offered.

24. *Cincinnati Enquirer*, December 17, 1927.

25. MME, "Mementoes on 3 sheets—4th sheet verifies—to be distributed by Isabella F. Hopkins when she wishes, either her lifetime or later by Charles J. Livingood," n.d., and CJL, "Mementoes [typed list of preceding], November 30, 1927, Steele Papers.

26. Rogers, *Randolph Rogers*, 202. According to Randolph Rogers's "Journal," J. Howard Emery ordered a replica of the reduction, or smaller size (36 inches), of *Nydia*, on February 22, 1868, for 127 pounds sterling. This example was exhibited at the Cincinnati Industrial Exposition, 1872, catalogue no. 4.

27. Gest to E. M. Sperling, October 15, 1927, CAMA. Sperling represented Kleinberger Galleries, New York.

28. "Record of Proceedings of the Incorporators, Stockholders, and Trustees of the Thomas J. Emery Memorial," 62, April 23, 1928, MPF.

29. "Proceedings of Incorporators, Stockholders, and Trustees of the Thomas J. Emery Memorial," January 9, 1931, MPF.

30. Thomas J. Davis, "Mary M. Emery Estate," October 5, 1931, MPF. Davis was chairman of the board of First National Bank, Cincinnati.

31. [Thomas Hogan, Jr.?], "Memorandum," October 8, 1931, MPF. The memorandum recounts Taft's visit with Thomas J. Davis, First National Bank, May 25, 1931. Attached to this memorandum is a "Statement of Assets," May 1, 1931, and signed "T. H. Jr." [Thomas Hogan, Jr.]. This document enumerates Emery assets of $18,101,276. These assets included: rental and saleable properties, $9,702,741; Thomas J. Emery Memorial assets, $5,401,035; and estate executor assets worth $2,997,500. The total value of the estate at this date should be compared with its value as reported to the Internal Revenue Service, noted earlier. Although Taft's involvement as lawyer for the Emery estate is known, he did not "supervise her estate," as Ross, indicates in her book on the Taft family (p. 23). That role was in CJL's hands.

32. "Proceedings of the Incorporators, Stockholders, and Trustees of the Thomas J. Emery Memorial," February 1, 1932, MPF.

AFTERWORD

1. Heilbrun, 131.

2. McCarthy, *Lady Bountiful*, x.

3. Horowitz, 65.

4. Ibid., 55.

5. Cahall, 431, discusses this extensively as a Cincinnati phenomenon.

6. Perry, 132. MME belonged to this association from its beginnings in 1877 to its dissolution in 1886.

7. Articles of Incorporation, Cincinnati Museum Association, February 15, 1881, signed by Joseph Longworth, Reuben R. Springer, David Sinton, Charles W. West, and Julius Dexter and recorded by the State of Ohio, February 18, 1881.

8. McCarthy, *Women's Culture*, 78–79.

9. Bumiller, 21.

BIBLIOGRAPHY

Unpublished materials, letters, and other documents pertaining to Mary M. Emery, with a few exceptions, are not recorded in this bibliography. The notes to the text indicate, where needed, the significant unpublished materials and newspaper references. The story of Mary Emery's planned community, Mariemont, and its beginnings will be told in a separate book by the present author that includes a complete bibliography on that masterpiece of town planning. Thus, the bibliography recorded below does not list the extensive references on the village designed by John Nolen and funded by Mary Emery.

Aaron, Daniel. *Cincinnati, Queen City of the West, 1819–1838*. Columbus, Ohio: Ohio University Press, 1992.

Baker, John D. "Mary Emery's Mariemont." *Cincinnati Magazine*, October 1973, 40–45, 72–75.

Behrman, S. N. *Duveen*. London: Readers Union, Hamish Hamilton, 1953.

Birmingham, Stephen. *The Grandes Dames*. New York: Simon and Schuster, 1982.

Brock, H. I. "The City Set at the Crossroads: A New Experiment in Town Planning to Fit the Motor Age." *New York Times Magazine*, August 24, 1924, 7–8.

Bumiller, Elizabeth. "Woman Ascending a Marble Staircase." *New York Times Magazine*, January 11, 1998, 18–21.

Cahall, Michael C. *Jewels in the Queen's Crown: The Fine and Performing Arts in Cincinnati, Ohio, 1865–1919*. Ph.D. dissertation, University of Illinois, 1991.

Caldwell, Wil F. "The Indians and the Early Settlers." *Mariemont Town Crier Special Edition*, July 12, 1991.

Carnegie, Andrew. *Miscellaneous Writings of Andrew Carnegie*. Garden City, N. Y.: Doubleday, Doran, 1933.

Cist, Charles. *Cincinnati in 1841*. Cincinnati: Privately printed, 1841.

———. *Cincinnati in 1851*. Cincinnati: W. H. Moore, 1851.

————. *Cincinnati in 1859*. Cincinnati: W. H. Moore, 1859.

Clubbe, John. *Cincinnati Observed, Architecture and History*. Columbus: Ohio State University Press, 1992.

Cook, S. H. *Half Century at Berry*. Rome, Georgia: Berry College, 1961.

Dabney, Wendell P. *Cincinnati's Colored Citizens*. Cincinnati: Dabney Publishing Co., 1926.

Devereux, Clara. *Mrs. Devereux's Blue Book of Cincinnati*. Cincinnati: the Author, n.d.

"Dr. John Nolen." *Architectural Forum*, April 1937, 94.

Drake, B., and E. D. Mansfield. *Cincinnati in 1826*. Cincinnati: Morgan, Lodge, and Fisher, 1827.

Edwards, Rev. George H. "Christ Church Parish House." *The Church Chronicle*, February 1909, 1.

Erhardt, William. "The Birth of Pediatrics: Children's Hospital in Its First Five Decades." *Queen City Heritage*, Fall 1983, 2–20.

Fischer, Martin. *Christian R. Holmes, Man and Physician*. Springfield and Baltimore: Charles C. Thomas, 1937.

Ford, Henry A., and Kate B. Ford. *History of Cincinnati, Ohio*. Cleveland: L. A. Williams, 1881.

Galbraith, John Kenneth. *The Affluent Society*. New York and Toronto: New American Library, 1958.

Giglierano, G. J., and D. A. Overmyer. *The Bicentennial Guide to Greater Cincinnati: A Portrait of Two Hundred Years*. Cincinnati: Cincinnati Historical Society, 1988.

Glenn, John M., and Lilian Brandt. *Russell Sage Foundation: 1907–1946*. New York: Russell Sage Foundation, 1947.

Goss, Charles F. *Cincinnati, the Queen City, 1788–1912*. Chicago: S. J. Clarke, 1912.

Greenbaum, Victor. "The Pediatrics Department of the College of Medicine." *University of Cincinnati Medical Bulletin*, June 1921, 38–43.

Greve, Charles T. *Centennial History of Cincinnati*. Chicago: Biographical Publishing Co., 1904.

Hammack, David C. *Power and Society: Greater New York at the Turn of the Century*. New York: Russell Sage Foundation, 1982.

Hancock, John L. *John Nolen and the American City Planning Movement: A History of Culture, Change, and Community Response, 1900–1940*. Ph.D. dissertation, University of Pennsylvania, 1964.

Harlow, Alvin F. *The Serene Cincinnatians*. New York: E.P. Dutton, 1950.

Heilbrun, Carolyn G. *Writing a Woman's Life*. New York and London: W. W. Norton, 1988.

Herrick, Warren C. *Frank H. Nelson of Cincinnati*. Louisville, Kentucky: Cloister Press, 1945.

Hooton, Earnest A. "Indian Village Site and Cemetery Near Madisonville, Ohio." *Papers of the Peabody Museum of American Archeology and Ethnology* VII, (1920) 1–137.

Horowitz, Helen L. *Culture and the City: Cultural Philanthropy in Chicago from the 1880s to 1917*. Lexington: University of Kentucky, 1976.

Howard, Ebenezer. *Garden Cities of To-Morrow* [First published as *To-Morrow: A Peaceful Path to Real Reform*, 1898; present title, 1902]. London: Faber and Faber, 1965.

Hurley, Daniel I. *One Child at a Time: A History of the Children's Home of Cincinnati*. Cincinnati: Children's Home of Cincinnati, 1990.

"John Nolen." *New York Times*, February 19, 1937.

"A July Phase of a Handsome Newport Garden." *Town & Country*, August 1919, 23–25.

Kimball, Fiske. "The Social Center, Part I, Commercial and Cooperative Enterprises." *Architectural Record*, May 1919, 417–40.

Landy, James. *Cincinnati Past and Present*. Cincinnati: Elm Street Printing Co., 1872.

Leavitt, Warren E. "The Romance of Mariemont." *Eastern Hamilton County Messenger*, April 19, 1973 [First published in *Mariemont Messenger*, March 19, 1926– November 26, 1926].

Leonard, Lewis A. *Greater Cincinnati and Its People, A History*. Cincinnati, New York, and Chicago: Lewis Historical Publishing Co., 1927.

Livingood, Charles J. "The New Town, A National Exemplar." Address to the Literary Club of Cincinnati, November 1, 1924.

Livingood, Charles J., and John Nolen. *A Descriptive and Pictured Story of Mariemont, A New Town: A National Exemplar*. Cincinnati: Mariemont Company, 1925.

Lyon, Robert A. *Benjamin Knox Rachford*. Cincinnati: Educational Horizons Publishers, 1972.

Mace, Ruth. "John Nolen." *Dictionary of American Biography*, Supplement II. New York: Charles Scribner's Sons, 1958.

"Madame X: Lady Bountiful." *Mariemont Town Crier*, March 1977, 4–5.

"Mariemont: A New Town, A Complete Residential Village Near Cincinnati, Ohio, Planned by John Nolen and Philip W. Foster, Associate, Town Planners." *Architecture*, September 1926, 247–74.

"Masterpieces of the Emery Collection." *Connoisseur*, January 1932, 70–71.

Maxwell, Sidney D. *The Suburbs of Cincinnati, Sketches Historical and Perspective*. Cincinnati: George E. Stevens, 1870.

Maxwell, Walter H. "The Emery Estate, A Commercialized Philanthropy." *Saxby's Magazine*, September 1909, 51–65.

McCarthy, Kathleen D., ed. *Lady Bountiful Revisited: Women, Philanthropy, and Power*. New Brunswick and London: Rutgers University Press, 1990.

———. *Women's Culture: American Philanthropy and Art, 1830–1930*. Chicago and London: University of Chicago Press, 1991.

Mc Auslin, William A. *Mayflower Index, Compiled and Edited for the General Society of Mayflower Descendants*. Clinton, Massachusetts: Colonial Press, 1932.

Metz, Charles L. "The Prehistoric Monuments of the Little Miami Valley." *Journal of the Cincinnati Society of Natural History*, October 1878, 119–45.

Morris, J. Wesley. *Christ Church, Cincinnati, 1817–1967*. Cincinnati: Cincinnati Lithographing Ohio Press, 1967.

Mowry, George E. *The Progressive Era, 1900–20: The Reform Persuasion*. Washington, D.C.: American Historical Association, 1972.

Mumford, Lewis. *The Culture of Cities*. New York and London: Harcourt, Brace, 1938.

Myers, Gustavus. *History of the Great American Fortunes*. [First published 1909] New York: Random House Modern Library, 1937.

Nichols, George Ward. "Private Picture Collections in Cincinnati." *Galaxy*, October 1870, 511–20.

Nolen, John. "Mariemont, Cincinnati District, Ohio." Address to the Commercial Club, Cincinnati, April 22, 1922.

———. "Mariemont, Ohio." *Architectural Forum*, March 1932, 245–48.

———. *New Towns for Old: Achievements in Civic Improvement in Some American Small Towns and Neighborhoods*. Boston: Marshall Jones, 1927.

Norman, Victoria L. "Cincinnati's Forgotten Philanthropist, Mary Muhlenberg Emery." Spring 1988. Rare Book and Manuscript Collection, Cincinnati and Hamilton County Public Library.

Parks, Warren W. "General Record of Work at Mariemont" in Diaries, 1–9, 1923–29, Cincinnati Historical Society.

———. *The Mariemont Story, A National Exemplar of Town Planning*. Cincinnati: Creative Writers and Publishers, 1967.

Parsons, Charlotte. "Summaries of Selected Projects. Prepared by Charlotte Parsons, Secretary to Mr. Nolen, 1913–1937." Carl A. Kroch Library, Cornell University.

Perry, Elizabeth W. *A Sketch of the Women's Art Museum Association of Cincinnati, 1877–1886*. Cincinnati: Robert Clarke, 1886.

Phelps, Harriet J. *Newport in Flower*. Newport, R. I.: Preservation Society of Newport County, 1979.

Richards, Caroline. "History of Stepping Stones." Cincinnati Historical Society, n.d.

Roe, George M. *Cincinnati: The Queen City of the West*. Cincinnati: *Cincinnati Times-Star*, 1895.

Rogers, Millard F., Jr. "Mary M. Emery: Development of An American Collector." *Cincinnati Art Museum Bulletin*, December 1986, 4–19.

———. *Randolph Rogers, American Sculptor in Rome*. Amherst, Mass.: University of Massachusetts Press, 1971.

Rogers, Millard F., Jr., and Lance Mayer. "Titian's Modello of Philip II." *Cincinnati Art Museum Bulletin*, April 1984, 5–10.

Ross, Ishbel. *An American Family, the Tafts, 1678 to 1964*. Cleveland and New York: World Publishing Co., 1964.

Ross, Steven J. *Workers on the Edge: Work, Leisure, and Politics in Industrialized Cincinnati, 1788–1890*, New York: Columbia University Press, 1985.

Shelton, Louise. *Beautiful Gardens in America*. New York: Charles Scribner's Sons, 1915, and revised edition, 1925.

Shine, Carolyn R., Mary L. Meyer, Elisabeth Batchelor, Beth Dillingham, and James B. Griffin. *Art of the First Americans* [Exhibition Catalogue]. Cincinnati: Cincinnati Art Museum, 1976.

Siple, Ella S. "Art in America, Notes on the Emery Collection in the Cincinnati Museum." *Burlington Magazine*, June 1930, 330–36.

Thomas, Louis R. *A History of the Cincinnati Symphony Orchestra to 1931*. Ph.D. dissertation, University of Cincinnati, 1972.

Veblen, Thorstein. *The Theory of the Leisure Class*. New York: MacMillan, 1899.

Venable, W. H. "Cincinnati, Historical and Descriptive." *The New England Magazine*, September 1888, 423–46.

Washington, Booker T. *Up From Slavery: An Autobiography*. New York: Doubleday Page, 1901.

Women's Art Museum Association. *Loan Collection Exhibition Prepared by the Women's Art Museum Association of Cincinnati, May 1878*. Cincinnati: A. H. Pugh, 1878.

INDEX

Page numbers in italics denote illustrations

SERIES ON OHIO HISTORY AND CULTURE

ABOUT THE AUTHOR

Millard F. Rogers, Jr. holds a M.A. in art history from the University of Michigan. He served 20 years as director of the Cincinnati Art Museum and currently serves as Director Emeritus. His previous publications include: *Randolph Rogers, American Sculptor in Rome*; *Spanish Paintings in the Cincinnati Art Museum*; *Favorite Paintings from the Cincinnati Art Museum*; and *Sketches and Bozzetti by American Sculptors, 1800–1950*.

ABOUT THE BOOK

Rich in Good Works was designed and typeset by Kachergis Book Design of Pittsboro, North Carolina. The typeface is Adobe Goudy which was designed by Frederic W. Goudy (1865–1947), a former Midwestern accountant who became probably the most prolific type designer in printing history.

Rich in Good Works was printed on sixty-pound Finch Opaque and bound by Sheridan Books of Ann Arbor, Michigan.